PROJECT CENSORED'S

STATE OF THE FREE PRESS 2023
The Top Censored Stories and Media Analysis of 2021–22

EDITED BY **Mickey Huff** AND **Andy Lee Roth**
WITH **Project Censored**

FOREWORD BY **Heidi Boghosian**

ILLUSTRATED BY **Anson Stevens-Bollen**

THE CENSORED
— PRESS —
SEVEN STORIES

Fair Oaks, CA • New York

PN
4784
'024
P76
2022

A JOINT PRODUCTION OF THE CENSORED PRESS
AND SEVEN STORIES PRESS

The Censored Press   Seven Stories Press
PO Box 1177   140 Watts Street
Fair Oaks, CA 95628   New York, NY 10013
censoredpress.org   sevenstories.com

ISBN 978-1-64421-237-0 (paperback)
ISBN 978-1-64421-238-7 (electronic)
ISSN 1074-5998

College professors and high school and middle school teachers
may order free examination copies of Seven Stories Press titles.
Visit https://www.sevenstories.com/pg/resources-academics
or email academics@sevenstories.com.

9 8 7 6 5 4 3 2 1

Printed in the USA

Book design by Jon Gilbert

DEDICATION

To Russ Kick
July 20, 1969 – September 12, 2021

Champion of information freedom and
government transparency.

Curator of The Memory Hole website
and *Graphic Canon* book series.

Challenger of official narratives
and political orthodoxies.

Contents

Fighting Words

HEIDI BOGHOSIAN

Journalists to police: "We're press, we're press!"
Police to journalists: "We don't care."[1]

Violence against American journalists is on the uptick. The vitriol underlying those physical attacks comes as much from private citizens as from law enforcement. In 2021, more than one in five television news directors reported attacks on newsroom staff.[2] Assaults caught on camera in 2020 numbered 593, an increase of nearly 1,400 percent from the prior year. Online threats to journalists have also skyrocketed.[3]

What does such violence have to do with censorship? Project Censored's definition of modern censorship includes, in part, manipulation of coverage due to political or legal pressures that impede the robust flow of information essential to a democratic society. Political and legal pressures also contribute to a climate of intimidating rhetoric that fuels violence. The chilling effects of violence—or the threat of it—on freedom of expression are undeniable.

Assaults and battery of reporters reflect the nation's growing acceptance of violence as a legitimate form of public expression.[4] Elected officials have fueled spasms of violence, sometimes with their own fists. When Greg Gianforte from Montana ran in a special 2017 election for a House seat, he grabbed a tape recorder from *Guardian* reporter Ben Jacobs, then slammed him to the floor. Donald Trump sang Gianforte's praises: "Any guy that can do a body slam, he's my guy!"[5] Gianforte won the House seat and in 2021 became governor.

When the president, other political leaders, and pundits impugn the integrity of reporters, they rile up the supplicant masses. For decades, conservative politicians and pundits have set the stage, poisoning public opinion against the "liberal press." Enter Donald Trump, stage right. He popularized disinformation and lies, vilifying the truth-telling press. Social media platforms such as Facebook, with engagement-maximizing algorithms that favor misinformation, controversy, and extremism over positive stories, further influenced people's mindset—negative, angry, seeking scapegoats.[6]

Sitting in a jail cell, fighting subpoenas in court, getting attacked by police at protests or at crime scenes, fearing for a source's safety, suspecting your home computer and phones are monitored by law enforcement—what treacherous terrain journalists trek in the digital era.

On June 28, 2018, Jarrod Ramos used his 12-gauge pump-action shotgun to spray terror in the *Capital Gazette* newsroom in Annapolis, Maryland. He killed five and injured more.[7] Ramos was angered over a 2011 article reporting that he was on probation.

In 2020, Cameron Shea, a leader of the neo-Nazi group Atomwaffen Division, was sentenced along with three co-defendants for hate crimes against journalists—many of color—who had filed reports on antisemitism.

Under Shea's direction, the group delivered posters featuring Nazi symbols, threatening language, and images of masked figures with guns and Molotov cocktails to the homes of journalists in Tampa, Seattle, and Phoenix.[8]

Journalists also face threats online. Digital harassment often takes the form of doxxing, the act of publishing, without permission, private information such as a person's home address and encouraging others to harass, threaten, or harm them. Slate journalist Amanda Hess experienced abusive tweets in 2014, threatening her with rape and decapitation.[9] She reported the abuse to the police, to no avail. Reporter Seung Min Kim did get support from her boss at the *Washington Post* when liberal Twitizens attacked her with racist and sexist tweets.[10] The aggressors cited a photo of Kim showing Senator Lisa Murkowski a critical tweet by Neera Tanden (President Biden's nominee for Budget Director). Seung Min Kim was seeking comment from the senator, a standard journalistic practice.

Set aside, for the moment, these *illegal* acts of physical violence and intimidation. The American legal system has *routinely* been used as a cudgel of censorship. Legal and law enforcement practices and policies are the new "fighting words" leveled at the press.

Journalists face legal obstacles each day they sit down to interview a source. Dodging subpoenas pressuring them to reveal sources—and sometimes going to jail for refusing to do so—is part of the job description. Sources often risk prosecution under the 1917 Espionage Act; witness the record number of whistleblowers prosecuted by the Obama Administration, as Project Censored has previously covered.[11] Espionage Act charges lay the groundwork for treating journalists who expose government misconduct as traitors. The indictment of WikiLeaks founder and transparency champion Julian Assange on seventeen espionage charges could be the final nail in the Fourth Estate's coffin.

Updates to Freedom of Information Act regulations make accessing "public" records more difficult than ever. And the folks issuing and pulling press passes throughout the nation? They would be the same police who handcuff "criminal" reporters covering protests.

Speaking of protests, when news bloggers, freelance reporters, and other independent journalists document them, they're now fair game for violence in direct view of the public. Take photojournalist Linda Tirado. At a 2020 Black Lives protest in Minneapolis, a foam bullet shot by police ripped through her protective goggles, permanently blinding her left eye. *Wall Street Journal* reporter Tyler Blint-Welsh, wearing his NYPD-issued press pass, was another victim. NYPD officers hit him in the face with their shield, breaking his glasses and pushing him to the ground.[12] As the U.S. Press Freedom Tracker documents, reporters are routinely tear-gassed, arrested, or detained just for trying to get their story.

Eroding public trust in the press undermines the delicate balance of power between the public and a government purportedly accountable to and in service of civil society. Add violence to the legal threats faced by reporters, and the cultural conditions for a free nation are imperiled: civil society can no longer keep government in check. Each time a reporter is arrested, pepper-sprayed, or beaten for doing their job, the free press gets a black eye, diminishing the likelihood of a well-informed public, the prospects for justice, and the outlook for the future of democracy.

The contest between the press and Americans who disdain truth is protracted and virulent. Our call to arms is continued resistance to legal and physical efforts to intimidate, discourage, or beat down the rare breed of independent and establishment journalists who aim to inform the public.

Fortunately, a number of organizational allies exist to help truth-seeking journalists and a truly free press to prevail, including the Freedom of the Press Foundation, the Committee to Protect Journalists, and Project Censored. The Project's stalwart commitment to highlighting important news stories that have been censored or marginalized illuminates the work of independent journalists, several of whom have endured legal, physical, and online attacks aimed at silencing them. The following pages contain many such stories and are testament to the featured journalists' courageous perseverance.

With each new assault—whether online or in person, in the courts or on the streets—the work of Project Censored assumes greater urgency.

HEIDI BOGHOSIAN is an attorney and co-host of *Law & Disorder Radio*. She is the author of *Spying on Democracy* (2013), *"I Have Nothing to Hide" and 20 Other Myths about Privacy and Surveillance* (2021), and the forthcoming *Democracy Games: The Epic Battle to Save Americans' Freedoms* (Beacon Press, 2023).

Notes

1. Kio Herrera, "More Than 50 Journalists Arrested or Detained While on the Job in the US in 2021," U.S. Press Freedom Tracker (Freedom of the Press Foundation), November 22, 2021.

2. "More Than 1 in 5 TV News Directors Say Their Journalists Were Attacked in 2021," Radio Television Digital News Association, May 5, 2022.

3. "Incident Database," U.S. Press Freedom Tracker, accessed June, 6, 2022.

4. Meryl Kornfield and Mariana Alfaro, "1 in 3 Americans Say Violence Against Government Can Be Justified, Citing Fears of Political Schism, Pandemic," *Washington Post*, January 1, 2022.

5. Christal Hayes, "Trump Praises GOP Congressman Who Assaulted Reporter: 'Any Guy That Can Do a Body Slam—He's My Guy,'" *USA Today*, October 10, 2018 (updated October 19, 2018).

6. Karen Hao, "The Facebook Whistleblower Says Its Algorithms Are Dangerous. Here's Why," *MIT Technology Review*, October 5, 2021.

7. Christine Hauser, "Gunman in Capital Gazette Shooting Is Sentenced to Multiple Life Terms," *New York Times*, September 28, 2021.

8. "Leader of 'Atomwaffen' Conspiracy Sentenced to Three Years in Prison for Threatening Journalists and Advocates," US Department of Justice, August 24, 2021.

9. Amanda Hess, "Why Women Aren't Welcome on the Internet," Pacific Standard, January 6, 2014 (updated June 14, 2017).

10. Lloyd Grove, "Liberal Twitter Mob Heaps Racist, Sexist Abuse on WaPo Reporter for Doing Her Job," Daily Beast, February 25, 2021.

11. Barack Obama's Justice Department charged or convicted eight people under the Espionage Act. See, e.g., Shannon Polvino, William Scanna-pieco, Kathryn La Juett, Justin Lewis, and Michael I. Niman, "Obama's War on Whistleblowers," in *Censored 2014: Fearless Speech in Fateful Times*, eds. Mickey Huff and Andy Lee Roth (New York: Censored Press, 2013), 72–75; and Peter Sterne, "Obama Used the Espionage Act to Put a Record Number of Reporters' Sources in Jail, and Trump Could Be Even Worse," Freedom of the Press Foundation, June 21, 2017.

12. Courtney Douglas, "Amid Black Lives Matter Protests, a Crushing Moment for Journalists Facing Record Attacks, Arrests at the Hands of Law Enforcement," Reporters Committee for Freedom of the Press, September 4, 2020.

State of the ~~Free~~ Billionaire Press

ANDY LEE ROTH and MICKEY HUFF

FRONT PAGE PROPAGANDA

The front page of *USA Today* on May 12, 2022, featured a set of stories that provides insight into the state of the free press, understood through the lens of the nation's third-largest circulating newspaper.[1] Above the fold, the day's headlines included "Blaming GOP May Backfire on Biden" and "Growing Outcry Over 'Mob Rule' Deepens Already Gaping Divide." Below the fold, but still prominently positioned, *USA Today* featured a report on inflation ("Is the Worst Over?") and a fourth story, "Russia's Not the First to Spew 'Firehose of Propaganda.'" The article examined propaganda as "a common tool . . . to justify conflict," looking back to British government propaganda during World War II and US government posters produced during World War I, before turning to "global condemnation" of Russia's use of "misinformation and censorship" to promote its invasion of Ukraine.[2]

Based on its report, *USA Today* evidently beholds propaganda as the proprietary domain of Russia, including its state-controlled media and "paid internet trolls"—but no more than a historic relic in the United States. This form of American exceptionalism is not limited to *USA Today*, but rather a defining trait of the US establishment press, as readers who follow the work of Project Censored or Fairness & Accuracy in Reporting will already understand.[3] In his pioneering study of news judgment at four major US news outlets, sociologist Herbert J. Gans identified ethnocentrism as one of the "enduring values" of establishment news.[4]

USA Today's take on propaganda was not only chauvinistic but also myopic. By focusing on *government* propaganda, the newspaper's report excluded consideration of propaganda originating from *corporate* sources—including, perhaps most tellingly, the newspaper's own reporting, that same day, on the roles of the Republican Party, Fox News, and conservative pundits in aggravating President Biden's inability to unite the country, and on the legitimacy of nonviolent, public protests in response to the Supreme Court's leaked draft opinion on a case that would overturn the Court's landmark ruling in *Roe v. Wade*.

A skeptic might dismiss the preceding example as a roll of the dice, putting too much critical emphasis on a single day's edition of just one newspaper. But similar conclusions could be drawn from examining other editions of *USA Today*, not to mention the daily coverage of additional, equally prominent US news outlets.[5]

USA Today is owned by Gannett, which became the nation's largest newspaper publisher in 2019 when it merged with GateHouse Media.[6] Gannet's CEO, Mike Reed, earned a reported $7.74 million in 2021, the same year the company cut 24 percent of its staff, according to official filings.[7] As rich and influential as Reed may be, the Gannett boss's wealth and clout pales in comparison to those of Jeff Bezos, Elon Musk, and Bill Gates, each of whom holds controlling interests in some of the nation's predominant media platforms.

BIG TECH, BIG BROTHER BILLIONAIRES SPELL BIG TROUBLE FOR FREE PRESS PRINCIPLES

Noting the inherent problems of an oligarchic class controlling an institution as vital to democratic self-governance as the free press is nothing new. The creation of Project Censored as a media watchdog, in 1976, was galvanized by the establishment press's delayed coverage of the Watergate scandal, which eventually toppled Richard Nixon's presidency. Although the Nixon administration successfully pressured the chair of CBS to scale back Walter Cronkite's coverage of the story, the White House failed to stop independent and alternative media coverage, which eventually led to Watergate becoming a major story.[8] This episode illustrates how elites often talk chiefly amongst themselves, influencing news coverage and even fostering self-censorship. However, as Project Censored's founder, Carl Jensen, noted, calling attention to pressures on the free press and sticking to dissonant stories that challenge the status quo can make a difference in the public interest.[9]

Over fifty years before Watergate, Upton Sinclair critiqued the wealthy owners of the press, including icons such as William Randolph Hearst, in his study of US journalism, *The Brass Check*.[10] In a 2002 article on Sinclair's book, media scholars Ben Scott and Robert McChesney rightfully recognized it as a "systematic and damning critique" of the robber barons' capture of the nation's media.[11] Scott and McChesney noted that Sinclair's title referred to chits issued to patrons at urban brothels, establishing "an analogy between journalists and prostitutes, beholden to the agenda, ideology, and policies of the monied elites that owned and controlled the press."[12] Sinclair's *Brass Check* sold more than 150,000 copies during the decade after he self-published it, without copyright—but it was almost entirely ignored by the press organizations and icons he assailed.[13]

A generation later, another muckraker, A. J. Liebling, who authored the *New Yorker*'s "Wayward Press" column for eighteen years, frequently called out the negative consequences for the public of for-profit journalism, in prose both acrid and eloquent. In one of his most widely cited articles, "Do You Belong in Journalism?" (published in 1961), he famously quipped, "Freedom of the press is guaranteed only to those who own one."[14]

Sinclair and Liebling paved the way for scholarly critiques of concentrated media power. These include now-classic studies by Ben Bagdikian, whose 1983 book *The Media Monopoly* anticipated a forthcoming wave of corporate media consolidation and warned against economic and political pressures on the integrity of news reporting; and by Edward Herman and Noam Chomsky, whose 1988 study *Manufacturing Consent* introduced their "propaganda model" of news to describe how ownership, advertising, elite sourcing, flak, and ideological bias produce "filtered" news in service of elite interests.[15]

Today, these critiques are arguably more relevant than ever, because consolidated corporate ownership of the legacy press is now augmented by the global scope of digital media giants such as Meta and Alphabet. History shows that consolidated media, controlled by a handful of elite owners, seldom serves the public interest. In pursuit of their own interests and investments, media tycoons past and present, again and again, appear to be conveniently oblivious to the main frame through which they filter news—that of class, including class structure and class interests.[16] Consequently, they often overlook (or ignore) conflicts of interest that implicate media owners, funders, investors, and advertisers, not to mention their business clients on Wall Street and in Big Pharma, Big Tech, and the military–industrial complex. This reality helps explain the lack of corporate news coverage on topics such as wage theft (which implicates the nation's largest employers), runaway inflation (partly the consequence of corporate consolidation), and the lack of investment in public transportation, as described in Chapter 1 of this book.

In recent years, many news executives, such as Gannett's Mike Reed, have come to seem like bit players compared to those on the increasingly long list of billionaires who have purchased legacy media outlets. These include Sheldon Adelson (casino owner, *Las Vegas Review-Journal*), Marc and Lynne Benioff (Salesforce founders, *Time*), Jeff Bezos (Amazon, the *Washington Post*), John W. Henry (investment manager, Boston Red Sox, the *Boston Globe*), Laurene Powell Jobs (Apple heiress, bought controlling shares of *The Atlantic*), Patrick Soon-Shiong (biotech, *Los Angeles Times* and *San Diego Union-Tribune*), and Glen Taylor (business magnate, *Minneapolis Star-Tribune*).[17] As Rodney Benson and Victor Pickard have noted, reporting by outlets owned by billionaires tends to favor their own class interests. While publications such as *The Atlantic* and the *Washington Post* enjoy public popularity as "the bright and shiny faces" of what Benson and Pickard characterize as "an increasingly oligarchic media system," they warn that the oligarchs' "values and priorities" conflict with democratic principles:

> Their business model—and definition of journalistic success—tends to exclude audiences or issues that cannot be monetized. High-end advertisers favor content that appeals to high-earning demographics, which can skew coverage away from concerns of the working class and poor. So instead of reaching out to underserved readers, these billionaire-owned news organizations may exacerbate economic and racial divides by privileging views and voices more in line with higher socioeconomic groups.... The biggest beneficiaries of a highly stratified economic system are unlikely to take the lead in addressing inequality.[18]

Pickard and Benson reiterate and update Sinclair's lamentations regarding the failures of the press a century ago, when he noted that "American journalism is a class institution serving the rich and spurning the poor."[19] As the titans of Silicon Valley revolutionize our ever-changing media systems by introducing new technologies, these same concerns persist and intensify.

Despite the promise of boundless access to information, Silicon Valley mirrors legacy media in its consolidated ownership and privileging of elite narratives. This new class of billionaire oligarchs owns or controls the most popular media platforms, including the companies often referred to as the FAANGs—Facebook (Meta), Apple, Amazon, Netflix, and Google (Alphabet).[20] Their

CEOs are routinely lionized in popular culture and the press as intrepid entrepreneurs, inventors of today's must-have tools for work and play, and stewards of the public square. They include, but are not limited to Bill Gates (Microsoft, Bill & Melinda Gates Foundation), Mark Zuckerberg (Meta, Facebook, Instagram), and Jeff Bezos (Amazon, the *Washington Post*)—all of whom are deeply involved and invested in computer software, social media platforms, and the worldwide web itself (e.g., Alphabet, the parent company of Google and YouTube).

Through the Bill & Melinda Gates Foundation, Bill Gates has provided $319 million to fund news outlets, journalism centers and training programs, press associations, and specific media campaigns around the world, an important but underreported story we cover in more detail in Chapter 1 of this volume. Elon Musk, the CEO of Tesla, who postures as a populist outsider and free speech absolutist, has caused a media storm due to his on-again, off-again effort to buy Twitter, proclaiming his desire to restore online freedom of expression. Never mind that Musk has a long history of censoring his critics and is deeply connected to the Pentagon and national security state, hardly the hallmarks of an outsider, much less a trustworthy custodian of free speech.[21] Zuckerberg hired "fact checkers" from the Atlantic Council (a NATO lobby group) and, in the name of combating online "misinformation," has stifled and deplatformed countless independent news voices, mostly those critical of US foreign policy, official narratives around COVID-19, and other controversial issues.[22]

Resembling previous generations of billionaires who owned legacy media outlets, today's digital tech titans blur the lines between journalism, entertainment, and consumption (of goods *and* information). They also increasingly partner with the military–industrial complex in service of "national security" and state surveillance. They not only peddle the kind of elite propaganda that Sinclair and Liebling previously decried, they also aim to collect and monetize any available information about the people who use their platforms. As critics including Shoshana Zuboff, Alan MacLeod, and Nolan Higdon have noted, Big Tech billionaires harvest and exploit our online data for profit, political influence, and social control, a power dynamic Zuboff calls "surveillance capitalism."[23]

POLICING DISINFORMATION—OR CENSORSHIP BY PROXY?

In the process, Big Tech giants and their oligarchic owners now engage in a new type of censorship, which we have called "censorship by proxy."[24] Censorship by proxy describes restrictions on freedom of information undertaken by private corporations, restraints that exceed limits on governmental censorship and serve both corporate and government or third-party interests.[25] Censorship by proxy is not subject to venerable First Amendment proscriptions on government interference with freedom of speech or freedom of the press.

Censorship by proxy alerts us to the power of economic entities that are not normally considered to be media "gatekeepers." For example, in 2022, the digital financial service PayPal (whose founders include Peter Thiel and Elon Musk) froze the accounts of Consortium News and MintPress News for "unspecified offenses" and "risks" associated with their accounts, a ruling that prevented both independent news outlets from using funds maintained by PayPal. Consortium News and MintPress News have each filed critical news stories and commentary on the foreign policy objectives of the United States and NATO; PayPal issued notices to each news outlet, stating that, in addition to suspending their accounts, it might also seize their assets for "damages." Joe Lauria, editor in chief of Consortium News, said he believed this was a case of "ideological policing."[26] Mnar Adley, head of MintPress News, warned, "The sanctions-regime war is coming home to hit the bank accounts of watchdog journalists."[27]

But PayPal's freeze on the accounts of MintPress News and Consortium News was not even the most glaring example of censorship by proxy in the past year. Instead, that (dis)honor goes to the Big Tech platforms and media companies that launched a massive campaign of online censorship in the fateful aftermath of Russia's attack on Ukraine in early 2022.[28] DirectTV, Roku, Sling TV, and Dish each dropped RT America from their platforms in protest against the Russian invasion.[29] In the name of fighting alleged Russian propaganda and disinformation (and following the lead of the European Union), YouTube disappeared entire Russian channels—including RT America and Sputnik—and those channels' archives, to great applause from various sectors of the American public, especially liberals.[30]

RT America was seen by many as anti-US propaganda, but as the French philosopher Jacques Ellul reminds us, the most potent propaganda is factual, if not totalizing.[31] Both views can be true—RT America purveyed propaganda *and* provided factual reporting and informed perspectives from many Western critics of US empire. It is also true that Russia's authoritarian government has undertaken horrendous crackdowns on press freedoms and civil liberties, and that, under President Vladimir Putin, the flow of news and opinion has long been influenced, if not outright controlled, by the state.[32] Anyone who opposes censorship, human rights abuses, and imperialism should be appalled by Putin's authoritarian rule; the regime's pervasive attacks on press freedom and journalists (which include bans on journalists' use of specific words, such as "war" and "invasion," backed by the threat of fifteen-year prison terms); its inhumane treatment of Russia's LQBTQIA+ community, including a "gay purge" in the Chechen Republic; and its latest crackdown, on citizens who publicly oppose their nation's assault on Ukraine—not to mention the illegal and immoral invasion itself.[33] However, the response in the United States to RT America and other media outlets whose reporting calls into question US foreign policy should not be to follow Putin's authoritarian approach of suppressing and criminalizing dissident perspectives. As journalist Matt Taibbi warns, that path leads to US citizens becoming the "doublethinkers" whom George Orwell's *1984* grimly portrayed.[34]

In an interview for *Democracy Now!*, after RT America shut down, Pulitzer Prize–winning journalist Chris Hedges, whose literary-focused interview program *On Contact* was broadcast by RT America, lamented the lack of a "functioning public broadcasting system" in the United States, telling host Amy Goodman, "The walls have just closed in.... There's less and less space for those who are willing to seriously challenge and question entrenched power."[35] Political comedian Lee Camp, whose RT America show *Redacted Tonight* was also scrubbed, raised similar concerns (see Chapter 5 of this volume for Camp's account of the affair).[36] From 2012 to 2015, before she launched *The Empire Files*, independent journalist Abby Martin's RT show, *Breaking The Set*, provided first-rate news coverage of topics and issues that legacy news outlets in the United States declined to cover, including US war crimes and journalistic hypocrisy. For a case study in censorship by proxy, look no further than YouTube's response to the closure of RT America: the popular video-hosting platform sent the archives of six years of Hedges's *On Contact* program, eight years of Camp's *Redacted Tonight*, and more than 500 episodes of Martin's *Breaking the Set* down the memory hole.[37]

TOWARD AN AMERICAN MINISTRY OF TRUTH?

There is already plenty of propaganda here in the United States, as exemplified in the preceding discussion of the *USA Today* headlines. But US propaganda is often disguised as "conventional wisdom" or "official accounts," or is embedded in a tech platform's guidelines for "community standards," which YouTube invoked to suppress content on Russia's invasion of Ukraine, as Kevin Gosztola of Shadowproof was quick to point out.[38] Other shadowy, self-appointed fact-checking organizations, such as NewsGuard, enlist former government officials, including Tom Ridge (the first director of Homeland Security) and Michael Hayden (who led the CIA during George W. Bush's presidency), to help determine who and what count as "trustworthy" information sources.[39] Microsoft even prepackaged its Microsoft Edge cross-platform web browser with NewsGuard to encourage its use, despite the fact that NewsGuard has bestowed its "green"rating—signifying "generally trustworthy"—on establishment news outlets (including Fox News) known to have published false or inaccurate information.[40]

If that's not enough, several high-profile Democrats, including former president Barack Obama, have publicly sounded alarms against the spread of "misinformation."[41] In April 2022, Obama gave the keynote address at a Stanford University symposium on "Challenges to Democracy in the Digital Information Realm." The former president called for increased efforts to control content and expression online through government regulation and tighter corporate controls.[42] This is exactly what YouTube, Roku, NewsGuard, and others are already doing, in the name of fighting misinformation and disinformation—but at the risk of engaging in censorship by proxy.

Although Big Tech corporations, quasi-governmental arbiters of news integrity, and prominent politicians present their efforts as necessary measures to police misinformation and protect the public, critics contend they are merely constructing their own Ministry of Truth.[43]

In April 2022, President Joe Biden's Department of Homeland Security (DHS) created the ominously named Disinformation Governance Board (DGB). The board's stated purpose is to protect national security by combating foreign sources of misinformation and disinformation, and by advising other DHS agencies—aims that have been widely criticized, across the political spectrum, for ambiguities in the definitions of the DGB's authority and jurisdiction, and doubts about the integrity of its leadership. Within a month, the Biden administration "paused" the DGB's operations, leading its first director, Nina Jankowicz, a proclaimed disinformation expert at the governmental-affiliated Wilson Center think tank, to resign in the wake of online criticism of her Democratic affiliations, and other personal attacks.[44] Jankowicz was replaced with a known neoconservative, Michael Chertoff, former head of DHS and co-author of the controversial USA PATRIOT Act, whose views on torture, unlawful detention, and surveillance have been roundly criticized by the American Civil Liberties Union (ACLU) and Human Rights Watch, among others. With Chertoff tapped to lead a "review and assessment" of the DGB's future, the newly created office drew another round of widespread (and deserved) condemnation.

According to DHS Secretary Alejandro Mayorkas, the DGB would continue its mission to monitor and counter disinformation, especially regarding border security, Russian propaganda, and other perceived threats to the nation's security.[45] Although DHS claimed the DGB had no operational capacity to control what Americans read or watched, such reassurances were hardly comforting in light of past revelations regarding mass surveillance of law-abiding citizens by other US government agencies.

With a wary eye on the billionaire tycoons who own more and more of the nation's most prominent news outlets, the digital tech titans who increasingly control the flow of information and the terms of public debate, and national agencies that aspire to "govern" disinformation, Project Censored and the contributors to *State of the Free Press 2023* advocate free speech, press freedom (including good old-fashioned muckraking), and critical media literacy as means to hold power accountable and to promote a more just, equitable, and inclusive society.

INSIDE *STATE OF THE FREE PRESS 2023*

A primary goal of Project Censored is to improve news coverage of important social issues. Chapter 1 features the most important but underreported news stories of 2021–2022. From investigative reports on the scope of direct and indirect subsidies received by the fossil fuel industry (a staggering $11 million *per minute*, as documented in this year's #1 story), to the number of members of Congress with substantial investments in fossil fuels (#4) and the increasingly pervasive and perverting influence of "dark money" in the political process (#5, #9, and #16), this year's Top 25 story list highlights vital reporting on fundamental public issues that corporate news media either marginalized or buried. The independent press also serves as an important check on the power of Big Media (see, for example, #12, on Facebook's "Dangerous Individuals and Organizations" blacklist) and the corporate press (as in #10, "Major Media Outlets Lobby Against Regulation of 'Surveillance Advertising'"). Overall, this chapter provides a clear picture of how independent journalists and news outlets provide crucial alternatives to corporate news reporting that is premised on narrow definitions of who and what count as "newsworthy."

Chapter 2, on Déjà Vu News, revisits five Top 25 stories from previous years. This year's chapter, by Mack Parlatore, Analisa Chudzik, Shealeigh Voitl, and Steve Macek, focuses on basic human needs, including eating and drinking, birthing and breastfeeding. Corporate power "has encroached on each and every one of these vital life processes," they write, and corporate news media have "largely failed to inform the public about this alarming state of affairs." This year, the Déjà Vu News chapter updates reporting on the prevalence of microplastics in seafood (and our bodies), from *State of the Free Press 2022*; the handful of giant companies who control the world's food system (from *Censored 2005*); the Project's 1994 report on the epidemic of cesarean sections in the United States; the push by multinational corporations to privatize water; and baby formula producer Gerber's efforts to suppress laws promoting breastfeeding (both from *Censored 2001*).

This year's Junk Food News chapter offers a buffet of the tropes and tripe that comprise the sensationalist, race-to-the-bottom, corporate coverage of news you *cannot* use, but are force-fed, nonetheless. In 1983, Project Censored founder Carl Jensen coined the term, likening Junk Food News to "Twinkies for the brain." Here, Jen Lyons, Gavin Kelley, Sierra Kaul, Marcelle Swinburne, and Mickey Huff take a look at what was on the Junk Food News menu this past year, including the trying relationships of celebrities, the billionaire space race, and NFL quarterbacks scrambling for their careers in a sports world gone wild (off the field). By the end of this mediocre monstrosity of a meal, sensitive readers may want to undertake an extended corporate media fast to revive their intellectual health.

In Chapter 4, Robin Andersen examines News Abuse with a focus on overlapping patterns in establishment news coverage of policing at home and war overseas. "State violence is promoted in both cases," she writes. "News Abuse"—the Project's term for distorted, misleading coverage of genuinely important news topics—is clearly evident when corporate news outlets peddle "copaganda," reporting that privileges the perspective and interests of law enforcement officials. And, against the backdrop of the withdrawal of US troops from Afghanistan and the Russian invasion of Ukraine, Andersen's chapter also examines the establishment media's perpetual reliance on defense industry spokespersons and former military officials as featured interviewees and commentators. In a textbook example of the slant that characterizes news abuse, such coverage typically omits any reference to such pundits' own financial ties to the defense industry, while also marginalizing (or completely excluding) the voices of informed experts who publicly oppose military solutions to political problems.

The book's final chapter highlights Media Democracy in Action, a concept developed in a chapter by that name in the Project's 2004 yearbook. The individuals and organizations featured here have dedicated themselves to educating and informing the public, defending freedom of expression, and resisting the chilling effects of surveillance. This year's contributors include Lee Camp, who hosted *Redacted Tonight* on RT America until it ceased operations; Sam Husseini of the Institute for Public Accuracy; Allison Butler, co-director of Mass Media Literacy; Nolan Higdon, representing the Critical Media Literacy Conference of the Americas, and Afsaneh Rigot of Article 19, reporting on Design from the Margins. As Mischa Geracoulis writes in the chapter's introduction, the featured authors offer readers "lucid direction for navigating this new era of polarization."

GLASS EYES, BLINDING LIGHTS—
AND CLEAR VISION

As *State of the Free Press 2023* goes to press, people around the world continue to grapple with the twin plagues of pandemic and misinformation. Just as the COVID-19 virus continues to mutate, impacting our daily routines and polarizing our politics, with no clear ending in sight, so too debates over information integrity, ethical journalism, and the public's sense of truth will almost certainly continue to shape our politics and vex our individual and collective spirits.

News, of course, plays a pivotal role in those debates. Despite the common admonishment to "figure it out for yourself," it is all but impossible to be an active, engaged citizen or community member without relying on some form of media for vital information and perspective.

Early in the 20th century, Upton Sinclair lamented the American press as "a class institution" that served the rich and spurned the poor.[46] Witnessing "a quickening decimation" of news outlets in the early 1960s, the *New Yorker*'s A. J. Liebling observed, "A city with one newspaper, or a morning and an evening paper under one ownership, is like a man with one eye, and often the eye is glass."[47] In 2017, historian Timothy Snyder observed that, when we abandon facts and embrace spectacle, "the biggest wallet pays for the most blinding lights."[48]

From Big Tech to big government, from Watergate to WikiLeaks, our society's most powerful institutions have prevailing interests in monitoring—if not controlling—the public's access to information. This becomes even more problematic when the interests of business and government align, as Sinclair, Liebling, and contemporary critics have all warned. Whether censorship is direct or by proxy, we oppose it—not necessarily to normalize or endorse the views of those subject to it, but because dissident views ought to be heard, considered, and debated if we seek to preserve (or establish) a truly free and equitable society.

As *State of the Free Press 2023* demonstrates, concentrated media ownership, corporate biases in who and what count as "newsworthy," and new forms of digital "gatekeeping" all make it more difficult than ever for ordinary people to see clearly, or to find viewpoints that permit sweeping sight of open vistas. Confronted with blinding lights controlled by the biggest wallets, it becomes too easy to close one's eyes or to look away, refocusing on less troubling subjects, while surrendering our own critical faculties to third-party providers such as NewsGuard, Homeland Security's Disinformation Governance Board, or some other incipient Ministry of Truth.

The alternatives are clear, but not easy. Project Censored's guiding principles suggest one approach, based on the premise that increasing the public's awareness of, trust in, and support for truly independent journalism is one essential dimension of every social justice movement.[49] Thus, the Project champions independent investigative journalism, fearlessly calls out corporate media when they fail to adequately inform the public, and advocates critical media literacy, including hands-on education for students, many of whom contributed research and writing to this book. We hope readers will find the media analysis and exemplary investigative journalism featured in this volume inspiring. May they guide your gaze behind the glassy-eyed headlines and past the blinding lights, beyond the biases and "front page propaganda" of the billionaire press, to the clarity of a free and truly independent press, in service of we the people.

Andy Lee Roth, Winthrop, Washington
Mickey Huff, Fair Oaks, California
June 2022

Notes

1. Third-largest circulation: Amy Watson, "Average Weekday Print Circulation of Selected Newspapers in the United States From October 2020 to March 2021," Statista, October 1, 2021.
2. Michael Collins, "Russia's Not the First to Spew 'Firehose of Propaganda,'" *USA Today*, May 12, 2022, 1A; published online as "Russia's 'Firehose of Falsehood' in Ukraine Marks Latest Use of Propaganda to Try to Justify War," *USA Today*, May 8, 2022 (updated May 11, 2022). Incidentally, *USA Today*'s treatment of Russian propaganda drew on a 2016 report by the RAND Corporation, which we critiqued in a previous edition of this yearbook. See Andy Lee Roth, "The Top *Censored* Stories and Media Analysis of 2017–2018," in *Censored 2019: Fighting the Fake News Invasion*, eds. Mickey Huff and Andy Lee Roth with Project Censored (New York: Seven Stories Press, 2018), 37–40.
3. See, e.g., Ari Paul, "Foreign Agents Designation Causes Media Cold War," Fairness & Accuracy in Reporting, February 28, 2022; Bryce Greene, "Calling Russia's Attack 'Unprovoked' Lets Us Off the Hook," Fairness & Accuracy in Reporting, March 4, 2022.
4. Herbert J. Gans, *Deciding What's News: A Study of CBS Evening News, NBC Nightly News, Newsweek and Time*, 25th anniversary edition (Evanston, IL: Northwestern University Press, 2004[1979]), 42–43.
5. Alan MacLeod, an independent journalist who reports for MintPress News, consistently provides critical analyses of major US news outlets' propagandistic headlines, via his social media feeds on Twitter @AlanRMacLeod.
6. See, e.g., Jon Allsop, "The Precarious State of Local News Giants," *Columbia Journalism Review*, November 20, 2019.
7. Don Seiffert, "Here's How Much Gannett CEO Mike Reed Made in 2021," *Boston Business Journal*, April 6, 2022.
8. Carl Jensen and Project Censored, *20 Years of Censored News* (New York: Seven Stories Press, 1997), 13–14.
9. Ibid., 18–19.

10.   Upton Sinclair, *The Brass Check: A Study of American Journalism* (Pasadena, CA: self-published, 1919). Sinclair did not copyright this book because he wanted it to be read far and wide. It can be accessed online at OpenLibrary.

11.   Ben Scott and Robert W. McChesney, "Upton Sinclair and the Contradictions of Capitalist Journalism," *Monthly Review*, May 1, 2002.

12.   Ibid.

13.   Ibid.

14.   A. J. Liebling, "The Wayward Press: Do You Belong in Journalism?" *New Yorker*, May 14, 1960, 105–112; Jack Shafer, "The Church of Liebling," Slate, August 25, 2004.

15.   Ben Bagdikian, *The Media Monopoly* (New York: Beacon Press, 1983); Edward S. Herman and Noam Chomsky, *Manufacturing Consent: The Political Economy of the Mass Media* (New York: Pantheon Books, 2002[1988]).

16.   News "does not often deal with income differences among people, or even with people as earners of income. . . . Journalists shun the term 'working class' because for them it has Marxist connotations." Gans, *Deciding What's News*, 23, 24.

17.   Rodney Benson and Victor Pickard, "The Slippery Slope of the Oligarchy Media Model," The Conversation, August 10, 2017; Ali Montag, "Jeff Bezos, Laurene Powell Jobs and Now Marc Benioff: Why Tech Billionaires Are Buying Media Companies," CNBC, September 17, 2018.

18.   Benson and Pickard, "The Slippery Slope."

19.   Sinclair, *The Brass Check*, 147.

20.   Nolan Higdon, "Elon Musk and the Oligarchs of the 'Second Gilded Age' Can Not Only Sway the Public—They Can Exploit Their Data, Too," The Conversation, April 27, 2022.

21.   Nolan Higdon, "Media Gets It Wrong on Elon Musk and Twitter: The Issue Is Oligarchy, Not 'Free Speech,'" Salon, April 24, 2022.

22.   Elliot Gabriel, "Facebook Partners with Hawkish Atlantic Council, a NATO Lobby Group, to Protect Democracy," MintPress News, May 22, 2018; Jake Johnson, "Alarming: Facebook Teams Up with Think-Tank Funded by Saudi Arabia and Military Contractors to 'Protect' Democracy," Common Dreams, May 18, 2018.

23.   Shoshana Zuboff, *The Age of Surveillance Capitalism: The Fight for a Human Future at the New Frontier of Power* (New York: Public Affairs, 2019); Alan MacLeod, "Elon Musk Is Not a Renegade Outsider—He's a Massive Pentagon Contractor," MintPress News, May 31, 2022; Nolan Higdon, "Elon Musk and the Oligarchs of the 'Second Gilded Age,'" The Conversation, April 27, 2022.

24.   Mickey Huff and Andy Lee Roth, "A Return to News Normalcy," in Project Censored's *State of the Free Press 2022*, eds. Andy Lee Roth and Mickey Huff (Fair Oaks, CA and New York: The Censored Press and Seven Stories Press), 5–6. See also Andy Lee Roth, avram anderson, and Mickey Huff, "Censorship by Proxy and Moral Panics in the Digital Era," in *Censorship, Digital Media and the Global Crackdown on Freedom of Expression*, eds. Robin Andersen, Nolan Higdon, and Steve Macek (New York: Peter Lang Publishing, 2023).

25.   Roth, Anderson, and Huff, "Censorship by Proxy and Moral Panics."

26. David Z. Morris, "Deplatformed by PayPal, Antiwar Journalists Speak Out," Coinbase, May 23, 2022.

27. Branko Marcetic, "PayPal Has Begun Quietly Shuttering Left-Wing Media Accounts," *Jacobin*, May 3, 2022.

28. Alex Weprin, "DirecTV Drops Russia-Backed RT Channel 'Effective Immediately,'" *Hollywood Reporter*, March 1, 2022.

29. Sara Fischer, "DirecTV Dropping RT America in Light of War in Ukraine," Axios, March 1, 2022; Hailey Fuchs, "Roku Boots RT From Its Global Platform," Politico, March 1, 2022; Weprin, "DirecTV Drops Russia-Backed RT Channel"; Phil Nickinson, "Roku Removes RT, for What That's Worth," Digital Trends, March 2, 2022; Phil Nickinson, "Dish and Sling TV Also Drop Russia Today Channel," Digital Trends, March 4, 2022.

30. "YouTube Blocks Russian State-Funded Media, Including RT and Sputnik, Around the World," France 24, March 12, 2022.

31. Jacques Ellul, *Propaganda: The Formation of Men's Attitudes* (New York: Random House, 1973[1965]).

32. Maya Vinokour, "Russia's Media Is Now Totally in Putin's Hands," *Foreign Policy*, April 5, 2022; Isaac Chotiner, "How Putin Controls Russia," *New Yorker*, January 23, 2020.

33. See. e.g., Anton Troianovski and Valeriya Safronova, "Russia Takes Censorship to New Extremes, Stifling War Coverage," *New York Times*, March 4, 2022; "Russia Bans Media Outlets From Using Words 'War,' 'Invasion,'" *Moscow Times*, February 26, 2022; Elene Kurtanidze, "Dismantling LGBT+ Rights as a Means of Control in Russia," Freedom House, April 30, 2021; Stephan Horbelt, "Chechnya's Horrific 'Gay Purge': A 4-Year Timeline of Abduction, Torture and Murder," Hornet, June 15, 2021; and Amy Goodman, interview with Vladimir Slivyak, "Russian Environmentalist Speaks Out on Putin's Attack on Antiwar Protesters & Independent Media," *Democracy Now!*, March 4, 2022.

34. Matt Taibbi, "Orwell Was Right," ScheerPost, March 13, 2022.

35. Amy Goodman, interview with Chris Hedges, "Disappeared: Chris Hedges Responds to YouTube Deleting His 6-Year Archive of RT America Shows," *Democracy Now!*, April 1, 2022; "Code Pink's Panel on Media Censorship of Voices for Peace Featuring Abby Martin, Lee Camp and Chris Hedges," *Project Censored Show*, April 6, 2022. Hedges' program was subsequently picked up by The Real News Network as "The Chris Hedges Show."

36. "Lee Camp on Censoring Anti-War Voices," Peoples Dispatch, April 5, 2022.

37. Maximilian Alvarez, "Abby Martin: How the Media Manufactures Bloodlust for War," Real News Network, March 8, 2022.

38. Kevin Gosztola, "Questions About YouTube's 'Community Guideline' for Removing Russia-Ukraine War Content," Facebook, March 11. 2022.

39. See Andy Lee Roth and Mickey Huff, "The Pandemic and the State of the Free Press," in Project Censored's *State of the Free Press 2021*, eds. Mickey Huff and Andy Lee Roth (New York: Seven Stories Press, 2020), 8-10.

40. Tom Parker, "The Most Outrageous Examples of Fake News from News-Guard's 'Trusted Sources,'" Reclaim the Net, January 25, 2019; Bruce Fein, "NewsGuard's Scarlet Letter," Consortium News, June 8, 2022.

41. Melissa De Witte, Taylor Kubota, and Ker Than, "'Regulation Has to Be Part of the Answer' to Combating Online Disinformation, Barack Obama Said at Stanford Event," Stanford News, April 21, 2022 [updated April 25, 2022].

42. The text of Barack Obama's speech is accessible as "Disinformation Is a Threat to Our Democracy," at Medium (April 21, 2022).

43. Matt Hampton, "How the Ministry of Truth Can Censor You Without (Technically) Censoring You," FEE Stories (The Foundation for Economic Education), May 6, 2022. Ministry of Truth, or Minitrue, was the name George Orwell used for the fictional propaganda and censorship department of Oceania in his dystopian classic *1984*.

44. Lev Golinkin, "Another Terrible Choice for Biden's 'Disinformation Board,'" *The Nation*, May 27, 2022; Editorial Board, "The Disinformation Governance Board Collapse Showcases the Problem," *Washington Post*, May 23, 2022.

45. Seth Smalley, "What We Know About the DHS' Disinformation Governance Board," Poynter, May 5, 2022.

46. Sinclair, *The Brass Check*, 147.

47. Liebling, "Do You Belong in Journalism?," 108.

48. Timothy Snyder, *On Tyranny: Twenty Lessons from the Twentieth Century* (New York: Tim Duggan Books, 2017), 65.

49. On Project Censored's guiding principles, see Roth and Huff, "The Pandemic and the State of the Free Press," 6-7.

CHAPTER 1

The Top *Censored* Stories and Media Analysis of 2021–2022

Compiled and edited by
SHEALEIGH VOITL, KATHLEEN MINELLI, AMY GRIM
BUXBAUM, STEVE MACEK, and ANDY LEE ROTH

INTRODUCTION

ANDY LEE ROTH AND STEVE MACEK

What does it consist in, this censorship
which dares not tell its name?

It means the ship doesn't sail
because there's no water in the sea.

—EDUARDO GALEANO[1]

In a 1977 article for the *Index on Censorship*, Uruguayan historian and journalist Eduardo Galeano used a simple metaphor to characterize censorship. "The ship doesn't sail because there's no water in the sea," he wrote. Galeano's basic point is clear, but we can appreciate its depth by asking, What does the ship represent?

Say the ship carries our best hopes for justice, democracy, and a vision of the future informed by a deep understanding of the past—all cardinal values of Galeano's lifework. All of this runs aground when information is blockaded and public deliberation diminished.

What, then, does the water stand for in Galeano's metaphor? It would include all the conditions necessary for justice and democracy, informed by historical perspective. The water necessary for the ship to sail would certainly comprise an understanding of the political process—including past abuses of it and present threats to it.

Historically, in the United States a free and independent press has been deemed essential to the public's understanding of the democratic political process and ability to participate effectively in it. Ideally, the press not only informs the public, but also acts as the "Fourth Estate," operating (in tandem with the executive, legislative, and judicial branches of government) as a watchdog on those with power.

Today, however, the establishment news media often fail to fulfill these fundamental duties. Consequently, too many Americans remain poorly informed about important public issues, because our most prominent news reporting organizations have blockaded or marginalized news coverage of them, a concern reflected in the Project's original, expanded definition of "censorship" as "the suppression of information, whether purposeful or not, by any method—including bias, omission, underreporting, or self-censorship—that prevents the public from fully knowing what is happening in society."[2]

This functional perspective alerts us that the outcome—defined as whether or not the public is likely to be well informed—ought to be paramount in our analysis. Whether news of some issue is subject to "prior restraint" by a government agency—as proscribed in the First Amendment—or subject to "censorship by proxy" by a corporate entity (which the First Amendment does *not* restrict), the primary concerns are the public's right to know and the integrity of democratic political processes.[3]

This broader orientation has important consequences. Returning to Galeano's metaphor, it suggests the ship can be prevented from sailing even when there's still *some* water in the sea. As we have previously argued, "the blockade of establishment news coverage need not be total in order for an issue to remain unknown to all but a small segment of the public that actively seeks reporting on that issue."[4] The public's right to know is compromised not only by total blockades on coverage, but also by partial coverage that omits important facts and perspectives, frames discordant news as "opinion," and minimizes the significance of an issue by subjecting it to isolated coverage.[5]

The independent news reporting included in Project Censored's 2021–2022 story list highlights corporate abuses of power, which threaten human health and dignity; collusion between corporate and government officials, which violate the spirit if not the letter of the law; and conflicts of interest, which often implicate the very news outlets charged with informing the public.

Corporate news outlets sometimes *do* cover stories such as these. For example, *New York Times* health and science reporter Pam Belluck and her colleagues deserve credit for deep, extended coverage of conflicts of interest and regulatory irresponsibility in the Food and Drug Administration's approval of the Alzheimer's drug Aduhelm.[6] And, in March 2022, Bloomberg's Jef Feeley reported that pharmaceutical company Johnson & Johnson funded a 1971 experiment in which incarcerated people were given injections of asbestos and talc in their backs.[7] Both the FDA's approval of Aduhelm and Johnson & Johnson's sponsorship of unethical experiments on prisoners were stories Project Censored monitored during the past year—but neither appears on this year's list of "Censored" stories, due to the quality and originality of the establishment press coverage noted here.

But, as this year's Censored story list shows, as often as not the establishment press failed to provide adequate coverage of stories that involved corporate misconduct, government-corporate collusion, conflicts of interest, and press censorship. It is simply stunning that the big commercial news outlets have not paid more attention to this year's top story, that the fossil fuel industry continues to be subsidized by governments around the world at a rate of $11 million per minute, even in the midst of a global climate crisis. And the fact that Palestinian journalists are routinely being arrested by Israeli defense forces and censored on social media at the request of the Israeli government, the #14 story on this year's list, ought to have gotten far more coverage than it did. The independent news reports featured in this chapter provide a crucial check on the omissions of the corporate news media.

The 207 students at ten college and university campuses across the United States who identified, vetted, and summarized several hundred independent news stories in 2021–2022 are the forty-seventh cohort in Project Censored's long-term effort—dating back to its founding by Carl Jensen at Sonoma State University in 1976—to document systemic gaps and slant in corporate news coverage.

Across six decades, and now extended to include a digitally networked coalition of college and university campuses, the Project's student researchers, faculty evaluators, and expert judges identify, vet, and summarize news reporting of critical importance in an effort to ensure that the ship continues to sail, despite the documented short-comings of the nation's corporate news media.

Students' hands-on engagement in the review process strengthens their critical thinking skills and media literacy, sharpens their alertness to the telltale signs of news bias in who and what count as "newsworthy," and enhances their appreciation for the role of a truly free press in the democratic process. As students develop expertise in and passion for the news stories they research, publishing their findings online and in the Project's yearbook gives them a public voice they might not otherwise have. They come to recognize all the ways the ship might be kept from sailing.

We hope this year's top *Censored* story list will provide readers with similar experiences, alerting you not only to important news stories the corporate news media missed or mixed up, but also to the vital role played by independent journalists and news outlets in assuring that the ship does sail, despite the often perilous conditions of the sea.

ACKNOWLEDGMENTS: Reagan Haynie, Jen Lyons, Marcelle Swinburne, and Gabriella Valdez provided invaluable research assistance during the final vetting of this year's top *Censored* stories. Thanks to Elizabeth Boyd for helpful suggestions on a previous version of this chapter's introduction.

A NOTE ON RESEARCH AND EVALUATION OF *CENSORED* NEWS STORIES

How do we at Project Censored identify and evaluate independent news stories, and how do we know that the Top 25 stories that we bring forward each year are not only relevant and significant but also trustworthy? The answer is that every candidate news story undergoes rigorous review, which takes place in multiple stages during each annual cycle. Although adapted to take advantage of both the Project's expanding affiliates program and current technologies, the vetting process is quite similar to the one Project Censored founder Carl Jensen established more than forty years ago.

Candidate stories are initially identified by Project Censored professors and students, or are nominated by members of the general public who bring them to the Project's attention.[8] Together, faculty and students evaluate each candidate story in terms of its importance, timeliness, quality of sources, and inadequate corporate news coverage. If it fails on any one of these criteria, the story is deemed inappropriate and is excluded from further consideration.

Once Project Censored receives the candidate story, we undertake a second round of judgment, using the same criteria and updating the review to include any subsequent, competing corporate coverage. We post stories that pass this round of review on the Project's website as Validated Independent News stories (VINs).[9]

In early spring, we present all VINs in the current cycle to the faculty and students at all of our affiliate campuses, and to our panel of expert judges, who cast votes to winnow the candidate stories from several hundred to twenty-five.

Once the Top 25 list has been determined, Project Censored student interns begin another intensive review of each story using LexisNexis and ProQuest databases. Additional faculty and students contribute to this final stage of review.

The Top 25 finalists are then sent to our panel of judges, whose votes rank them in numerical order. At the same time, these experts—including media studies professors, professional journalists and editors, and a former commissioner of the Federal Communications Commission—offer their insights on the stories' strengths and weaknesses.[10]

Thus, by the time a story appears in the pages of *State of the Free Press*, it has undergone at least five distinct rounds of review and evaluation.

Although the stories that Project Censored brings forward may be socially and politically controversial—and sometimes even psychologically challenging—we are confident that each is the result of serious journalistic effort and deserves greater public attention.

THE TOP *CENSORED* STORIES AND MEDIA ANALYSIS OF 2021–2022

Fossil Fuel Industry Subsidized at Rate of $11 Million per Minute

Damian Carrington, "Fossil Fuel Industry Gets Subsidies of $11M a Minute, IMF Finds," *The Guardian*, October 6, 2021.

Eduardo Garcia, "Fossil Fuel Companies Receive $11 Million a Minute in Subsidies, New Report Reveals," Treehugger, October 21, 2021.

Student Researcher: Annie Koruga (Ohlone College)

Faculty Evaluator: Robin Takahashi (Ohlone College)

A comprehensive study of 191 nations, published by the International Monetary Fund in September 2021, found that globally the fossil fuel industry receives subsidies of $11 million per minute, the *Guardian* and Treehugger reported in October 2021. Fossil fuel companies received $5.9 trillion in subsidies in 2020, with support projected to rise to $6.4 trillion by 2025, according to the IMF report.[11]

Some of these subsidies are direct, including government policies that reduce prices (representing 8 percent of total fossil fuel subsidies) and provide tax exemptions (6 percent). But the biggest benefits to fossil fuel companies include what the IMF report calculated as indirect subsidies, including lack of liability for the health costs of deadly air pollution (42 percent), damages caused by extreme weather events linked to global warming (29 percent), and costs resulting from traffic collisions and congestion (15 percent). In effect, fossil fuel companies do not cover the damages their products cause, thereby artificially reducing the costs of fuels and leaving governments and taxpayers to pay the indirect costs.[12] As Eduardo Garcia reported for Treehugger, when government taxes on fossil fuels produce inadequate revenues, the consequences include a combination of higher taxes in other areas, increased government deficits, and decreased spending on public goods.

Pricing fossil fuels to cover both their supply and environmental costs would result in what the IMF study called the "efficient price" for fossil fuels. However, as the IMF found, not one national government currently prices fossil fuels at their efficient price. Instead, an estimated 99 percent of coal, 52 percent of road diesel, 47 percent of natural gas, and 18 percent of gasoline are priced at less than half their efficient price.

These subsidies are not evenly distributed across the globe. Just five countries—the United States, Russia, India, China, and Japan—are responsible for two-thirds of global fossil fuel subsidies. In the United States, the IMF estimated that the US government provided $730 billion in direct and indirect subsidies to fossil fuel companies in 2020. According to a July 2021 study by the Stockholm Environment Institute and Earth Track, continued US subsidies and exemptions "could increase the profitability of new oil and gas fields by more than 50% over the next decade," with nearly all of the subsidies serving to increase companies' profits.[13] If Congress were to stop providing tax breaks to the industry, the drilling of new oil wells in the US would decrease by about 25 percent, according to a September 2021 E&E News report citing an estimate by the industry's American Exploration & Production Council.[14]

The IMF study behind this independent reporting explained that "underpricing of fossil fuels is still pervasive across countries and is often substantial." As the *Guardian* reported, ending fossil fuel subsidies would "prevent nearly a million deaths a year from dirty air and raise trillions of dollars for governments."

"It's critical that governments stop propping up an industry that is in decline," Mike Coffin, a senior analyst at Carbon Tracker, told the *Guardian*. Necessary change "could start happening now, if not for government's entanglement with the fossil fuels industry in so many major economies," added Maria Pastukhova of E3G, a climate change think tank. In September 2021, Oil Change International announced that more than 200 civil society organizations from more than forty countries called on international leaders to end public finance for coal, oil, and gas.[15] Laurie van der Burg of Oil Change International noted, "It's an utter disgrace that rich countries are still spending more public money on fossil fuels than on climate [protection] finance."

Eliminating fossil fuel subsidies could lead to higher energy prices and, ultimately, political protests and social unrest. But, as the *Guardian* and Treehugger each reported, the IMF recommended a "comprehensive strategy" to protect consumers—especially low-income households—impacted by rising energy costs, and workers in displaced industries. As Ipek Gençsü told the *Guardian*, public information campaigns would be essential to counter popular opposition to subsidy reforms. He said ending fossil fuel subsidies could allow governments to redistribute savings "in the form of healthcare, education and other social services."

As of May 2022, no corporate news outlets had reported on the IMF's report, though a few industry publications such as Power Technology have done so.[16] In November 2021, the *New York Times* published an opinion piece focused on the claim by John Kerry, US special envoy for climate change, that government fossil fuel subsidies that artificially lower the price of coal, oil, and gas are "a definition of insanity."[17] But the *Times'* coverage was framed as opinion, and the editorial did not address the significant indirect subsidies identified in the IMF study, as reported by the *Guardian* and Treehugger. In January 2022, CNN published an article that all but defended fossil fuel subsidies.[18] CNN's coverage emphasized the potential for unrest caused by rollbacks of government subsidies, citing "protests that occasionally turned violent."

Wage Theft: US Businesses Suffer Few Consequences for Stealing Millions from Workers Every Year

Alexia Fernández Campbell and Joe Yerardi, "Ripping off Workers without Consequences," Center for Public Integrity, May 4, 2021.

Student Researcher: Annie Koruga (Ohlone College)

Faculty Advisor: Robin Takahashi (Ohlone College)

Thousands of US companies illegally underpay workers yet are seldom punished for doing so, Alexia Fernández Campbell and Joe Yerardi reported for the Center for Public Integrity in May 2021. Since its initial report, the Center has documented extensively that employers who "illegally underpay workers face few repercussions, even when they do so repeatedly. This widespread practice perpetuates income inequality, hitting lowest-paid workers hardest."[19]

Wage theft includes a range of illegal practices, such as paying less than minimum wage, withholding tips, not paying overtime, or requiring workers to work through breaks or off the clock. It impacts service workers, low-income workers, immigrant and guest workers, and communities of color the most, according to the Center for Public Integrity's "Cheated at Work" series, published from May 2021 to March 2022. An Economic Policy Institute study from 2017 found that just one form of wage theft—minimum wage violations—costs US workers an estimated $15 billion annually and impacts an estimated 17 percent of low-wage workers.[20]

Based on their independent analysis of fifteen years of reports from the US Department of Labor's Wage and Hour Division, Campbell and Yerardi concluded that companies engaging in wage theft "have little incentive to follow the law." In 2019 alone, the Department of Labor cited more than 8,500 employers for stealing approximately $287 million from workers. Major US corporations—including Halliburton, G4S Wackenhut and Circle K Stores—are among "the worst offenders," Campbell and Yerardi reported.

The labor department's Wage and Hour Division, which is charged with investigating federal wage-theft complaints, "rarely penalizes repeat offenders," Campbell and Yerardi explained. Between October 2005 and September 2020, the agency fined "only about one in four repeat offenders." In just 14 percent of the documented cases, companies were ordered to pay workers cash damages, and since 2005, the agency has allowed more than 16,000 employers to avoid paying more than $20 million owed in back wages.

Lack of resources at the federal level is blamed for lax enforcement. As of February 2021, the Wage and Hour Division employed only 787 investigators, a proportion of just one investigator per 182,000 workers covered by the Fair Labor Standards Act, Campbell and Yerardi noted. For comparison, in 1948 the division employed one investigator per 22,600 workers, or eight times the current proportion. Insufficient federal enforcement is "especially problematic" for workers in states that lack their own enforcement agencies: some fourteen states "lack the capacity to investigate wage theft claims or lack the ability to file lawsuits on behalf of victims," according to the 2017 Economic Policy Institute report.

Strong state and local laws can help to protect workers and could offset weak federal enforcement. Campbell and Yerardi's report mentioned local successes in Chicago (2013), Philadelphia (2016), and Minneapolis (2019), for example. But, as the reporters also noted, workers' rights advocates continue to seek federal reforms, appealing to Congress to allocate funding to double the number of federal investigators. Terri Gerstein observed in May 2021, writing for the Economic Policy Institute, that in lieu of federal enforcement, and in response to "widespread, entrenched, and often egregious violations of workplace laws, an increasing number of district attorneys and state attorneys general have been bringing criminal prosecutions against law-breaking employers."[21]

Nonetheless, wage theft appears to be on the rise. A September 2021 study by One Fair Wage and the University of California, Berkeley, Food Labor Research Center found that 34 percent of workers in the service sector reported experiencing more violations of their rights—including wage theft—in 2021, compared to 2020. Some 35 percent of surveyed service workers reported that tips plus additional wages did not bring them up to their state's minimum wage, and 46 percent reported that employers did not compensate "time and a half" for working overtime.[22]

Since May 2021, a handful of corporate news outlets, including CBS News, covered or republished the Center for Public Integrity's report on wage theft.[23] Corporate coverage tends to focus on specific instances involving individual employers, but otherwise pays little attention to wage theft as a systemic social problem or to anemic federal enforcement.[24] For example, a September 2021 NBC News report framed wage theft cases as "disputes" involving "dueling claims that are difficult to verify."[25] Verifying systemic wage theft has become easier, however, thanks to the Center for Public Integrity's March 2022 decision to make the data and code used in their yearlong "Cheated at Work" investigation available to the public.

The story may gain more traction now that Congress is starting to pay attention. In May 2022, US House lawmakers introduced H.R. 3712, known as the "Wage Theft Prevention and Wage Recovery Act of 2022," which would amend the Fair Labor Standards Act to protect workers from wage theft, according to Ariana Figueroa of the *Virginia Mercury*.[26] Minnesota congressperson Ilhan Omar said, "It is clear more DOL [Department of Labor] funding and additional federal reforms are needed in our localities in order to protect our most vulnerable workers."[27]

EPA Withheld Reports on Dangerous Chemicals

Sharon Lerner, "EPA Withheld Reports of Substantial Risk Posed by 1,240 Chemicals," The Intercept, November 1, 2021.

E. A. Crunden, "EPA's Failure to Disclose Chemical Health Risks Draws Ire," E&E News, January 5, 2022.

Student Researcher: Zach McNanna (North Central College)

Faculty Evaluator: Steve Macek (North Central College)

Since January 2019, the Environmental Protection Agency (EPA) has received more than 1,200 legally required disclosures about chemicals that present a "substantial risk of injury to health or the environment." All but one of the EPA's reports on these chemicals have been withheld from the public, as reported by Sharon Lerner in a November 2021 Intercept article.

According to Lerner, the EPA received at least 1,240 substantial risk reports since January 2019, but only one was publicly available. The undisclosed reports documented "serious harms, including eye corrosion, damage to the brain and nervous system, chronic toxicity to honeybees, and cancer in both people and animals" as well as environmental risks.

The reports include notifications about highly toxic polyfluoroalkyl substances (PFAS), chemical compounds that are known as "forever chemicals" because they build up in our bodies and never break down in the environment. The Environmental Working Group explains that "very small doses of PFAS have been linked to cancer, reproductive and immune system harm, and other diseases. For decades, chemical companies covered up evidence of PFAS' health hazards."[28]

Chemical companies are required by law to provide the EPA with any evidence that a chemical may pose a "substantial risk" to public health or the environment. It had been the EPA's regular practice to publish these "section 8(e)" reports, named for a section of the Toxic Substances Control Act (TSCA), in a searchable public database called ChemView. The EPA typically posted hundreds of these reports per year but quietly discontinued this practice in early 2019. In response to questions from the Intercept, the EPA blamed its inaction on resource and staffing constraints initiated during the Trump administration.

Even internally, the EPA's own staff had difficulty accessing the substantial risk reports, according to two EPA scientists, because they had not been uploaded to the databases most used by chemical risk assessors. "As a result, little—and perhaps none—of the information about these serious risks to health and the environment has been incorporated into the chemical assessments completed during this period," Lerner reported. "Basically, they are just going into a black hole," according to one EPA whistleblower Lerner interviewed. "We don't look at them. We don't evaluate them. And we don't check to see if they change our understanding of the chemical."

Claiming confidential trade secrets and intellectual property rights, chemical companies have long resisted policies that promote public disclosure. Lerner conveyed that "close observers of the industry believe that pressure from companies that held this [stance] was likely what led the Trump EPA to decide to stop publicly posting the reports." As Eve Gartner, an Earthjustice attorney quoted in the Intercept article, stated, "It is not easy to keep selling your chemicals when people know they likely cause cancer or other serious disease."

A few legal and industry-related publications have focused on a lawsuit filed in January 2022 by Public Employees for Environmental Responsibility (PEER) to compel the EPA to disclose TCSA section 8(e) reports. E. A. Crunden of E&E News first reported that PEER filed the complaint after the EPA failed to respond to a Freedom of Information Act request seeking information about the missing reports. However, Crunden reported,

"EPA has committed to posting real-time information for industry members regarding the chemical approval process for their products, even as sharing the 8(e) reports has fallen by the wayside." Kyla Bennett, PEER's science policy director, who previously worked for the EPA, told Crunden, "It is incredible that EPA has funds to post real-time data about the regulatory status of new chemicals for industry's convenience but does not have funds to alert workers and consumers about substantial health and environmental hazards of these same chemicals."

Despite the concerns expressed by the EPA whistleblowers, the concealment of 8(e) substantial risk reports to appease chemical industry pressure has been mostly ignored by the corporate media. Apart from "EPA Exposed," the Intercept's extensive nine-part investigation of the EPA's dangerous conduct, toxic culture, and tendency to yield to industry pushback, only a handful of niche publications have reported on the matter. Bloomberg Law covered the story in December 2021, citing the Intercept's reporting.[29] However, the article downplayed the role of chemical industry pressure, instead pointing out that "businesses might need the information to decide whether to purchase a chemical, design an alternative, or improve its health and safety measures."

Notably, the *National Law Review* reported on January 8, 2022, that PEER's original Freedom of Information Act request was "built upon information reported in a November 2021 article in The Intercept."[30] PEER's subsequent lawsuit asked the court "to enter an order declaring that EPA wrongfully withheld requested documents and to issue a permanent injunction directing the EPA to disclose all wrongfully withheld documents."

Just weeks after PEER's complaint was filed, the EPA announced in a press release on February 3, 2022, that it would resume publishing 8(e) substantial risk reports in ChemView.[31] Clearly, independent journalism contributed significantly to this outcome. Had it not been for the work of investigative journalist Sharon Lerner at the Intercept, EPA whistleblowers would not have had a platform to share concerns that ultimately led the agency to resume these critical public disclosures.

At Least 128 Members of Congress Invested in Fossil Fuel Industry

David Moore, "Senators Cling to Fossil Fuel Stocks as World Heats Up," Sludge, November 5, 2021.

David Moore, "GOP Rep Picks up Millions in Pipeline Stock," Sludge, December 10, 2021.

David Moore, "At Least 100 House Members Are Invested in Fossil Fuels," Sludge, December 29, 2021.

Julia Rock and Andrew Perez, "Lauren Boebert's Anti-Climate Legislation Is a Self-Enrichment Scheme," *Jacobin*, September 13, 2021.

Student Researcher: Annie Koruga (Ohlone College)

Faculty Evaluator: Robin Takahashi (Ohlone College)

A series of Sludge articles written by David Moore in November and December of 2021 reported that at least 100 US Representatives and twenty-eight US Senators have financial interests in the fossil fuel industry.

According to Moore, some seventy-four Republicans, fifty-nine Democrats, and one Independent have interests in the fossil fuel industry. In both chambers, more Republicans than Democrats are invested in the industry, and the ten most heavily invested House members are all Republicans. However, the first- and third-most-invested senators, Joe Manchin (WV), who owns up to $5.5 million worth of fossil fuel industry assets, and John Hickenlooper (CO), who owns up to $1 million, are Democrats. Additionally, Senate Democrats own up to $8,604,000 in fossil fuel assets, more than double the Senate Republicans' $3,994,126 in fossil fuel assets. Aside from Senator Manchin, and Representative Trey Hollingsworth (R-IN), who owns up to $5.2 million worth of stock in oil and gas pipelines, many of the other deeply invested congressional leaders are Texas Republicans, including Representative Van Taylor, who owns up to $12.4 million worth of fossil fuel assets.

Besides directly owning stock or industry assets, members of Congress also profit from the fossil fuel industry in other ways. For example, as Julia Rock and Andrew Perez reported in a September 2021 article for *Jacobin*, the household of Representative Lauren Boebert (R-CO) received at least $938,987 from the fossil fuel industry in 2019 and 2020 through her husband's employment as a consultant for Terra Energy Partners, an oil and gas company that drills on federal lands. Boebert initially failed to report her husband's income as a fossil fuel consultant on her 2019 congressional financial disclosure forms.

Many of these congressional leaders hold seats on influential energy-related committees. In the Senate, Manchin is chair of the Energy and Natural Resources

Committee, Tina Smith (D-MN) chairs the Agriculture Subcommittee on Rural Development and Energy, Tom Carper (D-DE) is chair of the Committee on the Environment and Public Works, and Susan Collins (R-ME) and Bill Haggerty (R-TN) both serve on the Appropriations Subcommittee on Energy and Water Development, to name some of the most prominent senators.

In the House, members serving on influential committees include Boebert, who serves on the House Committee on Natural Resources, and Kelly Armstrong (R-ND), a member of the Energy and Commerce Committee. Armstrong owns up to $10.6 million in fossil fuel assets, including hundreds of oil and gas wells. Nine of the twenty-two Republican members of the Energy and Commerce Committee are invested in the fossil fuel industry.

As Project Censored detailed in the #4 story on the Top 25 list two years ago, these individuals' personal financial interests as investors often conflict with their obligation as elected legislators to serve the public interest.[32] Senator Manchin cut the Clean Electricity Performance Program, a system that would phase out coal, from President Biden's climate bill, and Representative Vicente Gonzalez (D-TX) delayed passage of the Democrats' budget bill when it included a clean-energy standard, according to Moore's December 29, 2021, article for Sludge.

The fossil fuel industry is deeply entrenched in Washington, lobbying to influence policy on crucial issues such as the transition to carbon-neutral energy and green infrastructure. According to OpenSecrets, the oil and gas industries spent $119.3 million on lobbying in 2021.[33] During the 2020 election cycle, the fossil fuel industry gave more than $40 million to congressional candidates, including $8.7 million to Democrats and $30.8 million to Republicans.[34]

Moore highlighted why these conflicts of interest are so deadly in his December 29, 2021, article: "In May, the International Energy Agency laid out an ultimatum to policy makers: for the world to have a 50/50 chance at reaching net-zero emissions by 2050, no new fossil fuel developments can be approved, starting immediately." And, yet, as Moore explained, production of oil and gas is projected to grow 50 percent by 2030 without congressional action. The fact that so many lawmakers have invested considerable sums in the fossil fuel industry makes it extremely unlikely that Congress will do much to rein in oil and gas production.

As of May 21, 2022, no corporate outlets had covered the full extent to which members of Congress are financially invested in the fossil fuel industry. Sludge ran a similar analysis of congressional fossil-fuel industry investments in 2020; that report also garnered no corporate coverage.[35] There have been only two articles by Business Insider that are tangentially related to members of Congress holding stocks in fossil fuel companies.[36] But only the independent media have detailed the exact dollar amounts that our legislators have sunk into the oil and gas business. Corporate news outlets have only reported on the fact that clean energy proposals are stalled in Congress, not the financial conflicts of interest that are the likely cause of this lack of progress.

Dark Money Interference in US Politics Undermines Democracy

Igor Derysh, "Dark-Money Groups Fighting Biden's Supreme Court Pick Also Funded Big Lie, Capitol Riot," *Salon*, March 8, 2022.

Student Researcher: Kira Levenson (University of Massachusetts Amherst)

Faculty Evaluator: Allison Butler (University of Massachusetts Amherst)

Conservative dark money organizations opposing President Biden's Supreme Court nomination also helped fuel conspiracy theories of election fraud after the 2020 election, as Igor Derysh reported for Salon in March 2022. Derysh summarized a recent report from the watchdog group Accountable.US, which revealed that organizations such as Judicial Crisis Network (JCN), the Federalist Society, and the 85 Fund had previously donated millions of dollars to groups involved in the January 6 Capitol riot. These same organizations, among others, were also responsible for funding vicious attack ads on Judge Ketanji Brown Jackson, Biden's Supreme Court nominee, arguing that Democrats were using Jackson as a pawn to promote a "woke agenda."

"It should worry us all that the groups leading the fight against Biden's historic nomination of Judge Jackson to the Supreme Court are tied to the Jan. 6 insurrection and efforts to undermine confidence in the 2020 election," Kyle Herrig, president of Accountable.US, told Salon.

"With American institutions and our democracy itself under constant attack from every direction, the importance of Judge Jackson's swift and successful confirmation cannot be overstated."

The influence of dark money—political spending by organizations that are not required to disclose their donors—presents a major challenge to the swift functioning of the judicial nomination and confirmation process, and the US government as a whole. In contrast to direct contributions to candidates, parties, and issue campaigns, which must be disclosed to the public, dark money contributions purposely hide donors' names from public view. As a result, dark money deeply influences political decisions in favor of select individuals' or groups' agendas rather than in support of the public's best interests.

According to a 2020 report by OpenSecrets, JCN also invested millions of dollars to help confirm Justices Gorsuch and Kavanaugh.[37] Most recently, dark money groups, including JCN, were heavily involved in the 2020 Supreme Court confirmation hearings of Judge Amy Coney Barrett, donating money to politicians such as Senator Lindsey Graham (R-SC), who were key players in advancing Judge Barrett's confirmation. Critics called Judge Barrett's confirmation process unusually quick, making the interference of dark money all the more unsettling.[38]

"Those wins [by dark money organizations] often come at the expense of regular Americans, stripping away protections for minority voters, reproductive rights, the environment, public health, and workers," Senator Sheldon Whitehouse (D-RI) wrote in a February 2022 *Washington Post* op-ed.[39] "And they often degrade our democracy: greenlighting gerrymandering, protecting dark money, and suppressing the vote."

Conservative dark money groups constitute a multi-million-dollar spider web. According to Accountable.US, the organization Donors Trust, supported by the Koch network, contributed at least $20 million to several groups that challenged the validity of the 2020 election.[40] That same year, Donors Trust also gave more than $48 million to the 85 Fund, then more than $700,000 to the Federalist Society.[41] In 2019 and 2020, the Bradley Foundation donated more than $3.5 million to groups connected to Leonard Leo, co-chairperson of the Federalist Society.[42] Cleta Mitchell, an attorney who serves on the Bradley Foundation's board, aided Trump's effort to get Georgia's Secretary of State to assist in an attempt to overturn Joe Biden's victory in the 2020 election.[43]

The role of dark money in politics, including opposition to Biden's Supreme Court nomination of Judge Jackson, has been a noteworthy topic in corporate media as recently as February 2022. However, coverage has focused on the political tensions erupting from Judge Jackson's nomination and dark money influence on previous Supreme Court nominations, largely ignoring the presence of dark money backing Trump's claims of voter fraud or supporting those implicated in the Capitol riot.

More recently, Republican and Democratic senators sparred over dark money alliances during Judge Jackson's confirmation hearings, according to NBC News.[44] Senator Chuck Grassley (R-IA) warned of "the troubling role [that] far left dark money groups" such as Demand Justice "have played in this administration's judicial selection process." Meanwhile, Senator Sheldon Whitehouse (D-RI) scoffed at Republican lawmakers' supposed concern over dark money, given that they have long pushed to protect laws that allow donors to make major campaign donations without disclosing their identities.[45]

In January 2022, the *New York Times* tracked the scale of dark money spending in the 2020 election, focusing on many new Democratic efforts to utilize dark money, in comparison to previous years when Democrats actively campaigned against the presence of dark money in politics.[46] In February 2022, Business Insider highlighted the surge in dark money donations from advocacy groups used to fight Judge Jackson's nomination and confirmation process.[47] Op-eds featured in both the *Wall Street Journal* and the *Washington Post* covered the discussion of dark money during Judge Jackson's confirmation hearings. A March 2022 *Mother Jones* report discussed JCN's influence on conservative politics and federal judicial nominations, and how dark money discourse played out shortly after Biden nominated Judge Jackson to the Supreme Court.[48] However, none of the articles featured in the corporate press covered dark money supporting Trump's Big Lie, the impact such funding had on promoting and reinforcing anti-democratic ideology, or the ramifications of how such dark money spending erodes public trust in government and the election process.

6. Corporate Consolidation Causing Record Inflation in Food Prices

Brett Wilkins, "New Report on 'Grocery Cartels' Details Exploitive Retailer Monopolies," Common Dreams, November 15, 2021.

David Dayen and Rakeen Mabud, "How We Broke the Supply Chain," *American Prospect*, January 31, 2022.

Kenny Stancil, "Corporate Greed the 'Real Culprit Behind Rising Prices,' Researchers Say," Common Dreams, October 14, 2022.

Nina Lakhani, Aliya Uteuova, and Alvin Chang, "Revealed: The True Extent of America's Food Monopolies, and Who Pays the Price," *The Guardian*, July 14, 2021.

Student Researchers: Mack Parlatore (North Central College) and Ethan Reiderer (Saint Michael's College)

Faculty Evaluators: Steve Macek (North Central College) and Rob Williams (Saint Michael's College)

Corporate consolidation is a main driver of record inflation in food prices, despite claims by media pundits and partisan commentators to the contrary. As the economy attempts to shake off the lingering impacts of COVID-19 and Americans struggle to stretch their dollars, many have blamed supply chain disruptions and the Biden administration's stimulus package for soaring prices. However, in an October 2021 article for Common Dreams, Kenny Stancil documents that food producers, distributors, and grocery store chains are engaging in pandemic profiteering and taking advantage of "decades of consolidation, which has given a handful of corporations an ever-greater degree of market control and with it, the power to set prices."

Stancil's article reported on new research by the Groundwork Collaborative that suggested price gouging was rampant in America's oligopoly-controlled food industry. In a paradigmatic case, the beef industry is simultaneously among the most consolidated and the most impacted by inflation. The study found that with only four conglomerates controlling 80 percent of the market, the cost of beef had risen a startling 12 percent since 2020. The egg industry also saw a dramatic increase in prices that sparked investigations and lawsuits across the country.

Record profits for food producers and grocers during the pandemic have raised questions about why these companies continue to shortchange their customers and employees. Kroger, the largest supermarket chain in the country, cited rising inflation as the reason for hiking prices in their stores even as they cut worker pay by 8 percent. Yet, as Stancil explained, Kroger's CEO publicly gloated that "a little bit of inflation is always good for business," a motto that many corporations seemed to adopt while making attempts to conceal high profit margins since the start of the pandemic.

A joint investigation by Food and Water Watch and the *Guardian* provides new details on the "market dominance" of the largest US food producers. In a July 2021 article for the *Guardian*, Nina Lakhani, Aliya Uteuova, and Alvin Chang reported that a handful of "food giants"—including Kraft Heinz, General Mills, Conagra, Unilever, and Del Monte—control an average of 64 percent of sales of sixty-one popular grocery items. Amanda Starbuck, a policy analyst at Food and Water Watch, told the *Guardian*, "It's a system designed to funnel money into the hands of corporate shareholders and executives while exploiting farmers and workers and deceiving consumers about choice, abundance and efficiency."

As an example of market consolidation and the illusion of consumer choice, the *Guardian* noted that three companies own 93 percent of carbonated soft drink brands; 55 percent of the market share in canned corn is controlled by four firms; and PepsiCo owns five of the most popular dip brands, including Tostitos, Lay's, and Fritos, controlling 88 percent of the market. Despite supermarket aisles full of shelves stacked with different breakfast cereals, just three companies—General Mills, Kellogg's, and Post—produce 73 percent of the cereals on offer. As for grocery stores themselves, Starbuck told the *Guardian* that supermarket mergers have eliminated smaller grocers and regional chains, and the nation has "roughly one-third fewer grocery stores today than we did 25 years ago."

A report for the *American Prospect* by Rakeen Mabud, chief economist at the Groundwork Collaborative, and David Dayen revealed that one of the most common inflation scapegoats, supply chain problems, is itself a consequence of consolidation. They argued that corporate-controlled supply chains were designed for "maximum profit rather than reliably getting things to people," ensuring that "the problems that arose in the pandemic folded in on themselves." Just three global alliances of ocean shippers are responsible for 80 percent of all cargo, allowing them to charge a premium even as delivery times soared during the pandemic. These shippers raked in "nearly $80 billion in the first three quarters of 2021, twice as much as in the entire ten-year period from 2010 to 2020," by increasing their rates as much as tenfold.

The establishment press has covered the current wave

of inflation exhaustively, but only rarely will discuss the market power of giant firms as a possible cause, and then usually only to reject it.

After the Biden administration identified consolidation in the meat industry as a cause of price increases in September 2021, the corporate media were overwhelmingly dismissive, treating administration attempts to link inflation to consolidation as a rhetorical move meant to distract from conservative critiques of Biden's stimulus program. One *New York Times* article, from January 2022, attempted to debunk consolidation as a factor in inflation, reasoning that "consolidation has been high for years, but inflation has been low for decades."[49] Another *Times* piece briefly touched on consolidation's role but went on to blame "broken supply chains and high demand for goods from consumers still flush with government-provided cash," and foregrounded perspectives from business lobbying groups such as the North American Meat Institute and the US Chamber of Commerce.[50] None of these articles presented the sort of detailed exploration provided by the *American Prospect* or the *Guardian* on the ways market structures and corporate power might contribute to rising food prices.

To its credit, in May 2022 the *Times* did publish an incisive commentary by the Groundwork Collaborative's executive director, Lindsay Owens, arguing that giant corporations are "using the cover of inflation to raise prices and increase profits" and pointing out that in industries such as meatpacking and shipping, "pricing power comes from concentrated market power."[51] In the same month, *Forbes* published a lengthy editorial by sustainable food advocate Errol Schweizer criticizing oligopolistic food companies for using the pandemic to reap windfall profits.[52] But these isolated opinion pieces were far outnumbered by the hundreds, even thousands, of reports and analyses by commercial media outlets that blamed everything *but* oligopolistic price gouging for the rising cost of groceries.

Concerns for Journalistic Independence as Gates Foundation Gives $319 Million to News Outlets

Alan MacLeod, "Revealed: Documents Show Bill Gates Has Given $319 Million to Media Outlets," MintPress News, November 15, 2021.

Student Researcher: Reagan Haynie (Loyola Marymount University)

Faculty Evaluator: Mickey Huff (Diablo Valley College)

The Bill and Melinda Gates Foundation has donated more than $319 million to fund news outlets, journalism centers and training programs, press associations, and specific media campaigns, raising questions about conflicts of interest and journalistic independence, Alan MacLeod reported for MintPress News in November 2021. "Today, it is possible for an individual to train as a reporter thanks to a Gates Foundation Grant, find work at a Gates-funded outlet, and to belong to a press association funded by Gates," MacLeod wrote.

Based on examination of more than 30,000 individual grants, MacLeod reported that the Gates Foundation provides funding for "many of America's most important news outlets"—including NPR (which has received $24.6 million in Gates funding), NBC ($4.3M), CNN ($3.6M), and the *Atlantic* ($1.4M)—and "a myriad of influential foreign organizations"—such as the *Guardian* ($12.9M), *Der Spiegel* ($5.4M), *Le Monde* ($4M), BBC ($3.6M), *El País* ($3.9M), and Al Jazeera ($1M). MacLeod's report includes a number of Gates-funded news outlets that also regularly feature in Project Censored's annual Top 25 story lists, such as the Solutions Journalism Network ($7.2M), The Conversation ($6.6M), the Bureau of Investigative Journalism ($1M), and ProPublica ($1M) in addition to the *Guardian* and the *Atlantic*.

Direct awards to news outlets often targeted specific issues, MacLeod reported. For example, CNN received $3.6 million to support "journalism on the everyday inequalities endured by women and girls across the world," according to one grant.

Another grant earmarked $2.3 million for the *Texas Tribune* "to increase public awareness and engagement of education reform issues in Texas." As MacLeod noted, given Bill Gates's advocacy of the charter school movement—which undermines teachers' unions and effectively aims to privatize the public education system—"a cynic might interpret this as planting pro-corporate charter school propaganda into the media, disguised as objective news reporting."

In addition to cause-focused grants, the Gates Foundation has also provided $12 million to directly fund press and journalism associations. One organization, the National Newspaper Publishers Association, which represents more than 200 outlets, received $3.2 million in Gates Foundation funding.

Additional Gates Foundation funds help to train journalists around the world "in the form of scholarships, courses, and workshops," MacLeod reported. Given Gates's known interests in the fields of education, health, and global development, the influence of Gates Foundation money on the training of journalists who will go on to work in those fields is another way that, in MacLeod's words, the Gates Foundation maintains a "low profile" with "long tentacles."

Although the Gates Foundation has often been lauded for its philanthropy, critics have warned about the ability of Bill Gates and other billionaires to use their extraordinary wealth to influence news and set the public agenda. From the acquisition of the *Washington Post* by Jeff Bezos, the wealthy Amazon founder, to Elon Musk's stake in Twitter, tech billionaires increasingly wield "clear and obvious forms of media influence," MacLeod wrote. (The publication of the MintPress News report predated the news that Musk sought to buy Twitter, a development that would only underscore the concerns raised by MacLeod.)

Noting that receiving Gates Foundation money does not make any media outlet "irredeemably corrupt," MacLeod nonetheless warned that Gates's money does introduce "a glaring conflict of interest whereby the very institutions we rely on to hold accountable one of the richest and most powerful men in the planet's history are quietly being funded by him."

No major corporate news outlets appear to have covered this issue. Independent journalist Matt Taibbi discussed it with Joe Rogan a few weeks after the publication of MacLeod's report.[53] The Grayzone republished the original MintPress News report, and Blaze Media published a story based on the MintPress story.[54] As far back as 2011, the *Seattle Times* published an article investigating how the Gates Foundation's "growing support of media organizations blurs the line between journalism and advocacy."[55]

CIA Discussed Plans to Kidnap or Kill Julian Assange

Zach Dorfman, Sean D. Naylor and Michael Isikoff, "Kidnapping, Assassination and a London Shoot-Out: Inside the CIA's Secret War Plans Against WikiLeaks," Yahoo News, September 26, 2021.

Student Researcher: Annie Koruga (Ohlone College)

Faculty Evaluator: Robin Takahashi (Ohlone College)

In late 2017, the Central Intelligence Agency (CIA), then under the direction of Mike Pompeo, seriously considered plans to kidnap or assassinate WikiLeaks founder Julian Assange, according to a September 2021 Yahoo News investigation. The Yahoo News report featured interviews with more than thirty former US officials, eight of whom detailed US plans to abduct Assange and three of whom described the development of plans to kill him. According to one former official, discussions of kidnapping or killing Assange occurred "at the highest levels" of the Trump administration. Yahoo News described the plans as "part of an unprecedented CIA campaign" against Assange and WikiLeaks. "There seemed to be no boundaries," according to the former senior counterintelligence official.

Potential scenarios proposed by the CIA and Trump administration officials included crashing into a Russian vehicle carrying Assange in order to grab him, shooting the tires of an airplane carrying Assange in order to prevent its takeoff, and engaging in a gun battle through the streets of London. US officials asked "their British counterparts to do the shooting if gunfire was required, and the British agreed," Yahoo News reported, on the basis of testimony by one former senior administration official. Senior CIA officials went so far as to request "sketches" or "options" detailing methods to kill Assange.

Some of the former officials interviewed by Yahoo News dismissed the planning as far-fetched. It was "unhinged and ridiculous," according to one former CIA official; another former senior counterintelligence official characterized the discussions as "just Trump being Trump." Nevertheless, at least one senior official noted that there were discussions of "whether killing Assange was possible and whether it was legal."

According to a 2020 Grayzone report, UC Global—a Spanish-based private security company hired by Ecuador to protect its London embassy, where Assange was living—spied on Assange and his contacts for the United States.[56] Its targets included Assange's legal team, US journalists, a US member of Congress, and the Ecuadoran diplomats whom UC Global had been hired to protect.

US plans to kidnap or assassinate Julian Assange have received little to no establishment news coverage in the United States, other than scant summaries by Business Insider and The Verge, and tangential coverage by Reuters, each based on the original Yahoo News report.[57] An October 2021 *New York Times* article made passing reference to the CIA's plot to kidnap or kill Assange, but noted this extraordinary point only as part of the argument made by Assange's lawyers to oppose his extradition to the United States.[58] The story received more coverage in the United Kingdom, including reports in the *Daily Mail*, the *Guardian*, and the Independent.[59] Al Jazeera ran an extensive story addressing the question, "Why isn't the CIA's plan to kidnap Julian Assange making more headlines?"[60] Among US independent news outlets, *Democracy Now!* featured an interview with Michael Isikoff, one of the Yahoo News reporters who broke the story, and Jennifer Robinson, a human rights attorney who has been advising Julian Assange and WikiLeaks since 2010.[61] *Rolling Stone* and The Hill also published articles based on the original Yahoo News report.[62]

New Laws Preventing Dark Money Disclosures Sweep the Nation

Alyce McFadden, "GOP Bill Would Codify IRS Rule Hiding 'Dark Money' Donors," OpenSecrets, May 27, 2021.

David Moore, "Florida Republican Introduces ALEC Bill to Protect Dark Money in Politics," Sludge, February 25, 2022.

Donald Shaw, "Laws Preventing Dark Money Disclosure Are Sweeping the Nation," Sludge, June 15, 2021.

Donald Shaw, "Noem Bill Would Make Dark Money Disclosure Illegal," Sludge, February 19, 2021.

Donald Shaw, "Omnibus Bill Contains Dark Money Riders," Sludge, March 10, 2022.

Student Researcher: Zach McNanna (North Central College)

Faculty Evaluator: Steve Macek (North Central College)

Across the United States, Republican lawmakers are pushing legislation modeled after a policy authored by the American Legislative Exchange Council (ALEC) that makes it illegal to compel nonprofit organizations to disclose the identity of their donors. In a June 2021 article for Sludge, Donald Shaw explained how these bills create a loophole allowing wealthy individuals and groups to pass "dark money" anonymously to 501(c) organizations which in turn can make independent expenditures to influence elections (or contribute to other organizations that make independent political expenditures, such as Super PACs), effectively shielding the ultimate source of political funds from public scrutiny. "These bills are about making dark money darker," Aaron McKean, legal counsel for the Campaign Legal Center, told Shaw.

As Shaw outlined, ALEC "brings together corporate activists, lobbyists, and state lawmakers to partner up on the crafting of rightwing legislation and other initiatives." The organization is commonly referred to as a "corporate bill mill" and has crafted other controversial laws, such as Stand Your Ground.

Legislation inspired by the ALEC bill that makes possible the silent transfer of political funds has been proposed, has passed, or is currently pending in Oklahoma, Arizona, Mississippi, Utah, West Virginia, Arkansas, Iowa, Tennessee, North Carolina, South Dakota, and

Florida. In South Dakota, Governor Kristi Noem, whose first gubernatorial campaign was supported by a Super PAC that received $95,000 in dark money donations, signed a version of the ALEC bill into law in early 2021. As Sludge reported on February 19, 2021, the South Dakota law passed by overwhelming majorities in both houses of the Republican-dominated state legislature, despite the fact that, in 2016, voters passed a ballot measure requiring disclosure of "the identity of donors who give more than $100 to organizations for the purpose of political expenditures," a requirement the legislature repealed a year later.

The impact of ALEC's model policy has extended beyond state legislatures. In a March 2022 article for Sludge, Shaw documented that the federal omnibus appropriations bill for fiscal year 2022 contained a rider exempting political groups that declare themselves "social welfare organizations" from reporting their donors, and another preventing the Securities and Exchange Commission from "requiring corporations to publicly disclose more of their political and lobbying spending."

Moreover, according to a May 2021 article from Open-Secrets, Senate Minority Leader Mitch McConnell (R-KY), Senator Mike Braun (R-IN), and forty-three other Republican senators have announced their support for the "Don't Weaponize the IRS Act," which would prevent the IRS from requiring that 501(c)(4) nonprofits disclose their top donors.

Beginning with the Supreme Court's 2010 decision in *Citizens United v. FEC*, a series of court rulings, Republican-backed laws, and executive orders has progressively insulated political spending by corporations and wealthy individuals from government regulation and reporting requirements. However, Democratic politicians and good government organizations have begun to push back, often citing bipartisan support for stronger enforcement of campaign finance laws and transparency in elections.[63] On April 27, 2021, thirty-eight Democratic senators sent a letter to Treasury Secretary Janet Yellen and IRS Commissioner Charles Rettig urging them to roll back an anti-disclosure rule put in place by the Trump Administration.[64] In addition, the Democrats' comprehensive voting-rights bill, the For the People Act, would have compelled the disclosure of all contributions by individuals who surpass $10,000 in donations in a given reporting period. The bill was passed by the House but died in the Senate.[65]

The Washington Post reported on Democrats pressuring the Biden administration to repeal Trump-era dark money rules, but made no mention of the wave of state laws designed to outlaw dark money disclosures.[66] The Associated Press reported on Governor Noem's defense of the South Dakota law shielding dark money donors, but failed to discuss ALEC's model bill or the other states considering similar legislation.[67] Outside of local reports appearing in regional papers such as the *Tampa Bay Times*, there has been little acknowledgment in the establishment press of the stream of ALEC-inspired bills passing through state legislatures that seek to keep the source of so much of the money spent to influence elections hidden in the shadows.[68]

Major Media Outlets Lobby Against Regulation of "Surveillance Advertising"

Lee Fang, "Major Media Outlets That Use Invasive User Tracking Are Lobbying Against Regulation," The Intercept, February 1, 2022.

Student Researcher: Christian Vogt (Saint Michael's College)

Faculty Evaluator: Robert Williams (Saint Michael's College)

The world's most popular social media apps and platforms—Facebook, YouTube, Instagram, TikTok—collect users' data and employ it to target them with tailored advertising. This sort of "surveillance advertising" has become a ubiquitous and extremely profitable practice. As Lee Fang reported for the Intercept in February 2022, the Biden administration's Federal Trade Commission (FTC) is now seeking to regulate the collection of user data. But lobbyists for online advertisers and their big media clients are pushing back.

The Interactive Advertising Bureau (IAB), a trade group that represents media outlets utilizing digital advertising, has strenuously opposed FTC efforts to restrict the collection and monetization of user data. As Fang wrote, the IAB represents CNN, the *New York Times*, NBC, the *Washington Post*, Fox News, and "dozens of other media companies."

The IAB argues that targeted advertising—and, by extension, the siphoning of user data—has become necessary due to declining revenues from print sales and subscriptions. Surveillance advertising sales have soared for most media conglomerates over the past decade as traditional ad sales have shrunk. Non-digital advertising revenue decreased from $124.8 billion in 2011 to $89.8 billion in 2020, while digital advertising revenue rose from $31.9 billion to $152.2 billion in the same period, according to Pew Research.[69]

A 2019 study by privacy researchers Timothy Libert and Reuben Binns found that "the democratic role of the press is being undermined by reliance on the 'surveillance capitalism' funding model." They concluded that "news sites are more reliant on third-parties than non-news sites, user privacy is compromised to a greater degree on news sites, and privacy policies lack transparency in regards to observed tracking behaviors."[70]

The personal information collected by online media is typically sold to aggregators, such as Oracle BlueKai and OpenX, that exploit user data—including data describing minors—to create predictive models of users' behavior, which are then sold to advertising agencies. The covert nature of surveillance advertising makes it difficult for users to opt out. For example, the New York Times Company's privacy policy openly states, "We don't currently respond to [browser-based 'Do Not Track'] signals."[71]

The user information collected by media sites also enables direct manipulation of public perceptions of political issues, as famously happened when the British consulting firm Cambridge Analytica tapped into personal data from millions of Facebook users to craft campaign propaganda during the 2016 US presidential election.[72] The mass transfer of user data to third-party aggregators also makes it virtually impossible to ensure that such data collection does not violate existing regulations protecting child privacy online. Indeed, the FTC fined OpenX $2 million in December 2021 for illegal collection of minors' location in violation of the commission's Children's Online Privacy Protection Rule.[73] Major news outlets chose not to cover the story, Fang wrote, because "they would have had to acknowledge an awkward reality," that they also use (or have used) OpenX to place targeted ads of their own.

In July 2021, President Biden issued an executive order on competition that included a directive for the FTC to develop rules regarding the "surveillance of users." In December 2021, the activist group Accountable Tech petitioned the FTC to prohibit surveillance advertising altogether. In response, the commission has begun crafting and taking public comments on regulations designed to rein in online data collection by digital advertisers. As Fang reported, the IAB responded by demanding that the FTC oppose any ban on surveillance ads, claiming that thousands of media outlets would be hurt by such a ban. According to OpenSecrets, the IAB spent $160,000 on lobbying efforts in 2021, much of it related to proposed legislation restricting the collection and exploitation of online personal data.[74]

The corporate media have reported the FTC's openness to new rules limiting the collection and exploitation of user data, but have generally not drawn attention to IAB lobbying against the proposed regulations. For example, in September 2021, the *Wall Street Journal* and the *Washington Post* ran articles on Accountable Tech's petition and the FTC's consideration of new regulations governing surveillance advertising.[75] However, neither outlet discussed IAB, its lobbying on this issue, or the big media clients the organization represents.

Wealthy Nations Continue to Drive Climate Change, with Devastating Impacts on Poorer Countries

Sonja Klinsky, "Climate Change Is a Justice Issue—These 6 Charts Show Why," The Conversation, November 3, 2021.

Tawanda Karombo, "These African Countries Are Among the World's Worst Hit by Climate Change," Quartz Africa, January 27, 2021, updated December 1, 2021.

Student Researcher: Lena Anderson (Diablo Valley College)

Faculty Evaluator: Mickey Huff (Diablo Valley College)

In a November 2021 article for The Conversation, Sonja Klinsky outlined how and why poorer regions are disproportionately affected by climate change. Wealthier nations, such as the United States, Canada, and Australia, release roughly 100 times the per-capita greenhouse gas emissions as many African countries, yet the responsibility for undoing this damage has long fallen on the shoulders of the most vulnerable victims of climate change.

Fossil fuels release carbon dioxide (CO_2) into the atmosphere, where it lingers for hundreds of years. CO_2 locks in heat, and its gradual buildup warms the planet, leading to the melting of polar ice caps, rising sea levels, and catastrophic natural disasters such as wildfires and floods. But the primary emitters of carbon are often not the ones bearing the brunt of the climate crisis. As sea levels rise, people in small island countries, such as Tuvalu and the Marshall Islands, will struggle to survive. In 2019, according to a Quartz Africa report by Tawanda Karombo in 2021, Mozambique, Zimbabwe, and Niger all experienced drastic, unpredictable changes in temperature and precipitation, causing food shortages, economic disasters, and hundreds of avoidable fatalities. "Many of these countries and communities bear little responsibility for the cumulative greenhouse gas emissions driving climate change. At the same time, they have the fewest resources available to protect themselves," Klinsky observed.

Only 5 percent of the world's population was responsible for 36 percent of the total greenhouse gas emissions from 1990 to 2015. The impoverished half of the global population accounted for less than 6 percent of all emissions in that period. But because greenhouse gases stay in the atmosphere for hundreds of years, it is misleading to consider only a twenty-year window. According to Klinsky, since the 1750s, the United States has emitted 29 percent of all global CO_2 emissions, or 457 billion tons, while the entire continent of Africa has emitted only 3 percent, or 43 billion tons.[76]

The 2015 Paris Climate Accords included a lofty promise by the United States to address the needs of low-income countries that suffer the disastrous effects of climate change.[77] The United States guaranteed that industrialized nations would contribute $100 billion a year to tackle climate change, beginning in 2020. However, they missed the mark that year and again in 2021. Even $100 billion, should it ever materialize, would not be sufficient to address the catastrophic impact of climate change in the Global South. According to Karombo, Zimbabwe required $1.1 billion to rebuild from just a single cyclone in 2019. And Mozambique has been experiencing average annual losses of about $440 million from cyclone-related floods.

Corporate outlets such as *Time* and the *New York Times* have started reporting on environmental racism in the United States.[78] Missing from this coverage, however, is the US role in speeding up the effects of climate change in the Global South. Last year, Project Censored's #4 story concerned the outsize contribution of the US and the Global North to the burgeoning climate crisis.[79] This broad topic is on our list once again, because corporate media still are not reporting on the situation in full; in particular, they are not covering adequately the egregious role played by the United States.

Facebook's Blacklist of "Dangerous Individuals and Organizations" Stifles Public Debate

Sam Biddle, "Revealed: Facebook's Secret Blacklist of 'Dangerous Individuals and Organizations,'" *The Intercept*, October 12, 2021.

Student Researcher: Jensen Giesick (San Francisco State University)

Faculty Evaluators: Amber Yang and Kenn Burrows (San Francisco State University)

Facebook's policy on "Dangerous Individuals and Organizations" (DIO) has become "an unaccountable system that disproportionately punishes certain communities," Sam Biddle reported for the Intercept in October 2021. The policy, he reported, includes a "blacklist" of more than 4,000 people and groups, "including politicians, writers, charities, hospitals, hundreds of music acts, and long-dead historical figures." The list, which Facebook employs some 350 specialists to maintain, is not public—despite calls for its release by legal scholars, activists, and Facebook's own oversight board, the Intercept reported.

The DIO policy not only bans specific individuals and groups from Facebook, it also selectively restricts "what other Facebook users are allowed to say about the banned entities," Biddle reported. The rules are "a serious risk to political debate and free expression," Faiza Patel, co-director of the Liberty and National Security Program at the Brennan Center for Justice, told the Intercept.

Facebook's DIO consists of three tiers of banned users. Tier 1, the most strictly limited group, includes alleged terror, hate, and criminal groups and their members. Facebook defines "terror" as "organizing or advocating for violence against civilians" and hate as "repeatedly dehumanizing or advocating for harm against" people with protected characteristics. The terrorist category comprises 70 percent of Tier 1 and "overwhelmingly consists of Middle Eastern and South Asian organizations and individuals," Biddle reported. Most of the entities listed in Facebook's terrorism category come "directly from" a government sanctions list of Specially Designated Global Terrorists. Facebook does not permit users to express "anything deemed to be praise or support about groups and people in this tier, even for nonviolent activities," Biddle wrote.

Tier 2 includes "Violent Non-State Actors," such as rebels who engage in violence targeting governments rather than civilians. Facebook users, Biddle reported, "can praise groups in this tier for their nonviolent actions but may not express any 'substantive support' for the groups themselves." Tier 3 consists of groups that engage in hate speech but not violence, that might soon become violent, or that violate the DIO policies repeatedly. This tier includes what Facebook calls "Militarized Social Movements," such as right-wing US anti-government militias. As Biddle noted, prohibitions on posts about predominantly white anti-government militias in the US are "far looser" than those on groups and individuals categorized as terrorists. Facebook uses terms such as "terrorist" and "Militarized Social Movement" in ways that make them "proxies" for racial and religious identities, Biddle reported, "raising the likelihood that Facebook is placing discriminatory limitations on speech."

With Biddle's report, the Intercept published a reproduction of Facebook's full list, with only minor edits.[80] In addition to numerous right-wing militias, the 100-page document lists a number of progressive-left organizations, such as the Elmer Geronimo Pratt Gun Club, which opposes police use of "no-knock" warrants and supports families of people murdered by the police, in addition to advocating for Black people's right to self-defense.[81]

In October 2021, Fox Business and *Newsweek* ran articles on Facebook's DOI list, based on the Intercept's original report.[82] The same month the *Wall Street Journal* ran a similar article, though it made no mention of the

Intercept report.[83] The *Wall Street Journal* article emphasized the perspectives of Facebook spokespersons, one of whom assured the *Journal* that Facebook had "confronted our toughest problems head-on."

"Smart Ocean" Technology Endangers Whales and Intensifies Climate Change

Koohan Paik-Mander, "Whales Will Save the World's Climate—Unless the Military Destroys Them First," BuzzFlash (via the Independent Media Institute's Local Peace Economy project), December 13, 2021.

Student Researcher: Jensen Giesick (San Francisco State University)

Faculty Evaluator: Amber Yang (San Francisco State University)

Joint military and industry efforts to develop new ocean technologies and infrastructure—which engineers and advocates call the "smart ocean"—will have lethal consequences for whales, significantly undermining their "indispensable role" in sequestering carbon and mitigating climate catastrophe, Koohan Paik-Mander reported in December 2021.

Whales "enable oceans to sequester a whopping 2 billion tons of carbon dioxide per year," Paik-Mander wrote. But "year-round, full-spectrum military practices" undertaken by the US Department of Defense have "fast-tracked us toward a cataclysmic environmental tipping point."

Whales have a symbiotic relationship with phytoplankton, which form the base of marine food webs. As whales dive and surface, their movements act as pumps, "bringing essential nutrients from the ocean depths" to the surface, "where sunlight enables phytoplankton to flourish and reproduce," Paik-Mander explained. This photosynthesis promotes carbon sequestration and oxygen production. "More whales mean more phytoplankton, which means more oxygen and more carbon capture," she summarized. An increase of 1 percent in phytoplankton productivity due to whale activity would "capture hundreds of millions of tons of additional carbon dioxide a year, equivalent to the sudden appearance of 2 billion mature trees," according to a 2019 report published in the International Monetary Fund magazine *Finance & Development*.[84]

The "smart ocean" envisioned by engineers and in the process of being weaponized by the US military depends on sonar, which can be lethal for whales. A March 2022 report in *Science* found that sonar triggers "the same fear response" in many whale species as calls emitted by killer whales, "their most terrifying predators."[85] In attempts to escape the perceived threat, many whales stop feeding, flee for their lives, or strand themselves in groups on beaches.

The developing "Internet of Underwater Things" will dramatically expand the scope of sonar use. Until now, sonar has been used primarily for military purposes, but data networks using sonar and laser transmitters will "saturate the ocean with sonar waves" to enhance civilian and military communications, according to Paik-Mander. The Department of Defense's Joint All Domain Command and Control system will interface with this sonar data network to connect aircraft, ships, and submarines in service of "satellite-controlled war," Paik-Mander wrote. The Pentagon has already sought bids from companies including Microsoft, Amazon, Oracle, and Google to manage the program's data storage cloud.

The Independent Media Institute project Local Peace Economy produced Paik-Mander's report, which was first published at BuzzFlash and subsequently republished by a number of independent outlets, including *CounterPunch*, *Monthly Review*, and Socialist Project. As early as 2017, Project Censored reported on the toll of US Navy training on marine wildlife.[86] A number of news outlets have covered scientific reports on the role of whales in capturing carbon and mitigating climate change.[87] But Paik-Mander's report is unusual in establishing how catastrophic declines in whale populations due to ongoing naval exercises will be worsened by the development of underwater data networks for both military and civilian applications, to the ultimate detriment of the world's climate.

Repression of Palestinian Media

Yuval Abraham, "Israel Charges Palestinian Journalists with Incitement—For Doing Their Jobs," The Intercept, April 5, 2022.

Nadda Osman, "Sheikh Jarrah: Activists Raise Concerns Over Deleted Social Media Content," Middle East Eye, May 7, 2021.

Ramzy Baroud, "How Israel's 'Facebook Law' Plans to Control All Palestinian Content Online," *Jordan Times*, January 18, 2022.

Student Researchers: Eli Rankin (Saint Michael's College) and Cem Ismail Addemir (Illinois State University)

Faculty Evaluators: Rob Williams (Saint Michael's College) and Steve Macek (North Central College)

The May 11, 2022, murder of Palestinian reporter Shireen Abu Akleh, evidently by Israeli soldiers, while she was covering one of their routine raids on a West Bank refugee camp sent ripples through journalistic circles and garnered extensive corporate press coverage. However, when it comes to repression of Palestinian media, Abu Akleh's killing is just the tip of the iceberg. Palestinian journalists routinely face harassment by Israeli defense forces, and the world's leading social media platforms have been quick to suspend, block, and restrict users who post pro-Palestinian content, including journalists.

Since 2020, twenty-six Palestinian journalists based in the West Bank have been imprisoned for attempting to cover Palestinian resistance to Israeli occupation. According to an April 5, 2022, report by Yuval Abraham in the Intercept, Palestinian journalists who post footage or comment on Israel's use of force are often placed in administrative detention for months at a time and experience harsh interrogations without ever being charged. After serving months of jail time, detainees are typically forced into entering guilty plea deals offered by Israeli military prosecution in order to be released.

Often, Palestinian journalists' social media posts are used against them by Israeli authorities. As Abraham detailed, journalist Hazem Nasser filmed a clash between Palestinians and Israelis that occurred on May 10, 2021, within the West Bank territory. He was confronted by Israeli soldiers on his way home, detained at a checkpoint, and then subjected to repeated interrogations about the incident for a month. In June, he was charged with incitement. The evidence of incitement presented in court consisted of some of Nasser's old Facebook posts rather than any of his journalism.

Between May 6 and May 18, 2021, the Arab Center for the Advancement of Social Media, 7amleh, documented 500 cases of digital rights violations targeting Palestinians.[88] These are cases in which social media platforms deleted stories, hid hashtags, and restricted or completely suspended accounts, often at the request of Israel's "Cyber Unit." Of those 500 violations, half involved Instagram and a third involved Facebook, both owned by social media giant Meta.

During spring 2021, Palestinians and pro-Palestine activists took to social media to condemn the evictions of Palestinian families from the Sheikh Jarrah neighborhood of Jerusalem. Subsequently, activists who condemned the evictions and journalists who covered them faced account suspensions and restrictions on social media, Nadda Osman reported for Middle East Eye. Mona Shtaya of

7amleh told Osman that these restrictions were part of a longstanding pattern: "Annually there are tens of thousands of requests that the Israeli cyber unit [sends] to social media companies in an attempt to silence Palestinians. The number of requests is increasing annually. In 2019 Israel made 19,606 requests from the cyber unit to social media companies regarding content takedowns."

Repression of Palestinian speech online could soon get much worse. In a January 18, 2022, article for the *Jordan Times*, Ramzy Baroud revealed that Israel's minister of justice, Gideon Sa'ar, is pushing legislation known as the "Facebook Law." The legislation would grant Israeli courts broad powers to remove online content deemed to be "inflammatory" or harmful to the security of the state from social media or "any website at all." Although the law ostensibly prohibits all violent, hateful rhetoric posted online, the Palestinian Digital Rights Coalition and the Palestinian Human Rights Organizations Council issued a statement opposing the legislation on the grounds that it would be used in a discriminatory manner and ultimately "increase the muzzling of Palestinian voices and advocacy for the Palestinian cause on social media platforms."[89]

Although Abu Akleh's murder was widely covered, the systematic repression of Palestinian journalists and the silencing of Palestinian expression on social media has been largely ignored by the establishment press. The arrest of dozens of Palestinian journalists detailed in Abraham's Intercept article never made it onto the corporate news media's radar. There have been scattered reports in the corporate press about censorship of Palestinian activists on social media. *The Washington Post* published a May 2021 article about Palestinians being blocked on social media.[90]

The same month NBC News reported on Palestinian accusations of censorship against social media platforms.[91] ABC News ran an October 2021 story about leaked Facebook documents recording its employees' concerns about restrictions on content about Palestine.[92] With the exception of publications focused specifically on Israel or the Middle East, there has been no discussion in the corporate media of Israel's so-called "Facebook Law."[93]

EARN IT Act Threatens Online Freedom of Expression Under Guise of Policing Child Pornography

Mathew Ingram, "A Resurrected Bill Troubles Digital Rights Advocates and Journalists," *Columbia Journalism Review*, February 17, 2022.

Kir Nuthi, "The EARN IT Act Would Give Criminal Defendants a Get-out-of-Jail-Free Card," Slate, February 11, 2022.

Student Researcher: Lily Callow (Saint Michael's College)

Faculty Evaluator: Rob Williams (Saint Michael's College)

Last introduced in 2020, the EARN IT Act (Eliminating Abusive and Rampant Neglect of Interactive Technologies Act) is back—and more threatening to online freedom of expression than before, according to recent independent news reports.

The EARN IT Act of 2022 aims to hold tech companies

responsible for the online spread of child pornography. As Mathew Ingram reported for the *Columbia Journalism Review* (*CJR*), the Act would establish a national commission to develop "best practices for the elimination of child sex-abuse material (CSAM)." Under the act, "online platforms hosting such material would lose the protection of Section 230 of the Communications Decency Act, which gives electronic service providers immunity from prosecution for most of the content that is posted by their users," the *CJR* reported.

The EARN IT Act could significantly impact freedom of expression on the internet far beyond its stated aim of policing child pornography. The *CJR* report quoted Riana Pfefferkorn, a research fellow at the Stanford Internet Observatory, who wrote that the act will result in companies "overzealously censoring lots of perfectly legal user speech just in case anything that could potentially be deemed CSAM might be lurking in there." The human rights organization Article 19 warned that the EARN IT Act would encourage platforms to engage in "overbroad censorship of online speech," targeting especially content created by "diverse communities, including LGBTQ individuals, whose posts are disproportionately labeled as sexually explicit."

The proposed Act would actually "undermine the fight against child predation online," Kir Nuthi reported for Slate in February 2022. Noting the "delicate constitutional balance that allows online platforms to voluntarily search for illicit and illegal material and report it to authorities without violating the Fourth Amendment," Nuthi wrote that the EARN IT Act could "end up giving criminals a way to challenge their convictions for child sexual abuse material." Nuthi added that, of course, it is "already a criminal offense to produce or distribute child sexual abuse content."

Because encryption is a potential red flag for CSAM content, the *CJR* reported, the EARN IT Act will likely pressure platforms to stop offering end-to-end encryption. In 2020, Stanford's Center for Internet and Society had characterized the then-current version of the EARN IT Act as a means to "ban end-to-end encryption without actually banning it."[94] The revised version of the legislation has "doubled-down" on anti-encryption, according to Stanford's Riana Pfefferkorn. But strong encryption is vital to many online users, especially members of marginalized communities. According to a 2020 analysis by the ACLU's Kate Ruane, "Strong encryption can be vital to many in the LGBTQ community who rely on the internet to access a support network, seek resources to combat discrimination and abuse, and find doctors and treatment to assist with transition, HIV prevention, and other health concerns."[95] Ruane noted that encryption also provides crucial safeguards for domestic violence victims, protest organizers, and journalists protecting confidential sources.

Since early 2022, the EARN IT Act has received limited coverage from major corporate newspapers such as the *Washington Post* and the *Wall Street Journal*.[96] A February 2022 editorial in the *Washington Post* reported on the bill's "dangerous tradeoffs," noting that concerns raised by privacy and speech advocates—including threats to end-to-end encryption and legitimate free expression—"have some merit."[97] A February 2022 report in the *Wall Street Journal* noted opposition to the EARN IT Act by "a coalition comprising more than 60 privacy

and human-rights groups" but emphasized a positive con-
sensus between Republican and Democratic lawmakers,
including Lindsey Graham (R-SC) and Dianne Feinstein
(D-CA).[98]

Dark Money Fuels Transphobic Opposition to the Equal Rights Amendment and Equality Act

Julia Peck, Ansev Demirhan, and Alyssa Bowen, "Dark Money 'Women's Groups' Are
Using Anti-Trans Scaremongering to Oppose ERA," Truthout, March 22, 2022.

Student Researcher: Mia Wood (San Francisco State University)

Faculty Evaluator: Amber Yang (San Francisco State University)

The Eagle Forum, Concerned Women for America
(CWA), the Independent Women's Forum (IWF), and
other women's groups leading the opposition to the Equal
Rights Act (ERA) and the Equality Act are funded by
dark money from a variety of right-wing interest groups,
Truthout reported in March 2022. Julia Peck, Ansev
Demirhan, and Alyssa Bowen wrote that the anti-fem-
inist legacy of Phyllis Schlafly, who pioneered resistance
to the ERA back in 1977, "very much lives on" through
the Eagle Forum, the CWA, and the IWF. Today, these
groups are using transphobia as a new tactic to mobilize
opposition to the ERA, a policy designed to guarantee
equal rights for all US citizens regardless of sex, and the
Equality Act, which would amend the 1964 Civil Rights

Act to prohibit discrimination based on sex, sexual orientation, and gender identity.

As Peck, Demirhan, and Bowen explained, "dark money"—funding used to influence policy, elections, and other significant political decisions whose precise donors are kept hidden from the public—"gives corporations and the wealthy undue sway in politics with little accountability." Many of the funders of the Eagle Forum are unknown, Truthout reported, but the Eagle Forum and its related Eagle Forum Education & Legal Defense Fund have received "tens of thousands over the years from the Bradley Foundation and Ed Uihlein Family Foundation, which are both massive foundations with deep connections to the far right."

Between 2010 and 2013, the CWA (and its partner organization, the Concerned Women for America Legislative Action Committee) received more than $11 million from groups associated with billionaire Charles Koch, including Freedom Partners, the Center to Protect Patient Rights, and TC4 Trust. The IWF, which began as Women for Clarence Thomas, also has links to the Koch brothers and the Bradley Foundation. According to the most recent IRS filings of the IWF and its partner organization, the Independent Women's Voice, the two groups received more than $4.75 million from these organizations since 2014.

Peck, Demirhan, and Bowen reported that anti-ERA groups such as the Eagle Forum, CWA, and IWF are "riding the recent wave of transphobia." Many of the nation's recently proposed anti-trans bills are rooted in erroneous and hateful anti-LGBTQ rhetoric, much like the Eagle Forum's opposition to the ERA. For example, in October 2021, a senior policy analyst at the IWF, Inez Stepman, told members of a House committee that the ERA would put women's physical safety at risk, highlighting an unsubstantiated claim that cisgender women are at a higher risk for violence when incarcerated with trans women. Yet, as Truthout documented, most incarcerated trans people are detained in facilities that align with the sex they were assigned at birth, and in fact, trans women imprisoned with men experience "high rates of extreme violence."

In the last year, sources such as the *Washington Post*, NBC News, and the *New York Times* have covered the recent rise in anti-trans legislation in the United States.[99] However, the corporate press has completely neglected dark money groups' continued support for conservatives leading the charge against the Equality Act and ERA.

Former Neo-Nazi Leader Now Holds DOJ Domestic Counterterrorism Position

Helen Christophi, "The Lone Wolf in the Henhouse," *The Progressive*, November 18, 2021.

Student Researcher: Annie Koruga (Ohlone College)

Faculty Evaluator: Mickey Huff (Diablo Valley College)

In a November 2021 *Progressive* magazine article, reporter Helen Christophi revealed that Brian P. Haughton, a former member of multiple racist skinhead bands and a past leader in the neo-Nazi movement, now holds an important counterterrorism position in the Department of Justice. Haughton serves as a law enforcement coordinator for domestic counterterrorism in the Middle Atlantic Great Lakes Organized Crime Law Enforcement Network of the Department of Justice's Regional Information Sharing Systems (RISS).

Michael German, a Brennan Center fellow who investigates neo-Nazis, told Christophi that it is "highly unlikely" that RISS or similar federal employers would have missed Houghton's neo-Nazi ties while conducting a background check. As Christophi reported, many other white supremacists likely hold powerful positions in law enforcement agencies, especially since neo-Nazi leaders are encouraging their followers to take jobs in the police or military.

In the 1980s and 1990s, Haughton played drums with the Arresting Officers, an influential neo-Nazi band, which was named for the belief that arresting officers had the best jobs since they could assault people of color. He also had connections to members of the Aryan Republican Army, a neo-Nazi gang that robbed twenty-two Midwest banks in the mid-1990s and is suspected of having helped to fund the Oklahoma City bombing. Haughton's involvement in the neo-Nazi skinhead scene ended around January 1995, when he joined the Philadelphia Police Department, where he worked until December 2017.

Although Haughton's ideological commitments could have changed since his days as a skinhead, Frank Meeink, a former neo-Nazi leader who knew Haughton and now conducts hate crime trainings, said, "I'm sure he still has these beliefs. You don't join the cops being racist and then get un-racist."

Georgetown law professor Vida Johnson told Christophi that police departments are overwhelmingly conservative and white and often give the benefit of the doubt to job applicants with racist or bigoted pasts. "Police underestimate white people as threats," Johnson said. German, the Brennan Center fellow, observed that a white supremacist "couldn't prosper in law enforcement agencies if the prosecutors didn't go along with it, if the judges didn't go along with it, if the government didn't go along with it."

The Federal Bureau of Investigation (FBI) has long been aware that white supremacists are infiltrating law enforcement agencies. In 2006, the Bureau disclosed that white supremacists were getting jobs as police officers in order to access intelligence and weapons training.[100] And, in 2015, an FBI counterterrorism policy directive referenced "active links" between white supremacists and law enforcement officials.[101] However, there is little evidence that law enforcement leadership did much in response to these revelations.

Although NPR, the *Washington Post* and the *New York Times*, among others, have reported on former or current police officers with ties to white supremacist organizations being charged in connection with the January 6 storming of the Capitol, only the *Progressive* appears to have reported on the alarming case of the neo-Nazi inside the DOJ.[102]

The Human Mind as "New Domain of War": NATO Plans for Cognitive Warfare

Ben Norton, "Behind NATO's 'Cognitive Warfare': 'Battle for Your Brain' Waged by Western Militaries," The Grayzone, October 8, 2021.

Student Researcher: Cem Ismail Addemir (Illinois State University)

Faculty Evaluator: Steve Macek (North Central College)

On October 5, 2021, the NATO Association of Canada (NAOC) sponsored a forum on what panelists described as the "weaponization of brain sciences" to exploit "vulnerabilities of the human brain" in service of more sophisticated forms of social engineering and control. As Ben Norton reported for the Grayzone, "with its development of cognitive warfare strategies," NATO has added a new, sixth level to the five operational domains—air, land, sea, space, and cyber—that the alliances' member nations have previously sought to control.

The NAOC panel discussion was part of NATO's Fall 2021 Innovation Challenge, hosted by Canada, which sought to enlist the expertise of private entrepreneurs and academic researchers "to help develop new tactics and technologies for the military alliance," Norton reported. (The NAOC, he noted, is technically a nongovernmental organization, but "its mission is to promote NATO.")

One panelist, Marie-Pierre Raymond, who represented

the Canadian Armed Forces' Innovation for Defense Excellence and Security Program, stated that "the rapid evolution of neurosciences as a tool of war" hinges on developments in artificial intelligence, big data, and social media. Raymond encouraged corporate interest in NATO's Innovation Challenge by telling potential applicants that successful innovators would receive "national and international exposure," cash prizes, and access "to a market of 30 nations." Another panelist, Shekhar Gothi, a military officer who works with Canada's Special Operations Force Command, assured corporate investors that "all innovators will maintain complete control of their intellectual property." As Norton noted, panelists representing NATO interests sought to ensure corporations that their shareholders would "continue to profit" from NATO's "imperial endeavors."

The panel's focus was guided by a 2020 NATO-sponsored study titled "Cognitive Warfare" and authored by François du Cluzel, who manages the NATO Innovation Hub and was one of the event's featured speakers. According to du Cluzel's report, the objectives of cognitive warfare are "to make everyone a weapon" and "to harm societies," rather than simply targeting an enemy's armed forces.[103] Furthermore, cognitive warfare is "potentially endless since there can be no peace treaty or surrender for this type of conflict."[104] For these reasons, "the human mind is now being considered as a new domain of war."[105] Du Cluzel emphasized that militaries "must work more closely with academia to weaponize social sciences and human sciences and help the alliance develop its cognitive warfare capacities," the Grayzone reported. The Grayzone's article also noted that NATO's desire to develop means of cognitive warfare came "at a time when member states' military campaigns are targeting domestic populations on an unprecedented level."

Since the Russian invasion of Ukraine in February 2022, the establishment press in the United States has published or broadcast hundreds of reports focused on NATO and the many contentious aspects of its role in that conflict. Many of these reports include explanations of NATO's goals, organization, and history. However, as of this book's publication, not one major US news outlet appears to have reported on NATO's efforts to develop its member nations' capacity for cognitive warfare, including the 2020 NATO study and the October 2021 NAOC panel.

Poor Infrastructure, a Legacy of Discriminatory Redlining, Inhibits Rural Black Americans' Internet Access

Avi Asher-Schapiro and David Sherfinski, "'Digital Divide' Hits Rural Black Americans Hardest," Thomson Reuters Foundation News, October 6, 2021.

Javeria Salman, "Racial Segregation Is One Reason Some Families Have Internet Access and Others Don't, New Research Finds," The Hechinger Report, October 14, 2021.

Student Researchers: Payton Blair, Milan Spellman, and Emmanuel Thomas (Loyola Marymount University)

Faculty Evaluator: Kyra Pearson (Loyola Marymount University)

Severe lack of infrastructure contributes to a "digital divide" in many southern states that most impacts rural Black Americans, according to an October 2021 study produced by the Joint Center for Political and Economic Studies (JCPES).[106] Avi Asher-Schapiro and David Sherfinski of the Thomson Reuters Foundation News and Javeria Salman of the Hechinger Report published pieces on this "digital divide" and the extent of its impact on Black Americans' lives and well-being.

Dominique Harrison, the JCPES study's author, told Asher-Schapiro and Sherfinski in October 2021 that "despite constant conversations about rural access to broadband in the US, most of it is focused on white rural residents." Harrison's study found that, across 152 counties in Alabama, Arkansas, Florida, Georgia, Louisiana, Mississippi, North Carolina, South Carolina, Tennessee, and Virginia, Black Americans were ten times more likely not to have internet access than white Americans in those same counties. Specifically, 38 percent of Black Americans in those counties reported that they lacked home internet access, while only 23 percent of white Americans in those same areas said the same.

The lack of infrastructure and financial resources available to these areas contribute to this digital divide. Hazel Levy of the University of Florida told the Hechinger Report that there were "actually access allocation issues. . . . That's not simply these access gaps that just naturally happen, that access is actually allocated."

Salman's Hechinger Report article outlined the historical background to these current access gaps. As she reminded readers, Depression-era federal housing policies denied mortgage guarantees to majority-Black neighborhoods by classifying them as "high risk," a practice known as redlining. Researchers from the University of Florida who examined the links between disparities in current broadband access and past discriminatory federal housing policies found that "despite internet service providers reporting similar technological availability across neighborhoods, access to broadband in the home generally decreases in tandem with historic neighborhood risk classification."[107]

Inadequate access to broadband can have dire consequences. Nicol Turner Lee, the director of the Center for Technology Innovation at the Brookings Institution, explained to Asher-Schapiro and Sherfinski that lack of broadband access "undermines everything [for the underserved], from those seeking jobs to those seeking public benefits to healthcare access—it's the whole nine yards."

Asher-Schapiro and Sherfinski noted that President Biden's infrastructure bill earmarks $65 billion for expanding broadband access, making it "the biggest broadband investment in our history to close the digital divide," according to Senator Michael Bennet (D-CO). On November 15, 2021, Biden signed the $1 trillion infrastructure bill into law.[108]

Although many news outlets have reported on America's digital divide, corporate news sources, such as the *New York Times* and CNN, have not addressed the deep historical roots of disparities in broadband access. *The Chicago Sun-Times* published a May 17, 2022, commentary about digital redlining of Chicago's Black neighborhoods.[109] But no big corporate news organizations appear to have covered digital redlining affecting Black communities in the South, even as it relates to the infrastructure bill.

States Hoard Federal Assistance Funding Amidst Record Poverty Levels

Eli Hager, "A Mother Needed Welfare. Instead, the State Used Welfare Funds to Take Her Son," ProPublica, December 23, 2021.

Eli Hager, "These Single Moms Are Forced to Choose: Reveal Their Sexual Histories or Forfeit Welfare," ProPublica, September 17, 2021.

Hannah Dreyfus, "States Are Hoarding $5.2 Billion in Welfare Funds Even as the Need for Aid Grows," ProPublica, December 29, 2021.

Adita Shrivastava and Gina Azito Thompson, "Policy Brief: Cash Assistance Should Reach Millions More Families to Lessen Hardship," Center on Budget and Policy Priorities, February 18, 2022.

Student Researcher: Zach McNanna (North Central College)

Faculty Evaluator: Steve Macek (North Central College)

Despite the national poverty rate making its largest upward jump in recorded history, Hannah Dreyfus reported for ProPublica that states had stockpiled $5.2 billion in undistributed funds from the federal Temporary Assistance for Needy Families program (TANF). Her report was part of a collection of articles published by ProPublica in 2021 that detailed the regulations allowing widespread denial of assistance and explored their impact on those in need.

Hannah Dreyfus reported in a December 2021 article that the number of approved applications for access to TANF funding has been cut in half since 2010 as guidelines to qualify become increasingly exclusionary, while reserved TANF funds have more than doubled in the same time period.[110]

Dreyfus profiled Bonnie Bridgforth, a single mother of four children, who was forced to work at just a dollar above Maine's minimum wage while pursuing her associate's degree to meet the "employment" qualification for TANF funding. However, Bridgforth was notified that her family no longer met the "deprivation" standard to receive aid after her estranged husband was released from prison. Dreyfus observed that "the same year Bridgforth was kicked off TANF, Maine was sitting on $111 million in unspent welfare dollars."

Bridgforth's story illustrates a larger problem stemming from the fallout of a 1996 welfare reform law passed by the Clinton administration allowing states to withhold assistance. The 1996 law awards states an up-front block grant each year, intending for the money to go toward helping the poor meet their basic needs. However, as Eli Hager explained in a December 2021 ProPublica article, states are allowed to spend this money in any manner they see fit, as long as it meets one of four very broad criteria.

Hager spoke with Arianna Bermudez about her experience with the state of Arizona, which "spent some of the same welfare funding that it could have used to provide her with direct assistance to instead help pay for a child protective service investigation into her emotional state." In a September 2021 article for ProPublica, Hager revealed that state investigators forced mothers to disclose information about their sexual histories as a condition of receiving aid.

Some state officials argue that the decline in applications for TANF money means states are moving families out of poverty. The Center on Budget and Policy Priorities has overwhelming data to suggest the opposite. Adita

Shrivastava and Gina Azito Thompson's February 2022 study shows that the TANF-to-poverty ratio hit an all-time low in the program's twenty-five-year history amid the COVID-19 pandemic.

The corporate media have helped states maintain their billions in undistributed welfare funds as a well-kept secret. Outside of a single January 2022 NPR story and coverage by independent journals such as Consortium News, which ran Dreyfus's original article, there has been no real coverage of the 1996 law allowing states to collect federal welfare funding without using it for its essential purpose.[111] *PBS NewsHour* has covered Hager's reporting about TANF's many failures as a safety net for poor women.[112]

School-Issued Technology Poses Surveillance Risks for Students

Nir Kshetri, "School Surveillance of Students via Laptops May Do More Harm than Good, The Conversation, November 9, 2021 (updated January 21, 2022).

Jessa Crispin, "US Schools Gave Kids Laptops During the Pandemic. Then They Spied on Them," *The Guardian*, October 11, 2021.

Student Researchers: Abigail Ariagno, Eliza Kuppens, and Ava Mullin (University of Massachusetts Amherst)

Faculty Evaluator: Allison Butler (University of Massachusetts Amherst)

To address inequities in technology access highlighted by the shift to remote learning since the onset of COVID-

19, school districts across the United States have doubled the number of laptops and tablets provided to students, according to a study published by the Center for Democracy & Technology in September 2021.[113] The problem, Nir Kshetri reported for The Conversation, is that "the vast majority of schools are also using those devices to keep tabs on what students are doing in their personal lives."

Software programs—including Bark, Gnosis IQ, and Gaggle—monitor students' technology use, including emails and private chats, with the promise of alerting school officials to hazards such as cyberbullying, drug use, or self-harm. As Jessa Crispin wrote in the *Guardian*, "It's not clear whether students are going to benefit from this surveillance, or if it is merely going to reduce schools' liability."

The surveillance tools used by schools cause students "emotional and psychological harm" and "disproportionately penalize minority students," Kshetri reported.

Surveillance makes students more cautious about what they say or search for online, potentially discouraging "vulnerable groups, such as students with mental health issues, from getting needed services," he noted. Tech-based surveillance especially impacts Black and Hispanic students, who are more likely to depend on school-issued devices and also more likely to be flagged for use of offensive language, due to biases in artificial intelligence programs. Surveillance tools also affect sexual and gender minorities: Gaggle, a program used by many schools, has flagged "gay," "lesbian," and other LGBTQ terms, ostensibly to track online pornography and protect LGBTQ students from bullying.[114]

The establishment press has not adequately covered

the privacy concerns raised by widespread use of surveillance technologies embedded in school-issued devices. In April 2020, the *Washington Post* published an article titled "School Closures Prompt New Wave of Student Surveillance," but this article focused specifically on software used by colleges and universities to monitor students taking exams.[115] In September 2020, the *New York Times* published a "Here to Help" column, "How to Protect Your Family's Privacy During Remote Learning," but its advice focused on concerns such as the "proactive role" of teachers in "building a safe space for students" and parents discussing with their children "when and how often to use the camera."[116] *The Wall Street Journal* published "How to Detect Your Child's Emotional Distress Before the School's AI Does."[117] These articles make no mention of specific software programs used to monitor students or how they hinder student privacy and development.

In May 2022, the Federal Trade Commission issued a policy statement on its intent to increase enforcement of educational technology vendors' responsibilities under the Children's Online Privacy Protection Act, a development the Center for Democracy & Technology lauded as "an important step toward improving privacy for students."[118]

US Transportation System "Fuels" Inequality

Basav Sen, "How the U.S. Transportation System Fuels Inequality," Inequality.org (Institute for Policy Studies), January 27, 2022.

Gabby Birenbaum, "The Bipartisan Infrastructure Bill Provides Historic Funding for Transit. It's Not Enough," Vox, August 23, 2021.

Lawrence Carter, "Inside Exxon's Playbook: How America's Biggest Oil Company Continues to Oppose Action on Climate Change," Unearthed, June 30, 2021.

Student Researcher: Zach McNanna (North Central College)

Faculty Evaluator: Steve Macek (North Central College)

The federal government disburses four times as much money for roadways as for public transit, a long-standing imbalance that has deprived the nation's poorest of basic mobility for decades, Basav Sen reported for the Institute for Policy Studies website, Inequality.org. Since 1990, the urban roadway system has grown by nearly 70 percent. At the same time, public transportation systems have accumulated an estimated $90–$176 billion in maintenance and repair backlogs.

According to Sen, this disparity disproportionately impacts Black and Latino communities, where personal vehicle ownership rates are much lower than in majority white communities. "Transportation policies prioritizing private vehicle use leave the poor and people of color behind," Sen reported.

The bias favoring automobiles in transportation policy is a result of corporate lobbying influence. "For the oil and gas industry in particular," Sen reported, "highway-centric transportation is a gift that keeps on giving." Political contributions by the oil and gas industry totaled $140 million in the 2020 election cycle alone, with hundreds of millions more since 2012.

In an August 2021 article for Vox, Gabby Birenbaum argued that, although the recent bipartisan infrastructure bill provided substantial funding for transit, the boost in federal funding was not enough to undo nearly fifty years of deferred maintenance. Full investment could "unlock a new era for transit," Birenbaum wrote, including increased public transportation services, expansion to new areas, and clean energy fleets. "But such an investment would need to be several times what has been allocated," she noted.

As Lawrence Carter pointed out in a June 2021 article for Unearthed, the outsize influence of the oil industry on US politics not only produces negative socioeconomic impacts, it also damages the environment. A senior lobbyist for Exxon told one of Unearthed's undercover reporters the company "had been working to weaken key aspects of President Joe Biden's flagship initiative on climate change, the American Jobs Plan." As Unearthed revealed, ExxonMobil targeted a number of moderate senators, seeking to influence them to "scale back the plan's ambition by scrapping the tax hikes that would pay for it."

Although some commercial news outlets such as Bloomberg have discussed how lack of funding for public transportation adversely affects the economy, the extent of the problem is significantly underreported by the establishment press.[119] Independent outlet Common Dreams covered Sen's Inequality.org report, and the magazine

Popular Science mentioned Sen's work in a story about "unsustainable cities," but none of the nation's most prominent news media appears to have reported his findings.[120] Absent widespread public awareness of these issues, the political influence of the oil industry will continue to shape transportation policy in ways that worsen existing inequalities.

Federal Safety Agency Underreports Deaths of Offshore Oil and Gas Workers

Sara Sneath, "Offshore Oil and Gas Fatalities Underreported by Federal Safety Agency," Southerly, August 18, 2021.

Student Researchers: Vincent Santilli and Noah Orser (SUNY Cortland)

Faculty Evaluator: Christina Knopf (SUNY Cortland)

In an August 2021 piece published simultaneously in four independent media outlets (Southerly, Drilled News, WWNO, and Energy News Network), environmental journalist Sara Sneath reported that the US Department of Interior's Bureau of Safety and Environmental Enforcement (BSEE) underreported offshore oil and gas worker fatalities from 2005 to 2019. BSEE's narrow reporting criteria excluded nearly half the offshore deaths that occurred, grossly distorting the level of danger inherent to the job.

The BSEE was created in response to BP's Deepwater

Horizon disaster in 2010—the largest oil spill in US history—in an effort "to improve safety and enforce environmental regulations in the offshore oil and gas industry." However, Sneath explained, BSEE's "inconsistent and missing data, as well as loopholes that allow some fatalities to go unreported, make the offshore industry appear safer than it really is."

In an analysis of BSEE data obtained through a Freedom of Information Act request, Sneath determined that "nearly half of known offshore worker fatalities in the Gulf of Mexico from 2005 to 2019 didn't fit BSEE's reporting criteria." The agency excludes "offshore fatalities that occur in state waters," "deaths that occur while workers are in transport to offshore facilities," and "deaths that happen on offshore platforms that aren't work related . . . even though the remoteness of offshore platforms makes it more difficult to seek medical attention."

More alarming is the fact that the fatality rate appears to be rising. Sneath reported that "even with missing data on fatalities, the number of reported deaths in 2019 is more than the previous five years combined, despite a drop in the number of people working offshore." A "shrinking workforce is one reason that the job is dangerous." Sneath quoted Mathew Shaffer, a Houston-based lawyer who represents offshore workers: "We see injuries because there wasn't enough crew. . . . A lot of those injuries are caused by the lack of manpower."

Although corporate media, including the *Washington Post*, covered the Trump administration's efforts to weaken offshore drilling regulations, none have reported this story.[121] Following a massive pipeline leak off the California coast in October 2021, the *Los Angeles Times* published a related story about inadequate inspections of critical infrastructure.[122] It noted that "critics in both the public and private sectors have been particularly harsh in their assessment of what they see as BSEE's failures to act as a robust regulative authority."

Indigenous Communities Using Data Sovereignty to Address Food Insecurity

Brian Oaster, interview with Toni Stanger-McLaughlin, "The First Answer for Food Insecurity: Data Sovereignty," *High Country News*, February 11, 2022.

Student Researchers: Emily Inman, Emma Stankiewicz, Maria Trifiro, and Kristina Vartanian (University of Massachusetts Amherst)

Faculty Evaluator: Allison Butler (University of Massachusetts Amherst)

The pandemic has compounded a host of systemic issues in the United States, including food insecurity in Indian Country. In an interview for *High Country News*, Brian Oaster spoke with the Native American Agriculture Fund's CEO Toni Stanger-McLaughlin (Colville) to learn more about the special January 2022 report "Reimagining Hunger Responses in Times of Crisis."[123] Supply-chain problems during the pandemic caused extreme delays in usual deliveries, meaning many went without access to basic necessities. In response, various Native organizations and self-governing communities are using data sovereignty to obtain federal funds that could transform local agricultural infrastructure.

"For the first time, we're going to take ownership of our data, and also the messaging and how the data is going to be interpreted," said Stanger-McLaughlin.

The Native American Agriculture Fund (NAAF) partnered with the Indigenous Food and Agriculture Initiative (INAI) and the Food Research & Action Center (FRAC) to research and develop the report in an effort to educate Congress about the importance of local agricultural production in indigenous communities. The report discovered that Native households go hungry at vastly higher rates than their white counterparts do. About 48 percent of more than 500 indigenous respondents shared that "sometimes or often during the pandemic the food their household bought just didn't last, and they didn't have money to get more."

NAAF, INAI, and FRAC discovered that Native communities more often turn to their tribal governments for help rather than access benefit cards, which are useless in rural areas where there are no nearby food stores. Farm-to-family direct sales became an increasingly popular way of acquiring food during the pandemic. Since the shift to producing and selling locally, instead of selling to stockyards, which then sell to processing plants, there have been reductions in transportation and storage costs. NAAF hopes that prioritizing Native-driven data collection will ultimately empower tribes that have waited too long on Washington leaders to make the right calls.

"We're asking tribes to reach out and engage with us if they're applying for federal funding, to use our work as a model of how we can all come together and actually leverage private and federal funding and expand and unify our mission, which is to feed our communities," said Stanger-McLaughlin.

Food insecurity has shown up in many recent corporate news headlines, most often related to global havoc inflicted by the pandemic or climate change. In August 2020, the *New York Times* covered food deserts among members of the Navajo nation; in December 2021, the *Washington Post* reported on farmers adapting indigenous peoples' sustainable farming efforts amidst dire water shortages.[124] However, one noticeable gap in all corporate coverage is indigenous communities' work to develop innovative solutions to historic inequity.

25. Injustice for Incarcerated Women in Maryland after State Defunds Prerelease Facility

Eddie Conway and Mansa Musa (Charles Hopkins), interview with Nicole Hanson-Mundell, "'It Is Torture': Women in Maryland's Prisons Have Nowhere to Turn," The Real News Network, February 14, 2022.

Student Researchers: Thomas Gruttadauria, Kate Horgan, and Lydia Jankowski (University of Massachusetts Amherst)

Faculty Evaluator: Allison Butler (University of Massachusetts Amherst)

Hundreds of incarcerated women in Maryland have been denied access to prerelease programs, which provide job opportunities and other vital re-entry services, Eddie Conway and Mansa Musa reported for the Real News Network in February 2022. Their report detailed the trajectory of Maryland's Gender-Responsive Prerelease Act, which would mandate the development of a dedicated prerelease facility for incarcerated women. The act was initially vetoed by Governor Larry Hogan in May 2020, and although the state legislature voted to override Hogan's veto, funding to construct the women's facility remained in jeopardy.

According to Out For Justice—a grassroots organization that advocates for reform of policies that adversely affect successful reintegration into society—Maryland maintains nine separate prerelease and minimum-security facilities for men, but none for women.[125] Although one in ten women at the Maryland Correctional Institution for Women is qualified for prerelease, as many as 30 percent of these women have not been assigned work opportunities.[126]

Nicole Hanson-Mundell of Out For Justice told the Real News Network how prerelease programs provide women within eighteen months of release with crucial opportunities to resume working, reconnect with family, and reestablish access to medical and mental health services.

In 2021, the state legislature appropriated $1.5 million for the Department of Public Safety and Correctional Services to construct a women's prerelease facility. However, as Hanson-Mundell described, Robert L. Green, the head of Maryland's Department of Corrections, "decided not to spend" the money the state legislature had allocated for the facility's construction. "That money went back into the general fund," she explained, because the prerelease facility "is not a priority for the Department of Corrections."

In April 2022, Maryland Matters reported that, after a two-year struggle to secure funding, the state legislature "passed a capital budget measure to funnel $2 million toward the planning and construction of a women's pre-release center."[127] The article quoted Out For Justice's Hanson-Mundell: "There is still more investment needed and much more work to do, but we believe our coalition and committed lawmakers will keep us moving forward."

Prior to this success, up-to-date news coverage regarding the lack of women's prerelease facilities in Maryland had been scarce. In January 2020, the *Washington Post* covered efforts to convert the Brockbridge Correctional Facility, a former maximum-security prison, into a "comprehensive prerelease, reentry, and workforce development facility" for both men and women.[128] At the time, women's advocates maintained that the coed design was unlikely to meet women prisoners' needs and reflected gender discrimination. That same month, the radio station WAMU, a Washington, D.C., NPR affiliate, produced a similar report.[129]

A key element in the Real News Network's report is its emphasis on organizers' repeated efforts to encourage Maryland officials to follow through with the Gender-Responsive Prerelease Act, despite opposition from the governor and corrections officials. In February 2020, the editorial board of the *Baltimore Sun* advocated for more services to help incarcerated Maryland women transition back to society, but the *Sun*'s editorial did not acknowledge the efforts by state senator Mary Washington, state delegate Charlotte Crutchfield, Out For Justice, the Maryland Justice Project, and others to shepherd this bill into law.[130]

Notes

1. Eduardo Galeano, "In Defence of the Word," *Index on Censorship*, Vol. 6 No. 4 (July 1977), 15–20, 16.

2. Carl Jensen, "Project Censored: Raking Muck, Raising Hell," in *Censored: The News That Didn't Make the News—and Why*, ed. Carl Jensen (Chapel Hill, North Carolina: Shelburne Press, 1993), 1-14, 7.

3. On "censorship by proxy," see Mickey Huff and Andy Lee Roth, "A Return to News Normalcy," in *State of the Free Press 2022*, eds. Andy Lee Roth and Mickey Huff (New York: Seven Stories, 2022), 5–6; and Andy Lee Roth, avram anderson, and Mickey Huff, "Censorship by Proxy and Moral Panics in the Digital Era," in *Censorship, Digital Media and the Global Crackdown on Freedom of Expression*, eds. Robin Andersen, Nolan Higdon, and Steve Macek (New York: Peter Lang Publishing, 2023).

4. Steve Macek, Analisa Chudzik, and Andy Lee Roth, "Introduction: What the Top 25 Story List Is, and What It Is Not," in *State of the Free Press 2022*, 21–29, 25.

5. Ibid., 25–28.

6. Pam Belluck and Rebecca Robbins, "Alzheimer's Drug Poses a Dilemma for the F.D.A.," *New York Times*, June 5, 2021 (updated October 20, 2021); Pam Belluck and Rebecca Robbins, "Three F.D.A. Advisers Resign Over Agency's Approval of Alzheimer's Drug," *New York Times*, June 10, 2021 (updated September 2, 2021); Pam Belluck, Sheila Kaplan, and Rebecca Robbins, "How an Unproven Alzheimer's Drug Got Approved," *New York Times*, July 19, 2021 (updated October 20, 2021); Pam Belluck, "Concerns Grow Over Safety of Aduhelm After Death of Patient Who Got the Drug," *New York Times*, November 22, 2021; Pam Belluck, "Medicare Proposes to Sharply Limit Coverage of the Alzheimer's Drug Aduhelm," *New York Times*, January 11, 2022.

7. Jef Feeley, "J&J's Controversial Prison Testing Resurfaces in Baby Powder Lawsuits," Bloomberg, March 7, 2022. The unethical experiments, which took place at Holmesburg Prison, outside Philadelphia, had been previously reported, but Feeley's report made public documents proving that Johnson & Johnson directly funded this experiment and at least one previous one on prisoners, in 1968.

8. For information on how to nominate a story, see "How to Support Project Censored" at the back of this volume.

9. Validated Independent News stories are archived on the Project Censored website.

10. For a complete list of the Project's judges and their brief biographies, see the acknowledgments at the back of this volume.

11. Ian Parry, Simon Black, and Nate Vernon, "Still Not Getting Energy Prices Right: A Global and Country Update of Fossil Fuel Subsidies," International Monetary Fund, September 24, 2021.

12. For one report on the deadly consequences of air pollution in the United States, much of which is driven by reliance on fossil fuels, see Lylla Younes, Ava Kofman, Al Shaw, Lisa Song, and Maya Miller, "Poison in the Air," ProPublica, November 2, 2021.

13. "US Subsidies Boost the Expected Profits and Development of New Oil and Gas Fields," Stockholm Environment Institute, July 29, 2021.

14. Timothy Cama and Lesley Clark, "Oil Lobby Targets Democrats in Fight Against Tax Plan," E&E News, September 10, 2021.

15. Laurie van der Burg and Lucile Dufour, "200+ CSOs Call on World Leaders to End Public Finance for Fossil Fuels in 2021," Oil Change International, September 23, 2021.

16. Zachary Skidmore, "IMF: Fossil Fuel Industry the Recipient of Subsidies of $5.9TN per Year," Power Technology, October 6, 2021.

17. Lisa Friedman, "John Kerry Says Fossil Fuel Subsidies Are the 'Definition of Insanity,'" New York Times, November 12, 2021.

18. Julia Horowitz, "Ditching Fossil Fuel Subsidies Can Trigger Unrest. Keeping Them Will Kill the Climate," CNN, January 20, 2022.

19. "Cheated at Work," Center for Public Integrity, May 4, 2021–March 11, 2022.

20. David Cooper and Teresa Kroeger, "Employers Steal Billions from Workers' Paychecks Each Year," Economic Policy Institute, May 10, 2017.

21. Terri Gerstein, "How District Attorneys and State Attorneys General Are Fighting Workplace Abuses," Economic Policy Institute, May 17, 2021.

22. "No Rights, Low Wages, No Service: How Increased Violations of Workers' Rights in 2021, Coupled with High Harassment, and Low Wages and Tips, Have Pushed Workers to Leave the Service Sector," One Fair Wage, September 2021.

23. "U.S. Companies Are Stealing Pay from Low-Wage Workers, Report Says," CBS News, May 4, 2021.

24. See, for instance, Gregory Yee, "Torrance Car Wash Ordered to Pay More than $800,000 in Stolen Wages Plus Fines," Los Angeles Times, April 28, 2022.

25. Gretchen Morgenson and Lisa Cavazuti, "The Hidden Scourge of 'Wage Theft': When Higher Profits Come out of Workers' Pockets," NBC News, September 6, 2021.

26. Ariana Figueroa, "U.S. House Panel Weighs Labor Law Amendment to Protect Workers from Wage Theft," Virginia Mercury, May 12, 2022.

27. Ibid.

28. "What Are PFAS Chemicals?," Environmental Working Group, undated [accessed July 8, 2022].

29. Sharon Lerner, "EPA Exposed" series, The Intercept, July 2, 2021–March 30, 2022; Pat Rizzuto, "EPA Stops Posting 'Critically Important' Chemical Risk Data," Bloomberg Law, December 13, 2021.

30. Lynn L. Bergeson and Carla N. Hutton, "PEER Files Suit against EPA Seeking TSCA Section 8(e) Reports," National Law Review, January 8, 2022.

31. United States Environmental Protection Agency, "EPA Re-initiates Publication of Chemical Health and Safety Notices to ChemView, Enhancing Public Accessibility," EPA.gov, February 3, 2022; Lynn L. Bergeson and Carla N. Hutton, "EPA Resumes Publishing TSCA Section 8(e) Notices to ChemView," National Law Review, February 5, 2022.

32. Cale Carpenter, Chris Valenzuela, Christopher Rodriguez, Steve Macek, Anna Gamboa, and Peter Phillips, "Congressional Investments and Con-

flicts of Interest," in Project Censored's *State of the Free Press 2021*, eds. Mickey Huff and Andy Lee Roth (New York: Seven Stories Press, 2020), 39–43.

33. "Industry Profile: Oil & Gas, 2021," OpenSecrets, April 22, 2022.

34. "Oil & Gas: Money to Congress, 2020," OpenSecrets, undated [accessed July 11, 2022].

35. Alex Kotch, "Members of Congress Own up to $93 Million in Fossil Fuel Stocks," Sludge, January 3, 2020.

36. Warren Rojas, Camila DeChalus, Dave Levinthal, and Madison Hall, "22 Democrats Hailed as Environmental Champions Have Personally Pumped Money into Companies That Rely on Fossil Fuels," Business Insider, December 13, 2021; Angela Wang and Madison Hall, "These Are the 50 Top Stocks That Members of Congress Own," Business Insider, December 14, 2021.

37. Anna Massoglia and Sam Levine, "Conservative 'Dark Money' Network Rebranded to Push Voting Restrictions Before 2020 Election," OpenSecrets, May 27, 2020.

38. Sarah Binder, "Barrett Is the First Supreme Court Justice Confirmed Without Opposition Support Since 1869," *Washington Post*, October 27, 2020.

39. Sheldon Whitehouse, "In the Federal Court Wars, the Right Has Jumped Through a Dark-Money Looking Glass," *Washington Post*, February 17, 2022.

40. "The Dark Money Groups Spending Big to Shape the Supreme Court Are the Same Groups That Spent Millions Pushing Trump's Big Lie and Funding Insurrectionists," Accountable.US, March 2022.

41. Ibid.

42. Ibid.

43. Ibid.

44. Sahil Kapur, "GOP Venting, 2024 Auditions and a Historic Moment: Highlights from Day 1 of Ketanji Brown Jackson Hearing," NBC News, March 21, 2022, updated March 22, 2022.

45. Ibid.

46. Kenneth P. Vogel and Shane Goldmacher, "Democrats Decried Dark Money. Then They Won With It in 2020," *New York Times*, January 29, 2022.

47   C. Ryan Barber and Dave Levinthal, "'Dark Money' Groups Are Mobilizing Around Biden's Nomination of Ketanji Brown Jackson to the Supreme Court," Business Insider, February 25, 2022.

48. Stephanie Mencimer, "With Little to Attack SCOTUS Nominee, Republicans Are Going Full Hypocrisy," *Mother Jones*, March 21, 2022.

49. Jeanna Smialek, "Democrats Blast Corporate Profits as Inflation Surges," *New York Times*, January 3, 2022.

50. Jim Tankersley and Alan Rappeport, "As Prices Rise, Biden Turns to Antitrust Enforcers," *New York Times*, December 25, 2021.

51. Lindsay Owens, "I Listened In on Big Business. It's Profiting From Inflation, and You're Paying For It," *New York Times*, May 5, 2022.

52. Errol Schweizer, "How Windfall Profits Have Supercharged Food Inflation," *Forbes*, May 10, 2022.

53. Joe Rogan, interview with Matt Taibbi, "#1745–Matt Taibbi," *The Joe Rogan Experience*, Spotify, December 2021. The relevant segment of the Rogan-Taibbi interview is also available via YouTube. See "Bill Gates Has Given $319 Million to Media Outlets," PowerfulJRE (YouTube), December 7, 2021.

54. Alan MacLeod, "Documents Show Bill Gates Has Given $319 Million to Media Outlets to Promote His Global Agenda," The Grayzone, November 21, 2021; Sarah Taylor, "Bill Gates Has Given $319 Million to Bankroll Select Media Outlets and Change the Public Narrative—And the Internet Has Receipts: Report," Blaze Media, November 18, 2021.

55. Sandi Doughton and Kristi Heim, "Does Gates Funding of Media Taint Objectivity?" *Seattle Times*, February 19, 2011, updated February 23, 2011.

56. Max Blumenthal, "'The American Friends': New Court Files Expose Sheldon Adelson's Security Team in US Spy Operation Against Julian Assange," The Grayzone, May 14, 2020.

57. Tom Porter, "The CIA Pitched Trump Officials Plans to Assassinate Julian Assange While He Was Hiding in a London Embassy in 2017, Report Says," Business Insider, September 27, 2021; Russell Brandom, "CIA Developed Plans to Kidnap Julian Assange, per Report," The Verge, September 27, 2021; Michael Holden, "Allegation of CIA 'Murder' Plot Is Game-Changer in Assange Extradition Hearing, Fiancee Says," Reuters, October 25, 2021.

58. Megan Specia, "British Court Hears Appeal in Julian Assange Extradition Case," *New York Times*, October 29, 2021.

59. Brian Stieglitz, "CIA 'Made Secret Plans to Kidnap or Assassinate Julian Assange After Wikileaks Published Sensitive Hacking Tools—and Even Plotted to Shoot Plane Tires If He Tried to Flee Embassy in 2017,'" *The Daily Mail*, September 26, 2021; Julian Borger, "CIA Officials Under Trump Discussed Assassinating Julian Assange—Report," *The Guardian*, September 27, 2021; and Eric Garcia, "Trump Denies Report He Considered Assassinating Julian Assange," *The Independent*, September 27, 2021. Notably, neither the BBC nor Channel 4 appears to have covered the story.

60. Michael Isikoff, Kevin Gosztola, Carrie DeCell, and Rebecca Vincent, "Kidnap or Kill: The CIA's Plot Against WikiLeaks' Julian Assange," Al Jazeera, October 2, 2021.

61. Amy Goodman, interview with Michael Isikoff and Jennifer Robinson, "The Plot to Kill Julian Assange: Report Reveals CIA's Plan to Kidnap, Assassinate WikiLeaks Founder," *Democracy Now!*, September 28, 2021.

62. William Vaillancourt, "CIA Reportedly Considered Kidnapping, Assassinating Julian Assange," *Rolling Stone*, September 26, 2021; Joseph Choi, "Trump Administration Mulled Kidnapping, Assassinating Julian Assange: Report," The Hill, September 27, 2021.

63. Sheely Edwards, "Bipartisan Poll Finds Voters Want Stronger Enforcement of Campaign Finance Laws, Increased Transparency in Elections," Campaign Legal Center, November 18, 2019.

64. Naomi Jagoda, "Democrats Press IRS To Reverse Trump-Era Rule Limiting Donor Disclosure," The Hill, April 27, 2021.

65. Grace Panetta, "Senate Votes Down Change to Its Filibuster Rules, Dealing the Fatal Blow to Democrats' Voting-Rights Push," Business Insider, January 19, 2022.

66. Olivier Knox, "The Daily 202: Senate Democrats Push Biden on 'Dark Money' Disclosures," Washington Post, April 27, 2021.

67. Stephen Groves, "Gov. Noem Defends 'Dark Money' Push as Privacy Protection," Associated Press, February 11, 2021.

68. Ana Ceballos and Samantha J. Gross, "Florida GOP Bill Would Further Shield Names of Dark Money Donors," Tampa Bay Times, January 20, 2022, updated January 22, 2022.

69. "State of the News Media—Digital News Fact Sheet," Pew Research Center, July 27, 2021.

70. Timothy Libert and Reuben Binns, "Good News for People Who Like Bad News: Centralization, Privacy, and Transparency on US News Sites," Proceedings of the 10th ACM Conference on Web Science, June 2019, 155–164. See, in particular, the quotation on page 155.

71. "The New York Times Company Privacy Policy," NYTimes.com, June 27, 2022.

72. Alexandra Ma and Ben Gilbert, "Facebook Understood How Dangerous the Trump-Linked Data Firm Cambridge Analytica Could Be Much Earlier Than It Previously Said," Business Insider, August 23, 2019.

73. "Advertising Platform OpenX Will Pay $2 Million For Collecting Personal Information From Children In Violation Of Children's Privacy Law," FTC.gov, December 15, 2021.

74. "Client Profile: Interactive Advertising Bureau," OpenSecrets, April 22, 2022.

75. John D. McKinnon and Ryan Tracy, "FTC Weighs New Online Privacy Rules," Wall Street Journal, September 29, 2021; Cristiano Lima, "Will the US Follow the EU Playbook to Crack Down on Silicon Valley Giants?" Washington Post, September 28, 2021.

76. Hannah Ritchie, "Who Has Contributed Most to Global CO_2 Emissions?" Our World in Data, October 1, 2019.

77. Somini Sengupta, "The Rich World's Promise of $100 Billion in Climate Aid Inches Forward," New York Times, October 25, 2021, updated October 27, 2021.

78. Justin Worland, "Why the Larger Climate Movement Is Finally Embracing the Fight Against Environmental Racism," Time, July 9, 2020; Margaret Renkl, "How to Fight the Poison of Environmental Racism," New York Times, August 16, 2021.

79. Sarah Uysal and Mickey Huff, "'Climate Debtor' Nations Have 'Colonized' the Atmosphere," in State of the Free Press 2022, eds. Andy Lee Roth and Mickey Huff (Fair Oaks, CA and New York: The Censored Press and Seven Stories Press, 2021), 46–49.

80. "Facebook Dangerous Individuals and Organizations List (Reproduced Snapshot)," The Intercept, October 12, 2021.

81. Josefina Morales, "Interview With Elmer Geronimo Pratt Gun Club, Black Self-Defense Group Listed as 'Hate Speech,' 'Dangerous' by Facebook," Tribune of the People, October 29, 2021.

82. Lucas Manfredi, "Leaked Facebook Document Reveals Blacklist of Dangerous Organizations, Individuals," Fox Business, October 14, 2021;

and Ewan Palmer, "Facebook's Leaked Blacklist Features 9 Pro-Trump Militia Groups," *Newsweek*, October 14, 2021.

83. Jeff Horwitz and Justin Scheck, "Facebook Increasingly Suppresses Political Movements It Deems Dangerous," *Wall Street Journal*, October 22, 2021.

84. Ralph Chami, Thomas Cosimano, Connel Fullenkamp, and Sena Oztosun, "Nature's Solution to Climate Change," *Finance & Development* (International Monetary Fund), Vol. 56 No. 4 (December 2019), 34–38.

85. Virginia Morell, "Why Whales Flee from Sonar—Sometimes to Their Death," *Science*, March 21, 2022.

86. Nora Kasapligil and Elaine Wellin, "The Toll of US Navy Training on Wildlife in the North Pacific," in *Censored 2018: Press Freedoms in a 'Post-Truth' World*, eds. Andy Lee Roth and Mickey Huff with Project Censored (New York: Seven Stories Press, 2017), 57–58.

87. See, e.g., Hannah Osborne, "Whales Removed an Abundance of Carbon from Earth. Then Humans Killed 3 Million of Them," *Newsweek*, November 3, 2021; and Jenny Morber, "Why Whale Poop Matters More Than You Might Think," Slate, November 4, 2021.

88. "The Attacks on Palestinian Digital Rights," 7amleh, May 21, 2021.

89. "The Palestinian Digital Rights Coalition and the Palestinian Human Rights Organizations Council Warn Against Passing the 'Facebook' Law in the Israeli Knesset and Its Repercussions on Palestinian Digital Rights," 7amleh, December 29, 2021.

90. Elizabeth Dwoskin and Gerrit De Vynck, "Facebook's AI Treats Palestinian Activists the Way It Treats Americans. It Blocks Them," *Washington Post,* May 28, 2021.

91. Olivia Solon, "Facebook Battles Reputation Crisis in the Middle East," NBC News, May 29, 2021.

92. Chris Looft, "Facebook Employees Questioned Apparent Restrictions on Palestinian Activist's Account: Documents," ABC News, October 29, 2021.

93. "Israel's 'Facebook Bill' Is a Serious Threat to Freedom of Expression," *Haaretz*, December 29, 2021.

94. Riana Pfefferkorn, "The EARN IT Act: How to Ban End-To-End Encryption Without Actually Banning It," Center for Internet and Society (Stanford University), January 30, 2020.

95. Kate Ruane, "The EARN IT Act Is a Disaster for Online Speech and Privacy, Especially for the LGBTQ and Sex Worker Communities," American Civil Liberties Union (ACLU), June 30, 2020.

96. Cat Zakrzewski, "A Bill Aiming to Protect Children Online Reignites a Battle Over Privacy and Free Speech," *Washington Post*, February 10, 2022; John D. McKinnon, "Websites Could Be Liable for Child-Sex-Abuse Content Under Bill Passed by Senate Panel," *Wall Street Journal*, February 10, 2022.

97. Editorial Board, "A Bill Taking Aim at Online Child Pornography Comes with Dangerous Tradeoffs," *Washington Post*, February 24, 2022.

98. McKinnon, "Websites Could Be Liable."

99. Kimberly Kindy, "GOP Lawmakers Push Historic Wave of Bills Targeting Rights of LGBTQ Teens, Children and Their Families," *Washington Post*, March 25, 2022; Matt Lavietes and Elliott Ramos, "Nearly

240 Anti-LGBTQ Bills Filed in 2022 So Far, Most of Them Targeting Trans People," NBC News, March 20, 2022; Eduardo Medina, "Utah Legislature Overrides Governor's Veto of Transgender Athlete Bill," *New York Times*, March 25, 2022.

100. Federal Bureau of Investigation, *Intelligence Assessment: White Supremacist Infiltration of Law Enforcement*, October 17, 2006.

101. Federal Bureau of Investigation, *Counterterrorism Policy Directive and Policy Guide*, April 1, 2015.

102. Tom Dreisbach, "A Capitol Police Officer Is Accused of Telling a Jan. 6 Suspect to Hide Evidence, " NPR, October 15, 2021; Spencer S. Hsu, "Current, Former Officers Charged in New Proud Boys Indictment in Capitol Riot," *Washington Post*, July 16, 2021; Neil MacFarquhar, "Efforts to Weed Out Extremists in Law Enforcement Meet Resistance," *New York Times*, May 11, 2021.

103. François du Cluzel, "Cognitive Warfare," Innovation Hub, November 2020, 25, 32.

104. Ibid., 7.

105. Ibid., 4.

106. Dominique Harrison, "Affordability & Availability: Expanding Broadband in the Black Rural South," Joint Center for Political and Economic Studies, October 6, 2021.

107. Benjamin Skinner, Hazel Levy, and Taylor Burtch, "Digital Redlining: The Relevance of 20th Century Housing Policy to 21st Century Broadband Access and Education," EdWorkingPapers.com, October 1, 2021.

108. Andrea Shalal and Steve Holland, "Biden Signs $1 Trillion Infrastructure Bill into Law," Reuters, November 15, 2021.

109. Tiffany Henyard, "Internet Providers Must Prioritize Minority Communities," *Chicago Sun-Times*, May 17, 2022.

110. *FY 2020 Federal TANF & State of MOE Financial Data*, Office of Family Assistance, US DHHS, 2021.

111. Mary Louise Kelly, Vincent Acovino, and Patrick Jarenwattananon, "Over $5 Billion in Welfare Spends Were Left Unspent by States," NPR, January 12, 2022; Hannah Dreyfus, "Hoarding Welfare Funds Amid Rising Need in the US," Consortium News, Janaury 11, 2022.

112. Stephanie Sy, interview with Eli Hager, "Why the TANF Program Fails as a Safety Net for Single Mothers, Other Vulnerable Americans," *PBS NewsHour*, December 29, 2021.

113. DeVan L. Hankerson, Cody Venzke, Elizabeth Laird, Hugh Grant-Chapman, and Dhanaraj Thakur, "Online and Observed: Student Privacy Implications of School-Issued Devices and Student Activity Monitoring Software," Center for Democracy & Technology, September 2021.

114. "Minneapolis Schools Are Spying on Queer Students & Outing Them to Teachers and Parents," LGBTQ Nation, October 16, 2021.

115. Drew Harwell, "Mass School Closures in the Wake of the Coronavirus Are Driving a New Wave of Student Surveillance," *Washington Post*, April 1, 2020.

116. Christina Caron, "How to Protect Your Family's Privacy During Remote Learning," *New York Times*, August 20, 2020, updated August 21, 2020.

117. Julie Jargon, "How to Detect Your Child's Emotional Distress Before the School's AI Does," *Wall Street Journal*, September 18, 2021.

118. Cody Venzke, "FTC to Prioritize Cybersecurity and Data Minimization Enforcement Under COPPA to Bolster Student Privacy," Center for Democracy & Technology, May 24, 2022.

119. Tiffany Chu and Daniel Ramot, "Fixing Transit Is More Than Just Infrastructure," Bloomberg, May 17, 2021.

120. Brett Wilkins, "New Report Shows How US Transportation System 'Fuels Inequality,'" Common Dreams, January 27, 2022; Jocelyn Timperley, "Urban Sprawl Defines Unsustainable Cities, But It Can Be Undone," Popular Science, May 3, 2022.

121. Juliet Eilperin and Dino Grandoni, "Trump Administration to Overhaul Safety-Monitoring Rules for Offshore Drilling," Washington Post, December 28, 2017.

122. Connor Sheets, Adam Elmahrek, Robert J. Lopez, and Rosanna Xia, "Federal Regulation of Oil Platforms Dogged by Problems Long Before O.C. Spill," Los Angeles Times, October 5, 2021.

123. Toni Stanger-McLaughlin, Sandy Martini, Geri Henchy, Katherine Jacobs, Erin Parker, and Valarie Segrest, "Reimagining Hunger Responses in Times of Crisis: Insights from Case Examples and a Survey of Native Communities' Food Access During COVID-19," Native American Agriculture Fund, January 2022.

124. Amelia Nicrenberg, "For the Navajo Nation, the Fight for Better Food Gains New Urgency," New York Times, August 3, 2020, updated May 21, 2021; Samuel Gilbert, "Native Americans' Farming Practices May Help Feed a Warming World," Washington Post, December 10, 2021.

125. "Women's Pre-Release," Out for Justice, undated [accessed May 26, 2022].

126. Ibid.

127. Hannah Gaskill, "Lawmakers Commit State Funding to Build Women's Pre-Release Center," Maryland Matters, April 20, 2022.

128. Alison Knezevich, "Inmates' Transition Site Called 'Not Enough,'" Washington Post, January 31, 2020.

129. Dominique Maria Bonessi, "Advocates Want Incarcerated Women in Maryland to Have Their Own Pre-Release Facility," WAMU (NPR), January 29, 2020.

130. Baltimore Sun Editorial Board, "Incarcerated Women Need Mores Services to Transition Back into Maryland Society," Baltimore Sun, February 11, 2020.

CHAPTER 2

Déjà Vu News
Eating and Drinking, Birthing and Breastfeeding—A Look Back at the Establishment Media's Failure to Report Corporate Interference with Basic Human Biology

MACK PARLATORE, ANALISA CHUDZIK,
SHEALEIGH VOITL, and STEVE MACEK

Some of the stories highlighted in Project Censored's annual Top 25 list of underreported news items eventually make their way onto the national news agenda. Others remain marginalized and ignored. Many of the Top 25 stories in any given year will witness significant new developments in the months and years after they are picked out as deserving of more public attention by the Project's international panel of judges. That is why every year we compile a Déjà Vu News chapter that reviews the fate of a select group of previous Top 25 stories.

Usually, the stories we update in the Déjà Vu chapter are less than five or six years old. And, normally, the collection of stories investigated in the chapter lack any kind of thematic connection. This year's Déjà Vu chapter is different.

In this year's chapter, we revisit Censored stories from a much wider swath of recent history, including some from more than two decades ago. In addition, the stories updated in this chapter share a common theme. Each of the previous top 25 stories we review here touches on the ways big business and the profit motive interfere with or disrupt key aspects of human biological life.

Human beings depend on healthy food and potable water for survival. Human infants do best when breastfed, at least in the early months of life. And the human species would not survive if women ceased giving birth. Yet, as this look at past Top 25 stories demonstrates, corporate power has encroached on each and every one of these vital life processes—eating, drinking, breastfeeding, and birthing—and the corporate news media have largely failed to inform the public about this alarming state of affairs.

From last year's list published in *State of the Free Press 2022*, we update story #5 about the prevalence of microplastics in the seafood so many of us consume. From *Censored 2005*, we look back at a story about the handful of giant companies who control the world's food system. Next, we revisit the top story from *Censored 2001*, which examined the push by multinational corporations to privatize water. From that same year, we also update a story about an effort by baby formula manufacturer Gerber to suppress laws promoting breastfeeding. Finally, we trace recent development concerning a 1994 story about the epidemic of cesarean sections in the US.

While a few of these stories have attracted a modest amount of media attention in the years and decades since Project Censored first identified them as overlooked—notably the story about microplastics—most have not received anything close to the coverage they deserve. The establishment news media have apparently determined that corporate disruption of human biological existence and life processes is just not that newsworthy.

Microplastics and Toxic Chemicals Increasingly Prevalent in World's Oceans

Robby Berman, "Study Found Plastic in Every Seafood Sample It Analyzed," Medical News Today, August 29, 2020.

Graham Readfearn, "More Than 14m Tonnes of Plastic Believed to Be at the Bottom of the Ocean," *The Guardian*, October 5, 2020.

Daniel Ross, "More Traces of Cancer-Causing PFAS in Arctic Raise Alarm Over Global Spread," Truthout, October 18, 2020.

Sharon Lerner, "PFAS Chemical Associated with Severe Covid-19," The Intercept, December 7, 2020.

Student Researcher: Eduardo Amador, Kolby Cordova and Natalia Fuentes (Sonoma State University)

Faculty and Community Evaluators: Peter Philips (Sonoma State University) and Polette Gonzalez

The #5 story on last year's Project Censored Top 25 list concerned a pair of scientific studies documenting that microplastics and a class of toxic chemicals known as polyfluoroalkyl substances (or PFAS) are becoming increasingly prevalent in the world's oceans and have begun to contaminate the global seafood supply.

According to a July 2020 study published in the scholarly journal *Environmental Science & Technology*, PFAS—a family of harmful chemicals used in a range of products including carpet, furniture, clothing, food packaging, and nonstick coatings—have now been found in the Arctic Ocean.[1]

Meanwhile, researchers at the University of Exeter and the University of Queensland's QUEX Institute have found microplastics in seafood sold in Australian markets, findings first published in *Environmental Science & Technology* and covered by Medical News Today in August 2020.[2] As Robby Berman reported for Medical News

Today, the new findings suggest that microplastics—small pieces of plastic, less than 5 mm long (about the size of a sesame seed), that result from the breakdown of larger plastics—have "invaded the food chain to a greater extent than previously documented."

The presence of PFAS in the Arctic Ocean is concerning for many reasons. As Daniel Ross reported in an October 2020 article for Truthout, PFAS chemical exposure is known to have serious impacts on human health, including causing certain cancers, liver damage, thyroid problems, and increased risk of asthma. People with elevated levels of PFAS chemicals are twice as likely to develop a severe form of COVID-19, since these chemicals are endocrine disruptors.[3]

Like PFAS compounds being found in Arctic waters, the discovery of microplastics in popular forms of seafood is alarming.

Microplastics' small size allows them to spread through "airborne particles, machinery, equipment and textiles, handling, and from fish transport." The research team at Exeter and Queensland found microplastics and polyvinyl chloride present in each of the seafood samples it studied. The study's lead author, Francisca Ribeiro, said that, for an average serving, a seafood eater could be exposed to "approximately 0.7 milligrams [mg] of plastic" when ingesting oysters or squid, and "up to 30 mg of plastic" when eating sardines. For comparison, a grain of rice weighs approximately 30 mg.

As Medical News Today reported in its August 29, 2020, article on the study, approximately 17 percent of the protein that humans consume worldwide is seafood. The findings suggest that "people who regularly eat seafood are also regularly eating plastic." According to Tamara Galloway, one of the study's co-authors, "We do not fully understand the risks to human health of ingesting plastic, but this new method will make it easier for us to find out."

In an October 5, 2020, article in the *Guardian*, Graham Readfearn reported that at least 14 million tons of microplastics are likely sitting on the ocean floor, "more than 30 times as much plastic ... than there is floating at the surface." As the *Guardian* report noted, "stemming the tide of plastic entering the world's waterways and ocean has emerged as a major international challenge." In September 2020, leaders from more than seventy countries signed a voluntary pledge to reverse biodiversity loss, an agreement that included a goal to stop plastic entering the ocean by 2050. The United States, Brazil, China, Russia, India, and Australia did not sign that pledge.[4]

Media coverage of both the study on microplastics in seafood and the research on PFAS in the Arctic Ocean came primarily from independent news outlets and those aimed at the scientific community. Most of the articles covering the presence of PFAS in Arctic waters simply summarized the findings of the research. However, Truthout and *Chemical & Engineering News* each took their reporting further by including professional opinions on the significance of the study.[5] Outside of coverage by the *Guardian*, no major commercial news outlet paid attention to the issue of microplastics in seafood.[6]

Update

Just days after the December 2021 release of *State of the Free Press 2022*, new scientific research was published revealing that "microplastics cause damage to human cells in the laboratory at the levels known to be eaten by people via their food." As reported by environmental editor Damian Carrington for the *Guardian*, the study—which was published in November 2021 by the *Journal of Hazardous Materials*—found that cell death, allergic reactions, and damage to cell walls were all caused by microplastics in laboratory conditions.[7]

The release of this study was followed by two even more startling scientific studies a few months later.

On March 24, 2022, scientists announced that they had for the first time ever detected microplastic particles in human blood. A study published in the journal *Environment International* found that seventeen of twenty-two anonymously donated adult blood samples contained microplastics, and some contained particles from three different kinds of plastic (PET, polystyrene, and polyethylene).[8] As the *Guardian* article about this study pointed out, these findings are especially concerning because microplastics latch onto the outer membranes of red blood cells, have been detected in the placentas of pregnant women, and have been shown to pass from pregnant rats to their fetuses.[9]

The blood study was followed by another shocking discovery, which found microplastic particles in healthy lung tissue taken from living adults for the very first time. Researchers identified the presence of microplastics in eleven of thirteen lung tissue samples taken from patients undergoing surgery. The report of these findings was published April 6, 2022, in the journal *Science of the Total Environment*, and Damian Carrington reported on the findings for the *Guardian*.[10] As Carrington explained, what makes this discovery particularly troubling is the potential connection between microplastics exposure and lung cancer. Studies of lung cancer patients have found that 97 percent of cancerous lung tissue samples were contaminated with plastic and other fibers (versus just 83 percent of non-cancerous lung tissue samples).[11]

The potential health hazard posed by microplastics is one reason why, in March 2022, 175 nations under the auspices of the United Nations Environmental Assembly agreed to develop a first-of-its-kind global treaty to limit plastic waste. International leaders have until 2024 to hammer out the details of the treaty.[12]

The establishment media have paid much closer attention to the recent wave of scientific findings about microplastics than they did to the tainted seafood story in 2020. *USA Today*, *Fortune*, and Bloomberg were just a few of the commercial outlets that since late March 2022 have reported that microplastics had been found in human blood.[13] And, after the story about microplastics being found in lung tissue broke, one influential news outlet after another covered it. NBC, *Newsweek*, *USA Today*, and NPR all carried reports on the story.[14] The corporate media have also covered the UN-sponsored treaty on plastic waste, with both the *New York Times* and the *Washington Post* running articles on the pact.[15] Whether this surge in media attention is an anomaly driven largely by the shocking new research on the degree to which microplastics permeate our environment and our bodies remains to be seen. For initiatives like the UN treaty on plastic waste to be successful, though, the media will have to do a much better job of informing the public about the health and environmental crisis being created by our addiction to plastic.

Global Food Cartel Fast Becoming the World's Supermarket

Hilary Mertaugh, "Concentration in the Agri-Food System," *Left Turn*, September 2003.

Student Researcher: Anna Miranda (Sonoma State University)

Faculty Evaluator: John Lund (Sonoma State University)

In 2003, the now-defunct magazine *Left Turn* published "Concentration in the Agri-Food System" about a growing global food cartel seizing control of the world's agricultural food system. According to the report, multiple acquisitions, mergers, joint ventures, and informal agreements had created a dangerous level of consolidation in agribusiness at every step, from seed to store. Project Censored highlighted the trend as its #19 *Censored* story of 2003–2004.

Censored 2005 warned that modern farmers were becoming increasingly subordinated to Big Agriculture. Due to consolidation among suppliers and processors, farmers were faced with little choice in whom to buy from or sell to, allowing a small collection of giant companies to charge them more and pay them less. With little control over the value of their crops, farmers were left in an even graver position by genetically modified seed varieties that allowed agribusinesses to claim ownership of the germplasm. The grip of these seed corporations was only becoming tighter as two of the largest companies, Monsanto and DuPont, agreed to share patents in 2002, forming a dubious "non-merger alliance" that gave them increasing market control while evading antitrust laws.

Meanwhile, the giant food producer Cargill was claiming a top-five spot in nine different markets for food products. Retailers, too, faced incredibly high levels of concentration. With a habit of buying out their rivals, ConAgra was the third-largest seller of retail food products in the world that year, despite a 2002 scandal for distributing 19 million pounds of *E. coli*–contaminated beef. Concerns about monopoly control over our food supply didn't stop there, with the top five supermarket chains capturing half the food sales in the United States, and companies such as Walmart providing cheap groceries at the cost of low wages and suppressed unionization rights.

Two decades ago, consolidation in the food industry had a bevy of threatening implications. Yet few Americans knew much about companies like ConAgra and Cargill or the growing threat they posed, in part because few news outlets were reporting about them. As these oligopolistic companies captured larger shares of their respective markets, the incentive for them to collude was only increasing, and the future of food seemed bleak.

Update

Over the past nineteen years, agribusiness giants have continued to merge, resulting in even more concentrated ownership and control over the world's food supply. By 2016, six global giants of the pesticide industry were about to become just three.[16] Dow and DuPont were finalizing a massive merger.[17] China National Chemical Corporation struck a deal to acquire the Swiss pesticide and seed company Syngenta AG, and Germany's Bayer had made an unsolicited bid to purchase Monsanto.[18] The scale of these mergers demanded both government and media attention.

In May 2016, the *Wall Street Journal* cautioned citizens about the potential risks of a merger between Bayer and Monsanto. Reports suggested that these mergers would result in just three companies controlling 83 percent of US corn seed sales and 70 percent of the global pesticide market.[19] Despite concerns over monopolistic control, the acquisition of Monsanto by Bayer was green-lit by the US Justice Department, as Brian Fung and Caitlin Dewey reported for the *Washington Post* in 2018.[20] While the DOJ had required Bayer to off-load $9 billion worth of assets as a condition for approval, many critics asserted that the move was insufficient to address antitrust concerns.[21]

The negative consequences of consolidation under-scored by the original *Left Turn* article remain. Mirroring the Cargill *E. coli* outbreak, the 2015 bird flu displayed how an overly concentrated industry can multiply the impact of disease. This epidemic quickly crippled the US egg and poultry industries.[22] As reported by the *Wall Street Journal*, the number of producers in the US commercial egg industry had dwindled from 10,000 companies in 1970 to less than 200 in 2015, and as a result, was the sector hardest hit by the bird flu outbreak.[23] With fewer companies, individual farms housed a greater percentage of the market's hens, creating the potential for a drastic increase in egg prices when even a single farm had to be taken out of production.[24] Consolidation enabled the bird flu to have a massive impact on the market, something that might have been avoided had the industry retained more small farms.

The dire impacts of concentrated ownership in agriculture are not limited to poultry or livestock. Story #11 in *State of the Free Press 2022* emphasized the way Big Agriculture's legal ownership of crop seeds and plant varieties threatens us all.[25] In response to a push by agribusiness to create protections that enforce seed monopolies, members of the seed sovereignty movement have been fighting to maintain the genetic variety necessary to ensure food security in the face of climate change.[26] Whether due to disease or global-warming-induced drought, a lack of diversity in world food supplies endangers the stability of our food systems. The impacts of the global COVID-19 pandemic further heighten concerns about concentrated ownership and industrial agriculture.[27]

In 2021, the *Guardian* conducted a joint investigation with Food & Water Watch into the "illusion of choice" that defines the American grocery industry.[28] The investigation analyzed consolidation in the industry and its impact on consumers, echoing the concerns featured in Project Censored's 2005 report. The study of more than sixty categories of everyday food items found that, despite a variety of lines and labels, nearly 80 percent were sold by four or fewer megafirms. Similarly, more than 80 percent of beef processing was found to be controlled by four multinational corporations.[29] *The Guardian* reported that these corporations had been increasingly paying farmers less and charging consumers more for beef over the last forty years, a direct impact of the consolidation that Mertaugh of *Left Turn* had warned against in 2003.[30] The 2021 study revealed that, on average, farmers receive only 15 cents of every dollar spent at the grocery store.[31] Amanda Starbuck, an analyst with Food & Water Watch, decried the entire system as one "designed to funnel money into the hands of corporate shareholders and executives while exploiting farmers and workers and deceiving consumers about choice, abundance and efficiency."[32]

Despite a slight increase in media attention about this issue, the corporate grip on our food system is not likely to loosen anytime soon. In 2020, President Biden appointed Tom Vilsack as Secretary of Agriculture despite Vilsack's record of coziness with agribusiness and laissez-faire attitude toward consolidation when he held the position during Obama's administration.[33] *The New York Times* warned that his appointment was unlikely to make Republican-leaning rural America any friendlier toward Biden.[34] In July 2021, Biden signed an executive order calling on Vilsack to "address the unfair treatment of farmers and improve conditions of competition."[35] However, recent consolidation, such as the Dairy Farmers of America's purchase of the country's largest milk processor, Dean, left small farmers skeptical that the new administration would bring about meaningful change.[36] One small dairy farmer was quoted in the *New Yorker* saying, "Vilsack's got a good story line this time around . . . but I don't have a lot of confidence."[37]

In the wake of the 26th Conference of the Parties (COP-26), an international conference aimed at addressing climate change, it seems even less likely that a solution is on the horizon. In a report by Consortium News, Vijay Prishad wrote that there was "no serious conversation about any transformation of the food system" at COP-26.[38] Meanwhile, there was talk among agricultural tech companies, such as Bayer, proposing drastic digital-agriculture methods that would gather data on farmworkers via online platforms and turn much of farming into gig work.[39]

Overall, the level of awareness and reporting around consolidation in the food and agricultural industries is growing. However, increased awareness has yet to translate into change, and the trend toward further consolidation of corporate ownership of our food system continues unabated. With the "Uber-ization" of agriculture on the horizon, the future of the food system remains precarious, and unless we act with haste, the industry will continue to be controlled by an increasingly powerful global food cartel.

Censored 2001 #1

World Bank and Multinational Corporations Seek to Privatize Water

Maude Barlow, *Blue Gold: The Global Water Crisis and the Commodification of the World's Water Supply*, International Forum on Globalization, June 1999 (Revised Edition, Spring 2001).

Jim Schultz, "Just Add Water," *THIS*, July/August 2000.

Jim Schultz, "Water Fallout: Bolivians Battle Globalization," *In These Times*, May 15, 2000.

Vandana Shiva, "Monsanto's Billion-Dollar Water Monopoly Plans," *Canadian Dimension*, February 2000.

Jim Schultz, "Water Fallout," *Canadian Dimension*, February 2000.

Daniel Zoll, "Trouble on Tap," *San Francisco Bay Guardian*, May 31, 2000.

Pratap Chatterjee, "The Earth Wrecker," *San Francisco Bay Guardian*, May 31, 2000.

Corporate News Coverage: *Globe and Mail*, May 11, 2000.

Student Researchers: Christina Van Straalen, Mike Graves, and Kim Roberts (Sonoma State University)

Faculty Evaluators: Tom Jacobson, Tom Lough, and Leilani Nishime (Sonoma State University)

In the years preceding Project Censored's 2001 book, independent journalism was spearheading reporting about an evolving water crisis. From December 1999 to

April 2000, a series of intense protests arose in Bolivia surrounding the World Bank's forced privatization of the country's water supply system in Cochabamba. The conflict became known as the Cochabamba Water War and sparked extensive reporting by alternative and independent news outlets revealing that the World Bank and predatory multinationals were moving to privatize water, our most precious resource, while corporate media remained silent.

At the time, trends in global water consumption had led to mounting fears about impending water scarcity. It was predicted that, by 2025, demand for fresh water would outpace supply by 56 percent. Multinational corporations were acutely aware of this and sought to monopolize the world's water supplies. Monsanto, for example, planned to accrue $420 million in revenue by 2008 from its water operations in India and Mexico. In addition, the corporation predicted water would soon become a multi-billion-dollar market.

Fears about corporations exploiting water scarcity in the future were substantiated by the experiences of Bolivians facing off against Bechtel. When the World Bank forced Bolivia to privatize Cochabamba's municipal water system, its management was contracted to Bechtel Enterprises. Under Bechtel's control water costs in Cochabamba skyrocketed to more than double the previous rate, igniting the intense protests of the Cochabamba Water War. Activists were arrested, a seventeen-year-old was killed, and unrest continued for four months until the Bolivian government finally ousted Bechtel. Bechtel then placed its subsidiary under Dutch registration to take advantage of a Bilateral Investment Treaty signed between the Netherlands and Bolivia and brought a lawsuit against the Bolivian government.

In a special report for the International Forum on Globalization, Maude Barlow warned that massive multinational corporations were operating "in collusion with the World Bank and the World Trade Organization ... to commodify and privatize the world's water."[40] Despite independent articles receiving high traffic online, Project Censored reported, corporate news coverage was mostly limited to reports by Peter McFarlane of the Associated Press, who echoed Bechtel by characterizing the protesting Bolivians as "narcotraffickers."

Update

Bechtel's lawsuit against the Bolivian government carried on for years. The massive multinational corporation was seeking $25 million in damages and another $25 million in lost profits from the government of Bolivia.[41] The case was met with protests around the globe when it was filed in November 2001.[42] Citizen activist groups from more than forty-three nations submitted a petition against Bechtel to the World Bank, and protests twice shut down Bechtel's San Francisco headquarters before the case finally came to a close.[43] In January 2006, Bechtel settled for a payment of just 30 cents.[44] Despite this symbolic victory, the fight against water privatization around the globe was far from over.

Over the years, Project Censored has repeatedly identified stories about water privatization as topics overlooked by the establishment press. Popular resistance to corporate water privatization continues to be underreported.[45]

In 2019, Project Censored highlighted a story by Doug Shields for *In These Times* that detailed the threat of public-private partnerships.[46] Shields revealed that Aqua America's purchase of Peoples Gas, Pittsburgh's local natural gas company, was a thinly veiled attempt to privatize the city's water supply.[47] In the months prior to the deal, Peoples Gas had been hammering out the details of a public-private partnership that would replace pipelines and build a new water treatment facility.[48] Shields wrote that the Pittsburgh Water and Sewer Authority (PWSA) was unlikely to be purchased outright by Aqua America, as the PWSA had already experienced disastrous results with privatization in the past, but that this partnership was sure to give Aqua America undue influence over the water utility in Pittsburgh.[49] It was, Shields wrote, "a form of privatization . . . that would leave Pittsburgh residents paying more while having less control over their future."[50] The future of Pittsburgh's PWSA remains on shaky footing, and Aqua America has continued to buy up water utilities around the country.

Concern over Aqua America is not without cause. From 2005 to 2016, Aqua America's subsidiary, Aqua North Carolina, had 170 instances of noncompliance with government contamination standards.[51] After an Aqua America takeover in Pennsylvania, water utility rates jumped 393 percent, and in Florida rates not only rose to double that of other local public utilities, but the company was hit with more than seventy-five water quality violations over safety concerns.[52] As of January 2022, Aqua America was attempting to acquire the water system in Chester, Pennsylvania.[53] In a move that Food & Water Watch dubbed "a hostile takeover," Aqua Pennsylvania made an unsolicited bid for ownership of the Chester Water Authority, a financially sound, award-winning water utility.[54] Having declared bankruptcy in 2020, the city of Chester views the potential sale of the Water Authority as a quick route to financial stability, but such a move would surely hurt Chester's residents in the long run.[55] Food & Water Watch is working with locals in Chester to oppose the sale; however, much as in Cochabamba, because the city has been under state financial oversight since the 1990s, ownership of Chester's water could be transferred to Aqua America by force.

Despite Chester's history and the concerning parallels to Cochabamba's struggles, a possible water crisis in Chester has gone unaddressed by the media, but for a few nonprofit sources such as the *Guardian* and PBS's WHYY.[56] Even more concerning, a provision designed to promote public-private partnerships was written into a draft of the Biden administration's 2021 infrastructure bill.[57] Inserted as part of a compromise with Republican lawmakers, the provision would have encouraged the sale of public water utilities to private companies in areas with struggling infrastructure, allowing companies to further exploit disadvantaged communities.[58] In a June 21, 2021, article published in the *American Prospect*, David Dayen dubbed the Senate's bipartisan infrastructure proposal a "stalking horse for privatization."[59] Public-private partnerships would contract out the management of public infrastructure to the highest bidder, a method that is, according to Dayen, a mere "euphemism for privatization."[60] More concerning, the bill would have allowed "asset recycling," by which water authorities and governments directly sell the ownership of existing public infrastructure to finance new infrastructure projects.[61] This proposal drummed up concern among water activists.

In July 2021, Food & Water Watch and its allies drafted a policy memo to several members of Senate leadership outlining the dangers of the Biden plan. They highlighted the fact that water privatization leads "to rate hikes on households already struggling to afford their water bills" and warned that "water privatization can trap communities in expensive deals."[62] The resistance of activists succeeded, and by the end of the month, water privatization was "stripped from the infrastructure package, with the remaining privatization incentives limited to transportation projects."[63]

Despite the fact that US citizens had narrowly avoided losing public control over their water utilities, corporate media paid scant attention to this story. Articles from sources such as CNN made mention of the bill financing new infrastructure and water utilities around the country, but offered no analysis of the proposed privatization provisions.[64] While an August 2021 article from *Forbes* discussed privatization as it pertained to the infrastructure bill, it did so to tout public-private partnerships as the solution, suggesting that the US sell off more utilities and "abolish antitrust regulations."[65] With corporate media remaining mostly silent, it was only thanks to activist groups such as Food & Water Watch and Corporate Accountability that the water privatization provision did not become law. Still, water systems in cities including Chester remain at risk of being taken over by big corporations, and the lessons of Cochabamba still go largely unreported by the establishment press.

Gerber Uses the WTO to Suppress Laws that Promote Breastfeeding

Peter Montague, "Corporate Rights vs. Human Need," Environment and Health Weekly, November 18, 1999.

Muddassir Rizvi, "Milking Profits in Pakistan," *Multinational Monitor*, September, 2000.

Student Researchers: Deanna Battaglia and Nathalie Manneville (Sonoma State University)

Faculty Evaluators: Suzanne Toczyski and Linda Novack (Sonoma State University)

Included in *Censored 2001* was a report about Gerber's effort to stifle a Guatemalan law encouraging mothers to breastfeed. As birth rates have dwindled in developed countries, baby formula makers have compensated by aggressively marketing their goods to women in the Global South. However, Guatemala's new law would have made it substantially harder for baby formula companies such as Gerber to peddle misleading information about their products.

In 1983, the Guatemalan government passed a series of regulations, slated to go into effect beginning in 1988, to better inform new mothers about the benefits of breastfeeding and risks associated with breast-milk substitutes. For example, formula manufacturers were not allowed to send out free samples or use images of "healthy, chubby" babies on their packaging. Most importantly, companies were prohibited from marketing to mothers in the hospital and were ordered to include disclaimers on product labels saying breast milk was "nutritionally superior."

By 1988, all domestic and foreign baby food manufacturers except Gerber had agreed to follow the Guatemalan government's new law. Still, Gerber refused to include the breastfeeding note on its labels or to remove the brand's signature smiling baby from its products. Negotiations between Gerber and the Guatemalan Ministry of Health were ultimately unsuccessful, and Gerber maintained its resistance to the law even after losing its appeal in 1993. When the World Trade Organization (WTO) was established in 1995, Gerber disputed Guatemala's law before a WTO tribunal and ultimately won. The Guatemalan government later changed the law's language to allow greater flexibility.

Update

Formula sales in the developed world have remained stagnant for years. This is in part due to declining birth rates and decades of compelling scientific research that suggests breast milk prevents a variety of health issues in infants.[66] Because of this, the formula industry has tried to expand in undeveloped countries and vulnerable US communities since as early as the 1970s.

After the publication of a 1974 investigative report titled "The Baby Killer," which detailed the formula industry's predatory marketing strategies in developing countries, an international boycott of the major formula producer Nestlé ensued.[67] Physicians were increasingly concerned by the company's dangerous messaging, which falsely claimed its milk substitutes were just as nutritious as breast milk. The report revealed how Nestlé, and companies like it, targeted poor families by framing baby formula as essential to a "modern" way of life. However, when women couldn't afford the rising cost of formula, they watered it down to make their supply last longer, which led to severe malnourishment of their babies.

As a response to the public outcry, the World Health Organization (WHO) rolled out a voluntary code in 1981 in an attempt to permanently stop the marketing of baby formula.[68] As a result, Nestlé was unable to promote its formula powder Nan in Mexico, which abided by the WHO code. Although the US also signed on to follow the WHO regulations, it left some glaring loopholes. Because the US never established laws aligning its policies with the agreement, formula corporations continued to enjoy free rein. From 2003 to 2005, the Department of Health and Human Services (HHS) organized a breastfeeding public service campaign, which initially featured striking images of insulin syringes and asthma inhalers capped with baby bottle lids. The ads were supposed to promote research showing lower rates of diabetes and respiratory issues as well as fewer infections in breastfed babies. In 2004, formula lobbyists convinced Dr. Carden Johnston, then-president of the American Academy of Pediatrics (AAP), to write a letter to the secretary of Health and Human Services, Tommy G. Thompson, concerning the possibility that the campaign might ostracize women who couldn't breastfeed, or chose not to do so.[69] Critics argued that the long-standing financial partnership between formula companies and the AAP caused the campaign's demise, not formula corporations' genuine concern about mom guilt.

The new, reformed ads, displaying benign photos of flowers and cherry sundaes, had little effect on the general public. At that time, breastfeeding rates in the US were still much lower than in most European countries. Before the ad campaign, according to Abbott Nutrition's 2002 Ross Mothers Survey, 70 percent of women breastfed their newborns in the hospital after giving birth. By 2006, the figure had sunk to 63.6 percent.[70]

Around the time the ads aired in 2004, Nestlé began marketing Nan, its leading Latin American formula product, in the United States with a bilingual label.[71] A 2002 report compiled by Ross Products, now Abbott Nutrition, found that 32.7 percent of Latina mothers and 19.2 percent of Black mothers breastfed their six-month-old babies, compared to 36 percent of white mothers. CDC data from 2019 suggests that the disparity stems from systemic bias and inequality. Lack of lactation resources in hospitals that serve minority communities, inflexible work schedules, and inability to take paid parental leave make breastfeeding difficult, if not impossible, for some Black and Latina mothers.[72] Things have improved slightly since Congress passed the Break Time for Nursing Mothers law in 2010.[73] The law requires employers to provide new mothers with a reasonable amount of time to pump during the workday and a designated nursing station that is not a bathroom. Still, the disparity persists.

New York mayor Michael Bloomberg announced a plan in 2012 to encourage New York City hospitals to keep track of their formula distribution.[74] Bloomberg was seemingly inspired by the Baby-Friendly Initiative, which was a similar series of hospital guidelines first developed in 1991. Participating Baby-Friendly facilities were required to abide by ten rules, including storing formula in a locked location, declining all free samples from corporations, and delivering lectures on the benefits of breastfeeding to any mother requesting breast-milk substitutes.[75]

These policies were meant to boost awareness about

the importance of breastfeeding before new mothers are discharged from the hospital. Like hospitals participating in Mayor Bloomberg's initiative, Baby-Friendly facilities were also required to keep a diligent record of the formula that had been signed out. In 1996, Evergreen Hospital Medical Center in Kirkland, Washington, became the first hospital in the US to receive an official Baby-Friendly designation.[76] Now, mothers can find a Baby-Friendly hospital or birthing center in any of the fifty states as well as the District of Columbia and Puerto Rico.

In 2018, United Nations delegations were set to discuss a resolution to prevent erroneous infant formula marketing claims.[77] A 2015 study found that, in developing countries, only 40 percent of babies younger than six months were breastfed.[78] Researchers project that doubling the proportion of breastfed children could prevent hundreds of thousands of infant deaths.[79] However, the $70 billion formula industry, largely controlled by the US companies Abbott and Mead Johnson, was less than thrilled. The US insisted that passages urging governments to "protect, promote and support breast-feeding" be completely removed from the resolution.[80] At the World Health Assembly in May 2018, the US threatened to impose tariffs and withdraw military aid from Ecuador, which was poised to introduce the resolution.[81]

In July 2018, then-president Trump took to Twitter to bash the *New York Times'* "fake" report on the Assembly meetings, claiming that although the US "strongly supports breastfeeding," baby formula must remain an option for women due to "malnutrition and poverty."[82] However, not only does breast milk contain essential nutrients that cannot be found in formula, but research also suggests that breastfeeding may save money by reducing long-term medical costs.[83]

If critics were already skeptical of the United States' concern for public health, Trump's baseless arguments cemented their doubts. Ultimately, Russia introduced the infant formula resolution at the UN Assembly with none of the United States' suggested changes.[84]

Corporate news outlets such as the *Los Angeles Times*, *Washington Post*, and *New York Times* have steadily covered breastfeeding news in the US for the past decade. However, the dire implications of the formula industry's marketing in low-income countries have received little establishment coverage in that time, aside from some attention to the Trump administration's crusade against the UN resolution in 2018.

Censored 1995 #19

Cesarean Sections Epidemic

Public Citizen Health Research Group, "Unnecessary Cesarean Sections: Curing a National Epidemic," *Health Letter*, June 1994.

Student Researcher: Jennifer Bums (Sonoma State University)

Faculty Evaluator: Carl Jensen (Sonoma State University)

In 1994, Public Citizen's Health Research Group released a report on the epidemic of cesarean sections, or C-sections, in the United States. A C-section is a surgical procedure in which a baby is delivered through an incision in the mother's abdomen. The rates of C-sections in the US had just begun to plateau after skyrocketing in the 1980s but were still significantly higher than in other advanced industrialized countries. As Project Censored noted in its summary of the report, although this procedure can sometimes be "a life-saving intervention for both mother and child," it can also "do significant harm to mothers without providing benefits to infants when performed outside of certain well-defined medical situations."

According to the report, about one in four pregnant women delivered via C-section in 1994, with the most frequently cited reasons for the procedure being breech presentation, a very slow birth, fetal distress, or that the mother had previously had a cesarean. Especially concerning was the fact that women who had had C-sections in the past were being discouraged from attempting vaginal birth, even though the American College of Obstetricians and Gynecologists recommended that "women with a previous C-section be given a chance to deliver naturally if possible."

The high number of C-sections performed in the US at the time of the study may have been caused by financial concerns on the part of hospitals and insurance companies. A study of hospitals grouped by ownership type found that for-profit hospitals had the highest rates of cesareans at 25.3 percent of all live births. It may also be the case that doctors ordered unnecessary C-sections to avoid malpractice lawsuits. Moreover, the report noted that research revealed an increase in the practice later in the evenings, when there tend to be fewer doctors on-site at most hospitals.

Public Citizen's research spotlighted the qualms of many within the medical community about the frequency of C-sections and urged a reevaluation of the reasons for conducting the procedure. Indeed, as Project Censored observed in 1995, one recognized authority on the topic, Dr. Emanuel A. Friedman, professor of Obstetrics and Gynecology at Beth Israel Hospital in Boston, believed that about 50 percent of cesareans for labor arrest disorders (dilation of the cervix and other standard stages in labor that either come to a stop or slow dramatically) "are unnecessary."

Moreover, the authors of the Public Citizen study pointed out that the epidemic of cesareans in the mid-1990s reflected a more general trend of substandard maternal health care in the United States.

Coverage of the report's findings was scarce at the time of its release, especially among corporate media. The *Los Angeles Times* published an article by Sheryl Stolberg that touched on the reports' results and controversy around the issue, but focused specifically on the prevalence of C-sections in Southern California.[85] The *Wall Street Journal* published a brief article, but only covered the report's finding of a small dip in the use of cesareans in 1992.[86]

Update

Since appearing on Project Censored's list of "Top Censored Stories of 1995," the issue of unnecessary cesareans has gotten significantly more attention from the corporate press as well as the medical establishment. This growing awareness has been part of a general public discussion about the need for improvements to maternal health care in the United States.[87] A variety of news outlets have carried articles on the issue, including a *Los Angeles Times* piece that examined plateauing cesarean rates in California and a *USA Today* report detailing a decision by the Joint Commission—the nation's oldest health care standards-setting body—to publicize C-section rates in an effort to prevent unnecessary procedures.[88] In 2010, the PRX radio program the *World* published a summary of World Health Organization research showing that some sixty-nine countries had excessive rates of birth via cesarean—defined as more than 15 percent of total births—and revealing that the United States had the third-highest rate of unnecessary C-sections of all the countries surveyed.[89]

In the past three decades, hospitals and medical providers in the United States have taken several steps to remedy these high rates. The nation overall has seen a slight decrease in total C-section rates from a peak of 32.9 percent in 2009 to 31.7 percent in 2019.[90]

California is one state that has committed to reducing unnecessary C-sections. After implementing a campaign that included "messaging to all hospitals from state agencies and health plans, annual public reporting of hospitals' C-section rates, and a quality improvement program targeting hospitals with the highest rates," California saw a drop in the number of C-sections.[91] The medical community has also reevaluated the once widely accepted requirement that women who have had a C-section avoid giving birth vaginally in subsequent pregnancies. In fact, some progress has been made toward a federal goal of increasing VBAC (vaginal birth after cesarean), although not as rapidly as officials had hoped.[92]

Still, it is concerning that the share of births by C-section continues to rise globally. A recent report by the World Health Organization documented that the rate of C-section delivery worldwide increased from 7 percent in 1990 to 21 percent in 2021.[93] Despite this alarming development, corporate media have tended to limit their coverage of the topic to the improvements in the United States. Moreover, the related problem of high levels of US maternal mortality—which most observers agree is connected to the prevalence of C-section births in this country—has still not received the corporate media attention it deserves; indeed, in 2017, Project Censored spotlighted the astronomically high incidence of maternal mortality in the US as one of the top censored news stories of 2017–2018.[94]

MACK PARLATORE graduated from North Central College with a bachelor's degree in Philosophy, Law and Society in 2022. His interest in environmental ethics drove his research around water privatization and food consolidation. As part of Berkeley Law's Class of 2025 he hopes not only to get in a few trips to California's Yosemite National Park but to pursue further research and action in the field of environmental justice.

SHEALEIGH VOITL graduated from North Central College in 2021. She was a co-author of the Déjà Vu chapter in last year's Project Censored volume. Shealeigh is currently working as a freelance journalist and Project Censored Research Associate.

ANALISA CHUDZIK is a graduating senior at North Central College with a major in Political Science and a minor in Gender and Sexuality Studies. Last year, she co-edited the Top 25 chapter of Project Censored's *State of the Free Press 2022*.

STEVE MACEK is Professor of Communication at North Central College and a frequent contributor to Project Censored's annual books. His op-eds and articles on the media, politics, and the First Amendment have been published in Truthout, Common Dreams, *Z Magazine*, Ms. Magazine Online, and assorted other newspapers and online publications.

Notes

1. Hanna Joerss, Zhiyong Xie, Charlotte C. Wanger, Wilken-Jon von Appen, Elsie M. Sunderland, and Ralf Ebinghaus, "Transport of Legacy Perfluoroalkyl Substances and the Replacement Compound HFPO-DA through the Atlantic Gateway to the Arctic Ocean—Is the Arctic a Sink or a Source?" *Environmental Science and Technology*, Vol. 54 No. 16 (2020), 9958–9967.

2. Francisca Ribeiro, Elvis D. Okoffo, Jake W. O'Brein, Sarah Fraissinet-Tachet, Stacey O'Brien, Michael Gallen, Saer Samanipour, Sarit Kaserzon, Jochen F. Mueller, Tamara Galloway, and Kevin V. Thomas, "Quantitative Analysis of Selected Plastics in High-Commercial-Value Australian Seafood by Pyrolysis Gas Chromatography Mass Spectrometry," *Environmental Science and Technology*, Vol. 54 (2020), 9408–9417.

3. Sharon Lerner, "PFAS Chemical Associated with COVID-19," The Intercept, December 7, 2020.

4. Lisa Cox, "Australia Joins US, China and Russia in Refusing to Sign Leaders' Pledge on Biodiversity," *The Guardian*, September 28, 2020.

5. Katherine Bourzac, "CFC Replacements Are a Source of Persistent Organic Pollution in the Arctic," *Chemical and Engineering News*, May 2, 2020.

6. Graham Readfearn, "It's on Our Plates and in Our Poo, but Are Microplastics a Health Risk?" *The Guardian*, May 15, 2021.

7. Damian Carrington, "Microplastics Cause Damage to Human Cells, Study Shows," *The Guardian*, December 8, 2021.

8. Heather A. Leslie, Martin J. M. van Velzen, Sicco H. Brandsma, A. Dick Vethaak, Juan J. Garcia-Vallejo, and Marja H. Lamoree, "Discovery and Quantification of Plastic Particle Pollution in Human Blood," Environment International, March 24, 2022.

9. Damian Carrington, "Microplastics Found in Human Blood for the First Time," *The Guardian*, March 24, 2022.

10. Lauren C. Jenner, Jeanette M. Rotchell, Robert T. Bennett, Michael Cowen, Vasileios Tentzeris and Laura R. Sadofsky, "Detection of Microplastics in Human Lung Tissue Using μFtir Spectroscopy," *Science of the Total Environment*, Vol. 831, 2022.

11. Damian Carrington, "Microplastics Found Deep in the Lungs of Living People for the First Time," *The Guardian*, April 6, 2022.

12. Hiroko Tabuchi, "The World Is Awash in Plastic, Nations Plan a Treaty to Fix That," *New York Times*, March 2, 2022.

13. Mike Snider, "Microplastics Have Been Found in Air, Water, Food . . . and Now Blood," *USA Today*, March 25, 2022; Sophie Mellor, "Tiny Particles of Plastic Have Been Detected in Human Blood for the First

Time. They Can't Be Filtered Out," *Fortune*, March 24, 2022; Kanoko Matsuyama, "Microplastics Found in Blood for the First Time, Study Says," Bloomberg, March 25, 2022.

14. Evan Bush, "Microplastics in the Human Body: What We Know and Don't Know," *NBC News*, April 11, 2022; Ed Browne, "What are Microplastics? Fragments Found in Human Lungs, Blood for the First Time," *Newsweek*, April 7, 2022; Wyatte Grantham-Philips, "Researchers Find Microplastics in the Lungs of Living People for the First Time, " *USA Today*, April 8, 2022; Rina Torchinsky, "For the First Time, Researchers Find Microplastics Deep in the Lungs of Living People," NPR, April 6, 2022.

15. Hiroko Tabuchi, "The World Is Awash in Plastic"; Michael Birnbaum and Min Joo Kim, "Plastic Production is Skyrocketing. A New UN Treaty Effort Could Cap It," *Washington Post*, February 8, 2022.

16. Jacob Bunge and Jesse Newman, "Bayer's Bid for Monsanto Faces Hurdles; Wave of Consolidation in Agricultural Sector would Give Significant Power to Three Companies," *Wall Street Journal*, May 19, 2016.

17. Ibid.

18. Ibid.

19. Ibid.

20. Brian Fung and Caitlin Dewey, "Justice Department Approves Bayer-Monsanto Merger in Landmark Settlement," *Washington Post*, May 29, 2018.

21. Ibid.

22. Kelsey Gee, "Egg Prices Jump as Bird Flu Spreads; Almost 39 Million Birds Dead; Industry Consolidation Compounds Problem," *Wall Street Journal*, May 21, 2015.

23. Ibid.

24. Ibid.

25. Taylor Greene and Kenn Burrows, "Seed Sovereignty Movements Challenge Corporate Monopolies," *State of the Free Press 2022*, eds. Andy Lee Roth and Mickey Huff (New York: Seven Stories Press, 2022), 74–78.

26. Ibid.

27. See, for example, another of the Project's Top 25 stories from 2020-2021: Emily Utsig and Elliot D. Cohen, "US Factory Farming a Breeding Ground for Next Pandemic," *State of the Free Press 2022*, 83–86.

28. Nina Lakhani, Aliya Uteuova, and Alvin Chang. "Revealed: The True Extent of America's Food Monopolies, and Who Pays the Price," *The Guardian*, July 14, 2021.

29. Ibid.

30. Ibid.

31. Ibid.

32. Ibid.

33. Alan Rappeport and Michael Corkery. "Biden's Choice of Vilsack for U.S.D.A. Raises Fears for Small Farmers," *New York Times*, December 21, 2020, updated January 19, 2021.

34. Ibid.

35. Dan Kaufman. "Is It Time to Break Up Big Ag?," *New Yorker*, August 17, 2021.

36.   Ibid. One month after Biden's executive order, Dairy Farmers of America was exposed as having purchased millions of dollars of milk made with prison labor.

37.   Ibid.

38.   Vijay Prashad, "COP26: Uberizing Farms to Save the Climate," Consortium News, November 19, 2021.

39.   Ibid.

40.   Maude Barlow, *Blue Gold: The Global Water Crisis and the Commodification of the World's Water Supply*, International Forum on Globalization, June 1999 (Revised Edition, Spring 2001).

41.   "Bechtel Surrenders in Bolivia Water Revolt Case," *Earthjustice*, January 19, 2006.

42.   Ibid.

43.   Ibid.

44.   Ibid.

45.   See, e.g., Antonio Arenas, Nguyet (Kelley) Thi Luu, and Kenn Burrows, "Popular Resistance to Corporate Water Grabbing," in *Censored 2016: Media Freedom on the Line*, eds. Mickey Huff and Andy Lee Roth with Project Censored (New York: Seven Stories Press, 2015), 48–52.

46.   Joseph Viso and Steve Macek, "Aqua America Seeks to Privatize Pittsburgh's Water," Project Censored, March 12, 2019.

47.   Doug Shields, "The Stealthy Corporate Scheme to Privatize Pittsburgh's Water System," *In These Times*, January 14, 2019.

48.   Ibid.

49.   Ibid.

50.   Ibid.

51.   Bruce Murphy, "8 Problems with Privatizing Water Utilities," *Urban Milwaukee*, February 2, 2016.

52.   Ibid.

53.   Nina Lakhani, "Corporate Vultures: How Americans Fearing Higher Water Bills Are Fighting Takeovers," *The Guardian*, January 25, 2022.

54.   Ibid.

55.   Ibid.

56.   Kenny Cooper, "What's at Stake in the Fight over the Chester Water Authority," WHYY, November 14, 2021.

57.   David Dayen, "Bipartisan Senate Infrastructure Plan Is a Stalking Horse for Privatization," *American Prospect*, June 21, 2021.

58.   Ibid.

59.   Ibid.

60.   Ibid.

61.   Ibid.

62.   "No Water Privatization in the Infrastructure Plan," Food & Water Watch, July 1, 2021.

63.   "NY Applauds Sen. Schumer as Water Privatization Appears Absent in Bipartisan Infrastructure Framework," Food & Water Watch, July 30, 2021.

64.   Katie Lobosco and Tami Luhby, "Here's What We Know So Far About the Bipartisan Infrastructure Deal," CNN, June 24, 2021.

65.   Clyde Wayne Crews Jr., "Republicans Should Kill the Bipartisan Infrastructure Bill and Do This Instead," *Forbes*, August 2, 2021.

66. David Dayen, "Kids' Health or Corporate Profits?" *Los Angeles Times*, July 10, 2018.
67. "A Baby Formula Blunder," *Washington Post*, July 16, 2018.
68. Miriam Jordan, "Nestlé Markets Baby Formula to Hispanic Mothers in US," *Wall Street Journal*, March 4, 2004.
69. Wendy Orent, "A Formula to Put Babies at Risk; the Bush Administration Squelched Ads That Promoted the Benefits of Breast-Feeding," *Los Angeles Times*, September 30, 2007.
70. Marc Kaufman and Christopher Lee, "HHS Toned Down Breast-Feeding Ads; Formula Industry Urged Softer Campaign," *Washington Post*, August 31, 2007.
71. Jordan, "Nestlé Markets Baby Formula."
72. Laura Santhanam, "Racial Disparities Persist for Breastfeeding Moms. Here's Why," *PBS News Hour*, August 29, 2019.
73. Ibid.
74. "Nursing Grudges: The Debate Over Public Breast-Feeding," *Washington Post*, August 9, 2012.
75. Jennifer Delgado, "Hospitals Take Baby Steps," *Chicago Tribune*, January 10, 2013.
76. "Celebrating Evergreen Hospital, Baby-Friendly Trailblazers," *Baby-Friendly USA*, May 31, 2019.
77. Editorial Board, "Why Breast-Feeding Scares Donald Trump," *New York Times*, July 9, 2018.
78. Ibid.
79. Ibid.
80. Andrew Jacobs, "Opposition to Breast-Feeding Resolution by U.S. Stuns World Health Officials," *New York Times*, July 8, 2018.
81. Ibid.
82. Ibid.
83. Jordan, "Nestlé Markets Baby Formula."
84. Kevin Horrigan, "Big Baby and the Triumph of Corporate America," *Chicago Tribune*, July 18, 2018.
85. Sheryl Stolberg, "Cesarean Birth Rate Leveling Off Health: Experts, Who Say Half the Procedures Are Unnecessary, Fear the U.S. Will Not Meet Its Goal of Lowering Surgeries to 15% of All Deliveries," *Los Angeles Times*, May 19, 1994.
86. "Caesarean-Section Births Eased in 1992, Data Shows," *Wall Street Journal*, May 19, 1994, B4.
87. Elizabeth Dawes Gay, "Congressional Briefing Puts U.S. Maternity on Exam Table," Women's eNews, April 15, 2016.
88. Jacqueline H. Wolf, "Too Many Caesareans, at Too Much Risk," *Los Angeles Times*, July 29, 2018, and Adrianna Rodriguez, "Unnecessary C-Sections Are a Problem in the US. Will Publicizing Hospital Rates Change That?" *USA Today*, December 21, 2020.
89. Tory Starr, "Why Are Cesarean Sections So Common When Most Agree They Shouldn't Be?" The World, May 12, 2014.
90. Maternal Safety Foundation, "Understanding Cesarean Rates," Cesarean Rates.org, undated [accessed February 17, 2022].
91. Erin Digitale, "California Campaign Lowers Statewide C-Section Rate, Study Reports," Stanford Medicine, April 27, 2021.

92.   Gaby Galvin, "The U.S. Rate of Vaginal Birth After C-Section Is Increasing, CDC Data Finds," *U.S. News & World Report*, March 5, 2020.

93.   Laura Keenan and Elizabeth Noble, "Caesarean Section Rates Continue to Rise, amid Growing Inequalities in Access," World Health Organization, June 16, 2021.

94.   Jane C. Hau, Hope Matheson, Andy Lee Roth, and Steve Macek, "Maternal Mortality Growing in the US," *Censored 2018: Press Freedom in a "Post-Truth" World*, eds. Andy Lee Roth and Mickey Huff (New York: Seven Stories Press, 2017), 59–61.

Junk in the Box:
Eat, Prey, Fight
Nothing Brings People Together (and Apart)
Like Junk Food News

JEN LYONS, SIERRA KAUL, MARCELLE SWINBURNE,
GAVIN KELLEY, and MICKEY HUFF

If I like a food, I'll eat it, even if I know it's not good for me.
—KIM KARDASHIAN

*It's also like if you go to a great restaurant, even if I'm a
shitty date, it's like at least the food was great.*
—PETE DAVIDSON

WHAT'S ON THE MENU?

Who's hungry? Craving something to fulfill your nutritional yearning, maybe something that's not the most well-balanced meal? Then this year's Junk Food News menu is for you!

"Junk Food News" is a term first coined by Project Censored founder Carl Jensen in 1983, defined as a category of sensationalist, inconsequential (but undeniably delicious in the moment) news stories that receive substantial coverage by corporate news outlets, thus distracting audiences from more significant, newsworthy stories.[1] While our past Junk Food News stories have been categorized as afternoon or midnight snacks, this year's lineup is a luxurious four-course meal. As COVID fatigue began to fade and the once-mandated masks came off, Junk Food News grew more abundant and filling than ever. However, after two years of those masks, social distancing, vaccine debates, and overall uncertainty associated with the global pandemic, it was as if Americans had completely forgotten how to behave at the dinner table! These crude table manners left viewers stuffed to the brim with subpar stories, distracting from the *real* news that could and should be filling the menu of the so-called public airwaves.

This year's *prix fixe* menu of Junk Food News is a four-course, Michelin-star meal of mediocrity and mendacity. Cocktail hour includes none other than Kimye's inevitable divorce and the infamous Kardashian rebound, Pete Davidson. The charcuterie board boasts cheeses, meats, sausages, and hints of *dicks in space*—billionaires outspending each other to catch a glimpse of the world turning and burning from above. The main course of the delicious lineup this year is a hearty serving of superstar gossip, including brawls between a multitude of celebrities and cable news networks alike. Ever *Heard* of it? We know Johnny Depp has—along with millions of Americans who couldn't turn away from the televised four-week, he-said, she-said defamation trial. To finish off this delectable meal there's a finger-licking discussion about on- and off-the-field headlines regarding NFL quarterbacks—including controversies surrounding their blushing brides and deciding whether to actually spend time with their families, all while sexual assault allegations hit double digits.

This year's Junk Food News menu, as copious as they

come, has also transitioned into fine dining. We all have to grow up eventually, don't we? This subcategory of news distraction did just that this past year. While Kanye West (now Ye) openly stalked his eventual ex-wife, Kim Kardashian, and her new beau, Pete Davidson (of *Saturday Night Live* fame), no actions were taken, even as Ye acted out and showed undeniable signs of committing domestic abuse while the cameras rolled and millions tuned in. Remember the Cold War Space Race between the former Soviet Union and the United States in the 1950s and 1960s? Jeff Bezos, Richard Branson, and Elon Musk went ahead and turned that into a modern-day dick-measuring contest, for lack of a better phrase, to see who could get there first for the longest. Their space outfits, extensively reported on by CNN Science, received more attention than the pollution caused by this narcissistic billionaire power competition, in which one rocket launch produced an estimated 300 tons of carbon dioxide in the upper atmosphere, where it can remain for years.[2] But, lord knows, corporate media wouldn't miss the chance to provide live updates as Musk tried to take over the fading social media platform of Twitter! Tweet, tweet.

Aside from the annual Keeping Up with the Kardashians banter and our growing collective disdain for mostly hand-me-down billionaires, additional celebrity gossip served as this year's Junk Food News main course. With daytime trash TV hosts Maury Povich and Jerry Springer officially retired, celebrities took matters into their own hands. Hollywood giant Will Smith kicked things off when he whacked comedian Chris Rock in front of the Academy Awards audience at this year's Oscars in what would become known as "the slap heard 'round the world." Spotify podcast giant and UFC front man Joe Rogan stepped into the Octagon to face off against CNN, while Whoopi Goldberg challenged the daytime television program *The View*. But a new group of drama kings emerged this year: NFL quarterbacks! From retiring for a total of forty days before a triumphant return, to a concerning number of sexual assault accusations, some of the highest-paid athletes in the United States made waves both on and off the turf. And, you guessed it, the media had a field day! Why report on US/NATO history as Russia invades Ukraine or the disappearing of an entire TV network from cable services and YouTube, when one could focus on the guaranteed $230 million contract of a known sexual predator?

We hope you came hungry for this year's Junk Food News chapter. The world has certainly transformed since last year's "return to normalcy," and Americans ate it up. Despite the upgrade to fine dining in this year's go-around, the kitchen never closes when it comes to Junk Food News. So, pull up a chair, imbibe your drink of choice, and enjoy the titillating idiocy of this year's top Junk Food News stories. *Bon appétit*!

KIMYE: CHAMPAGNE MARRIAGE AND A BEER BUDGET DIVORCE

Of course, one of the biggest junkets from the past year was perhaps more contagious than any of the COVID variants spreading: Kimye. Got. Divorced. The family whose names nearly utilize the entire compass finally went their separate directions: Kim Kardashian West's relationship with Kanye West went south (no mention of how North

West, their firstborn, is doing). Less than a year after their separation Kanye (now known simply as "Ye") reportedly bought the house directly across from Kardashian, paying nearly ten times the asking price so he could be near his children.[3] This sparked a range of internet jokes, including, "This is how Gatsby got shot" and "Do you think he'll try holding up a boombox outside?" Others seem to think it's a way for him to keep an eye on his ex-wife's new beaus, and perhaps intimidate them.

Meanwhile, in another shocking twist, Kardashian began dating the walking embodiment of what twelve-year-olds think is cool, the champagne of beer, Miller Low Life, Pete Davidson. As a popular recent *Saturday Night Live* alumnus, Davidson was known for a myriad of things, including, according to CNN Business, leaving the popular show.[4] Before that, he was known for his very public relationship with Ariana Grande that ended in 2018, and his hit song with Timothée Chalamet, "Yeet." Davidson has become relatively infamous for his capability to pull in such attractive, rich women, which was cause for an even bigger avalanche of jokes, but not at Davidson's expense. Rather they were aimed at all other men: examples include "Maybe Pete just texts back at a normal rate" and "He probably doesn't use a 2-in-1 shampoo conditioner combo," and the best for last: "Maybe he asks Kim what she wants to do."

No matter what traits Davidson has that could be considered green flags for a partner, the internet certainly was enthralled with whether their relationship is a strange conspiracy, perhaps set up by Momager Kris Jenner? Could it be that their whole relationship was a long plot devised by Davidson as revenge for having to pick up a hefty Nobu dinner tab that West (Ye) had racked up one birthday celebration?[5] Diving deeper into the rabbit hole, Ye recently started dating actress/model Julia Fox, who once modeled as the Barbie to Pete Davidson's Ken in a photoshoot for *Paper* magazine.[6] Coincidence? Twitter users with too much time on their hands say it's not. Supposedly, Ye is so unhappy and jealous of his ex-wife dating Davidson that he went immediately to spoiling the nearest woman connected to Davidson that he could—Fox.[7] Never mind that Fox and Davidson never dated, nor ever showed any romantic inclination toward each other, Ye quickly moved in for the kill after meeting Fox on New Year's Eve 2021 and was already in a committed relationship before the end of the first week of 2022. Since we finished typing that sentence (less than a few months after the start of the relationship), Fox and Ye broke up, with Ye already starting a new relationship with a beauty influencer who looks remarkably like his ex. Basically, Ye is developing new relationships faster than COVID develops new variants.

But the worst part of it all is the extensive news coverage of the whole farce. Ye and Kardashian seem to be everywhere—once confined to gossip columns of *People* magazine and E! television, the trash TV icons have reinvented themselves to appear as regulars on the streaming platform Hulu, as well as make headlines for CNN, BBC, and even the award-winning *San Jose Mercury News*. But what these news outlets and others have missed is that Ye is openly stalking his ex-wife, and no one seems to care.

With his Twitter rants and recent raps dissing every new addition to Kardashian's life (including a bizarre Claymation music video in which he appears to behead Davidson),

Ye has been engaging in undeniably questionable behavior toward his estranged wife. According to the National Network to End Domestic Violence, "stalking is a serious issue affecting more than six million people each year.... [I]t is often one of many tactics that abusers use in order to maintain power and control over a current or former intimate partner."[8] Stalking partners is especially evident in pop culture, with this situation being no exception.

In fact, the National Network to End Domestic Violence also notes, "All too often, messages in the media portray stalking as an extreme, even desirable, display of love and devotion. Or, the behavior is minimized and normalized, attributed to a change in social norms that we should accept." The Network goes on to say, "While it may seem harmless, the more we normalize and accept these messages, the harder it can be for victims of stalking to identify the harm they're experiencing, to be believed if they disclose it, and to be supported if they choose to reach out for help."[9] Although we laugh at the vapid nature of many celebrities, it cannot go unnoticed that Kardashian's safety is on the line in a very real way. And in this specific case, both parties may have bitten off more than they can chew.... With this being only the first course, it is going to be a long meal. Some of you may want to grab the antacids and a critical thinking textbook, stat, and possibly open another bottle of *whine*.

DICKS IN SPACE: BILLIONAIRES PUSHING THE BOUNDARIES OF TASTE

It was the "year of space tourism," "the year of the billionaires," the year space became "sexy all over again." Between summer 2021 and spring 2022, there were hundreds of news stories across corporate media outlets celebrating and/or criticizing the billionaire space race. While this rich dude bratwurst dish appears filling, it turns out that all this news is about as nourishing as a tin of Vienna Sausages.

The news of the billionaire space race launched in the summer of 2021 with Amazon's Jeff Bezos, Twitter's aspiring stepdad, Elon Musk, and Sir Richard Branson of Virgin Group boldly going where no one could afford to go before—all vying to buy a spot in history. CNN was one of the main media outlets covering this new space race in detail, centering its reports on the dick-measuring contest between the three magnates. In its business pages, CNN covered the sword fight between Bezos and Branson vying to be the first to launch themselves into Earth's upper atmosphere, with Branson scooping Bezos by nine days to be the first of the billionaires to take a suborbital flight, via his company Virgin Galactic, on July 11, 2021.[10] Not only was Bezos's Blue Origin flight upstaged by Branson, but Bezos also lost a $2.9 billion government contract from NASA to build the next lunar lander module, prompting Bezos to go to court to cry about it. If we're taking out the old measuring tape and doing this, SpaceX's Inspiration4 flight in September 2021, bankrolled by another man with too much money, did measure bigger and longer than both Bezos's and Branson's suborbital flights, going higher than the International Space Station and orbiting Earth several times in a three-day period. Musk's SpaceX has since transported astronauts to the International Space Station, while Bezos's Blue Origin has mostly made news for shuttling PR-grubbing celebrities and rich brats into space for mere minutes. Since the failures and mistakes reported in Branson's short flight, the media have reported that Branson plans to fly next on a SpaceX vessel,[11] while also scolding the vassals back on Earth to slow down while driving to decrease European fuel demand from the West's continued and renewed Cold War enemy, Russia.[12]

Of particular interest to the *New York Times* was Star Trek's William Shatner launching into space in October 2021, on Bezos's Blue Origin flight. *The New York Times* alone published stories on October 4 and October 7, several on October 13, and another on October 14 on this specific topic. News outlets gushed as the famous "Captain Kirk," known on television in the 1960s for his own virility and libido in space, became the oldest man to journey into real-life space. Also wasting fellow Earthlings' time and attention was the news that Pete Davidson was pulling out of a relatively quiet plan that would have seen the first comedian in space.[13] Any of us normies offered a flight may fear the safety of these billionaire-funded endeavors, but Davidson had the added worries of rocket sabotage by Ye and/or the likelihood of Kim Kardashian moving on to her next beau while he was briefly off-planet. Fox News reported that comedian Ricky Gervais, while on the *Tonight Show Starring Jimmy Fallon*, said that he had also turned down an offer to do a short comedy set in space.[14] That's a double whammy, in that we got a news report about a celebrity comment made on a late-night show about an event that wasn't going to happen.

Throughout this modern-day, privatized space race, there have been a multitude of stories regarding what these billionaire astronauts were wearing. These news pieces weren't confined to Entertainment and Style sections but often appeared on the Science and Technology pages of historic publications. For example, the *New York Times* Science pages offered a story about the designs of the uniforms worn by self-styled space cowboy Jeff Bezos and his crew. Any chance those space diapers can be retrofitted for your Amazon workers and delivery drivers denied bathroom breaks, Jeff?[15] Talk about averting a modern Triangle Shi[r]twaist Factory fire! We also learned that Elon Musk hired the costume designer for movies like *Batman v Superman* and *The Avengers* to create functional space suits worthy of Hollywood red carpets. He realizes those are movies, right? Bringing sexy back, indeed.

The billionaire space race has not been without its criticisms, from realistic analyses of the dangers of space travel in the hands of civilians to warnings from the *New York Times* and *Washington Post* against the further expansion of unregulated Big Tech into space. Joining critics of this "cosmic country club," notable silver-spoon monarch Prince William weighed in, earning himself several fawning news pieces by Fox News and the *Wall Street Journal*. But with the royal family's history of environmental exploitation and degradation, it doesn't appear that Prince William has a third leg to stand on. We get that you were a "real" pilot, but if you want to enter this contest, you'll need to whip out something bigger than the private jets you normally charter. Only one independent news source, Truthout, reported on a Media Matters for America study that found that morning TV shows gave as much airtime to Bezos's 2021 space launch as they did to *all climate crisis news* in 2020.[16] Maybe Prince William forgot his place in the global elite, the top 1 percent, that Oxfam showed in late 2020 emitted more than double the carbon pollution of 3 billion of the world's poorest people.[17] The Oxfam study was actually well reported on by a panoply of sources—some even mainstream-corporate—that included CNN, *Forbes*, CNBC, BBC, the *Guardian*, and even government-owned news outlets in William's home country, the UK, no?

While Bezos bobs around in space, the behemoth creature he left behind, the Amazon corporation, made its own news as its package-packed vans swarmed across the Earth. Legacy media outlets such as the *New York Times* have covered the battle between the Amazon corporation and its employees. We know of the years-long new stories about the *pissy* labor conditions of delivery driving for Amazon, but more recent news has focused on the efforts of warehouse workers to unionize in Alabama and New York. A *New York Times* report published around the time of Bezos and Shatner's little voyage headlined a story "How Amazon Crushes Unions."[18] We're truly living in a post-apocalyptic movie, one that feels like it was written by Mike Judge (*Idiocracy*, *Beavis and Butt-Head*) and directed by John Carpenter (*They Live*). Corporations are allegedly persons before the law, but ones with limitless protections. The rich are cosmonauts escaping Earth to people new planets. Meanwhile, the rest of us will be left here on Earth eating Soylent Green, which, if you didn't know, is made out of people.

In the meantime, corporate media (*Fortune*, CBS, the *Guardian*, Fox Business, CNBC) have been discussing the rising pay of CEOs through the pandemic. What goes unmentioned in so-called mainstream news is that the top 1 percent dodge upwards of $160 billion in taxes a year.[19] According to the Institute on Taxation and Economic

Policy, because of Amazon's tax breaks, it avoided over $5 billion in federal taxes.[20] Also escaping the attention of corporate media are the stories covering the potentially $10 billion Congressional participation trophy—rather, bailout of Blue Origin—so Bezos could build a lunar lander, after losing his court challenge to NASA, which decided to go with Musk's SpaceX for the job. So, American taxpayers essentially helped pay for executive chair Bezos to cosplay as Bruce Willis in *Armageddon* and go joyride in space. It is the public subsidizing these wealthy ego trips into space. Why can't these billionaires pay for their own phallic flights to the moon (and perhaps take up residence there)?

If we had to choose a winner in this space race so far, it would undoubtedly be Elon Musk's SpaceX. That's SpaceX, mind you, not Musk himself. Musk has become bogged down in negative press, covering everything from his loud, scammy squawking about buying out Twitter in the name of free speech, to his intimate ties with the embroiled Amber Heard and Johnny Depp—did you hear that they divorced and that we were all a part of it? Meanwhile, SpaceX has continued in 2022 to launch rockets and Starlink satellites to ferry real astronauts back and forth to the International Space Station, causing no scandals in the media whatsoever. Actually, no so-called mainstream news as of mid-May 2022 had turned toward Business Insider's report that SpaceX paid $250,000 in 2018 to settle a sexual harassment claim by a corporate jet flight attendant stemming from a 2016 incident in which Musk bared his human penis and offered the flight attendant/licensed massage therapist a horse in exchange for an erotic massage.[21] Regardless of how the story pans out, it has already blasted off with the corporate media's undivided attention.

In the midst of all this cosmic melodrama, scientific sources have remained concerned (some since the 1990s) over the increase of space junk orbiting Earth, pieces of debris abandoned over years of space exploration. *Scientific American*, *Nature*, *New Scientist*, and even the *Washington Post* have reported on "space junk" and the dangers space debris poses to the world's space stations and satellites in 2022. An article from The Hill in November 2021 featured a science team's prediction that this space junk would eventually form Saturn-like rings around Earth.[22] While proponents of the billionaire space race argue that it will make space travel cheaper and more advanced in the long run, more reputable sources such as *New Scientist* report on the damage done by increased space junk on astronomical studies years in the making.[23] Then there are the physical, potentially fatal, risks facing astronauts on the International Space Station (ISS), who had to delay a spacewalk in November 2021 because of the threat of space debris.[24] One would think that 20,000–30,000 pieces of dangerous space junk would be the focus of the news media, particularly as these pieces of junk interfere with real-life scientific endeavors and crash into bodies like the Moon. But warning the worldwide public that Musk is a misogynistic massage creep (which is also an issue) has taken and will continue to take higher priority than the ever-growing possibility that space debris might hit the Earth, the ISS, future rocket flights, and more. Literal space junk food news around men catapulting their junk into orbit. It remains all too convenient to blame debris falling to Earth on China, as was the case in May 2021 and May 2022.[25]

In addition, many scientists worry about the long-term effects this modern-day space race may have on future Earthlings. According to a recent study by the National Oceanic and Atmospheric Agency (NOAA) covered in *Popular Mechanics*, the increase of black carbon being put into the atmosphere because of rocket fuel will likely increase the temperature of the stratosphere by up to 4 degrees Fahrenheit. The report notes this temperature rise could dampen the ozone layer and alter atmospheric circulation.[26] In short, this is not good news.

Also less reported than the schadenfreude-infused stories about the characters of Musk and Bezos are the ones about possible solutions to cleaning up space junk created by China, the US, Russia, and India. There have been only a handful of establishment media stories about these efforts, or at least, the need for efforts such as these to exist.[27] Humanity has penetrated space and ejaculated our dangerous litter. Take it from there, NASA and Space Force and … real scientists. But, unlike here on Earth with the climate crisis, we can't possibly be blaming space pollution on the world's individuals when it's only the largest corporations, the military–industrial complex, and the wealthiest humans assaulting our orbital space to bring their massage-and-cowboy-couture culture up into the cosmic country club. We can only hope the media won't add to this corporate-sponsored blame game and continue to shrug off stories about the climate crisis.

All of this news hasn't been fruitless, however. We commend the phallic memes created over the course of the billionaire space race. We also commend the entrepreneurs out there like the porn website that created a line of sex toys called the "Billionaire Flesh Rocket" series. In a way, this exploration has not been in vein—sorry, vain. In Branson's case, space is no longer Virgin. And as the billionaire space race continues, so in turn will the massive, girthy attention paid to it by corporate news media as the world burns.

UNHAPPY HOUR: APPS 'N' SLAPS FOR THE TABLE

Meanwhile, down here on the ground, the ultimate undefeated Junk News champion that captures our imagination (and most importantly, attention) is a circle jerk that only celebrities can provide! We all know that some of the most widely viewed programs on television are live, from the Super Bowl to the Academy Awards. However, those events are essentially one-offs that can't maintain a distracted public for more than their allotted 180-minute airtime.

But the elite in the entertainment world know that truly sustainable distractions are the soap operatic lives of the celebrated rich and infamous, as they war in court, on talk shows, or over social media. So much like the pastie nip slip seen round the world when Justin Timberlake ripped Janet Jackson's top off during the 2004 Super Bowl halftime show (no wardrobe malfunction, just misogyny as entertainment), Will Smith's right-hand strike across Chris Rock's left cheek during the live presentation of the Academy Awards became the headline-grabbing slap heard 'round the world. As ever, substantive stories of the Russian invasion of Ukraine or the United States' own twenty-year war on terrorism would fall off the front pages, if not off every page, to make room for such hot goss.

Yes, for the absolute purest form of uncut Junk News look no further than the intersection of celebrities and news-types fighting for all our First Amendment rights (because we all know the fight to regulate guns challenging the Second Amendment will not come between conservative senators and their economic love affair with the NRA, no matter how many innocent members of the public are sacrificed in the meantime). Or, more specifically, fighting for our attention as they hammer out who among them has the right to say what. These media types are judge and jury, inviting us to be the executioners, doling out punishment in the form of public shaming, extended coverage, hashtags, and slaps.

Professional megastars, who earn their multimillions through the art of mindless entertainment, ripped a chapter out of Jerry Springer's book circa 1995, as they fought for their right to grab headlines and trend through no-holds-barred shocktainment. Oscar winners, comedy legends, podcast royalty, talk TV celebrities, and legacy media pundits all jumped into the ring (or, in UFC front man Joe Rogan's case, the Octagon) this year, as they faced off in a war over who had the right to say what, while seeking to enlist us, the American consumer audience, to take up arms in the form of our social media handles. And did we ever!

Going full tactical nuclear with our hashtags, we left no celebrity freedom-of-junk-speech fight unscathed in the clashes of Chris Rock vs. Will Smith, Joe Rogan vs. CNN, Whoopi Goldberg vs. *The View,* Sam Elliot vs. Jane Campion's chaps, and Campion vs. the Williams sisters, not to mention Amber Heard vs. Johnny Depp, revealing poorly worded sexts for the world to see—celebrities really are like us! The divisiveness and resulting outrage become a full-time job: tweeting and retweeting in a thirsty search for likes pulls us away from real-world nuclear war concerns and US foreign policy hypocrisy. Did you hear about the plan to redeploy US troops in Somalia with a "persistent presence"?[28] Sorry, as you can tell from these last few pages, we've been distracted.

In this massive grab for ratings and subscriptions, the new king of talk, Spotify's podcast majesty Joe Rogan, reigns over legacy media. In response, rather than doing what the podcaster does with his haphazard interviews—exploring topics that might not otherwise see the light of a monetized platform—the hired hands of CNN and others go on the attack. So, whether we turn on Spotify or a cable network, we find ourselves transfixed by different angles of the same story. Are the pundits who rush to their split screens to express their shock and awe for thirty seconds sincere in their overzealous diatribes? Audience members have to wonder if said pundits are truly concerned about Rogan's questionable questions or whether they're just trying to pull viewers back into the legacy media's fold. If it trends, it leads.

Meanwhile in Hollywood, Sam Elliott, Oscar winner and co-star of the 1989 homoerotic *Roadhouse*, went on Marc Maron's WTF podcast and attacked *Power of the Dog* director Jane Campion for the overuse of chaps and the implications of that wardrobe choice. Campion clapped back, calling Elliott a "B-I-T-C-H" on a red carpet.[29] Fast-forward a few days, and the white Campion let African American tennis pros Serena and Venus Williams know that they didn't confront the type of adversity

Campion herself faced in the Best Director–nominated Oscar pool that saw her face off against only men. But we were told not to worry about that one—it was just a joke that didn't land, unlike Chris Rock's joke that landed him the "slap heard 'round the world" from Will Smith. Not live, mind you, as ratings for the Academy Awards were down this year, but the seemingly innocuous joke by the comedy veteran about Jada Pinkett Smith's hair and the slap back that followed by her husband, Will Smith, took over social media, legacy media, and even the Joe Rogan podcast, grabbing headlines far and above the peace summit that was taking place in Turkey between Russia and Ukraine.

Not to be outdone by Smith vs. Rock, Johnny Depp and his posse of bodyguards took the bout against his ex-wife, Amber Heard, to the courts, seeking a payoff that would make even World Boxing champion Floyd "Money" Mayweather blush. There's nothing quite like a month-long trial (coming after years of buildup) filled with sordid details to grab sustained headlines and spawn a whole slew of fanboys who weaponize YouTube with their daily excerpts from the trial, persuading fans who can't tune in for four-hour testimonies how they should feel. Good thing we were able to watch this live stream of a former celebrity couple trading blows, but we haven't heard a word on the trial regarding the partner of the late serial molester Jeffrey Epstein, Ghislaine Maxwell. Meanwhile, millionaire and megastar Depp will emerge millions richer from the trial. Surely, he won't make the same mistake his former domestic partner did by not following through on a pledge to support organizations dealing with victims of domestic abuse.

Doubt that the headline-grabbing celebrity circus is pure uncut distraction? Ask yourself, "What are the two most memorable quotes of 2022?" Surely, it's somewhere between Mr. Smith's "Keep my wife's name out your f—king mouth" and Ms. Heard's "My dog stepped on a bee." Those quotes will certainly be remembered more by the public than President Joe Biden's "gaffe" when he said that Russian president Vladimir Putin "cannot remain in power" or former president George W. Bush's epic Freudian slip in a talk he was giving at his presidential center in Dallas. Bush "mixed up" his own murderous regime's illegal invasion of Iraq in 2003 with Putin's current war in Ukraine when he quipped it was the "decision of one man to launch a wholly unjustified and brutal invasion of Iraq." Bush then quickly made a joke of it, muttering under his breath, "Iraq, too, anyway," as he corrected himself to awkward laughs from the audience.[30] Perhaps it's our presidents who should take some advice from Smith, and keep the names of foreign countries they want to invade, and leaders they want to undermine or eliminate, out their f—king mouths.

FINGER LICKIN' BAD: WAGS BLITZ THE QUARTERBACKS

When life gets crazy and things feel uncertain, it is always nice to have one constant to rely on: watching two teams of grown adult men trying to absolutely kill each other every autumnal Sunday, Monday, and now Thursday and sometimes even Saturday, via the National Football League (NFL). And now, insatiable Americans that we are, we have even added one more game to the regular season schedule. This way, the Detroit Lions and Jacksonville Jaguars fans can feel included for a whole extra week! Aside from the grotesque multimillion-dollar contracts that could solve world hunger and the grueling injuries that leave 300-pound men knocked out cold, members of the NFL made headlines for a multitude of reasons this season, both on and off the field.

First, Satan himself, quarterback Tom Brady, announced his retirement. And thank God. Creeping up on forty-five years old, Brady is married to an ultra-rich supermodel, has won more Super Bowls than any NFL franchise, and is considered one of, if not *the* greatest quarterback of all time. In February, he announced he would be hanging up his cleats for good, and rival fanbases shared a collective sigh of relief. But after nearly six whole weeks off the field, Brady had evidently spent more time with his family than he could handle. The quarterback announced via Twitter that he had changed his mind, would be unretiring, and would return for his twenty-third NFL season.[31] Brady proves that some men can have it all.

But some men can't. In contrast to Brady, Green Bay Packers quarterback Aaron Rodgers positioned himself as public enemy number one, midseason. After he claimed he was "immunized" to COVID-19, it was revealed that Rodgers had lied about his vaccination status to the media, and liberals had a field day.[32] Despite going on to win the 2021 Most Valuable Player award and signing a record-breaking $200 million four-year contract in the off-season, Rodgers received a mountain of backlash for opting to take Ivermectin, which liberals derisively call a "horse dewormer" (the use for which the drug is mostly known), to treat a virus that caused a global pandemic.

Rodgers was forced to isolate for ten days, causing the star quarterback to miss a key week-thirteen matchup against the Kansas City Chiefs. Not only that, but the mounting mass media pressure ultimately caused Rodgers and inarguably the world's most exciting actress, rumored fiancée Shailene Woodley, to split. I guess we can't all be Tom Brady.

Yet the want-to-be NFL power couple that caused the most off-the-field ruckus was Kansas City Chiefs quarterback Patrick Mahomes and his now-wife, Brittany Matthews. Aside from giving birth to the couple's first child, Sterling Skye, the WAG (a term often used for an athlete's wife and/or girlfriend) was making headlines for exuberant sideline celebrations at Arrowhead Stadium in Kansas City with then-future brother-in-law Jackson Mahomes. Things heated up when a tiff between Patrick and Brittany was caught on camera at a Texas Tech University basketball matchup, as Patrick reportedly told his future wife, "No more resting bitch face," triggering an immediate reaction.[33] But Mrs. Mahomes faced severe backlash when a viral tweet showed her spraying champagne on Kansas City fans in 37-degree weather after the team defeated the Buffalo Bills in the AFC divisional round of the 2021 playoffs. The future Mrs. faced so much criticism for her actions, she began selling T-shirts with the slogan "Free Brittany" in her defense. However, the twenty-six-year-old's life isn't all bad—she and high school sweetheart Patrick tied the knot in early March. The new Mrs. Mahomes wore a custom-made Versace dress, paired with an 8-carat engagement ring that is rumored to have cost well over $150,000. Husband Patrick signed a blockbuster deal in 2021 that led to an average annual salary of $45 million a season—second only to, you guessed it, Aaron Rodgers. So, despite the accountability poor Brittany faces for her public actions, she can use hundred-dollar bills to wipe her tears.

But one of the biggest off-season headlines was about a fourth NFL quarterback, Deshaun Watson. Watson was signed by the Cleveland Browns for a blockbuster fully guaranteed, five-year contract for $230 million.[34] Proud recipient of the most ensured money in NFL history, Watson sat out all of the 2021 season, due to trade-offer standoffs with the Houston Texans and, oh yeah, *twenty-four* outstanding sexual assault and misconduct cases.[35] Recently, the NFL quarterback settled twenty of these civil lawsuits, paying off a plethora of massage therapists who accused Watson of pressuring them to touch him sexually.[36] Still, the NFL is adamant about an *indefinite* suspension for the Cleveland Browns Quarterback.[37] According to the *Baltimore Sun*, "A person familiar with the case told the AP the league believes it presented evidence to warrant keeping Watson off the field this season [and that] he would be required to undergo counseling before returning."[38] Despite the turmoil his off-field behavior has created, Watson's contract remains fully guaranteed, a rarity in the NFL.

As these quarterbacks, including Watson, make headlines across the sports world, news outlets continue to ignore sexual assault survivors while promoting their abusers. An article by Rachel Thompson of the *Guardian* notes, "research suggests that it can take years—sometimes decades—for some survivors to realize or accept that their experience amounts to sexual assault or rape."[39] Thompson goes on to say that a US survey estimated "a staggering 60 percent of female university students have experienced unacknowledged rape," and that "between 30 percent and 88 percent of all sexual assaults go unacknowledged by survivors."[40] These horrifying numbers leave many survivors of sexual violence questioning their sanity and actions, especially with such little support and so few resources. So, while ESPN, SportsCenter, and the local networks celebrate abuser Deshaun Watson's record-breaking NFL contact, an astounding number of victims and survivors of sexual assault continue to suppress their experience, for their own personal sanity. With that in mind, are you ready for some football?

CONCLUSION: LET THEM EAT JUNK!

Americans have faced an upward battle since the world decided the COVID-19 pandemic was over. Sky-high inflation, a fuel crisis while attempting to avoid an all-out World War III, supply chain shortages on everything—material, produce, labor, even baby formula. Can't find what you need at the store to feed your infant baby? Inflation so high that the cost of living is becoming unattainable for a large percentage of the middle class? American leaders today mirror Marie Antoinette, telling their people to eat junk, instead. Because, as the "post-COVID" society pushes forward in an uncertain world, Junk Food News remains constant.

Unfortunately, however, that seems to be just the problem. Americans look to these Junk Food News stories and truly believe this is all that is going on in the world. Monica Lewinsky—yes, that Monica Lewinsky—describes a recent Junk Food News story, the *Depp v.*

Heard trial, perfectly: "a pure car wreck: accessible, tawdry, and immediately gratifying. We dispense with critical thinking and substitute the cheap thrill. Such scattershot consumption hasn't allowed for real comprehension."[41] As we witness the bits and pieces of these narratives, we begin to actually identify with these stories, torn between our "relationships" with celebrities—as if we actually know them ourselves! Again and again, we line up for the buffet of junk food—or, in this year's case, a *prix fixe* menu—and devour the mundane mediocrity of mainstreamed stories. Unfortunately, we, as Americans, continue this pattern with no signs of slowing down.

So, as you make your daily drive down the information superhighway of corporate-controlled public airwaves, social media, podcasts, and streaming services, rest assured there is an ample supply of conveniently packaged breaking, and broken, junk news to consume. Distractions, one after the other, streaming into our cerebral cortex, make network executives jealous at the 24/7 programming. The junk food counter is open with seemingly tacit coordination between all the talking heads, knowing when to jump off one distraction to the next: just as Ye fades, Bezos pops up. As Musk wanes, Will Smith slaps back. As the Super Bowl concludes, Brady unretires. Analysts, podcasters, YouTubers, and the consuming public jump on board, battling amongst themselves over Junk Food News stories. Rewards for privileged misbehavior are high, with the true cost being a well-informed public and civic engagement.

These concrete patterns of Junk Food News reinvent and reintroduce themselves to American audiences every year. And, as if Americans have never witnessed them before, we gorge ourselves on these unvarying stories, each echoed by nearly every so-called mainstream outlet. These accounts can no longer act as a façade to the reality of our current societal state. It is one thing to enjoy Junk Food News as a guilty pleasure—but when stories of this quality are all that are regularly presented to and digested by the American public, there just might be a problem that goes beyond the menu. We need to look at who and what is cooking in the kitchen.

JEN LYONS is a history instructor at Diablo Valley College and the University of Nevada, Reno. She earned her MA in history from the University of Nevada in 2020. Her research focuses on the United States in the 20th and 21st centuries, especially the ways various forms of communication directly impact Americans. In her free time, Lyons spends her time caring too much about the Las Vegas Raiders and other trivial constituents.

MARCELLE SWINBURNE teaches women's, California, and US history at Diablo Valley College and Solano Community College. Her passions include gender politics, K-12 special education, travel, comedy, and "other hot-girl stuff."

SIERRA KAUL is a senior at UC Davis, majoring in history and minoring in museum studies. When she isn't discussing conspiracies in history with classmates, she can be found at a coffee shop having yet another iced coffee. If you want to reach out, please don't, she's probably trying to nap.

GAVIN KELLEY is a graduate of Cal State Long Beach with a degree in creative writing. He wields his pen as an arts organization administrator and is currently director of operations for the Colburn School's dance program. A kung fu practitioner and a martial arts movie podcaster and fan, Gavin developed a keen eye for Junk Food News after years of studying straight-to-video B movies. He co-hosts the *Martial Arts Mania Podcast*.

MICKEY HUFF is director of Project Censored and president of the Media Freedom Foundation. He is also a professor of social science, history, and journalism at Diablo Valley College, where he co-chairs the history area and is chair of the Journalism Department. He has co-edited and contributed to Project Censored's annual books since 2009. Junk Food News analysis has long been one of his guilty pleasures.

Notes

1. Terelle Jerricks, "In the Time of Pandemic Junk Food News," Random Length News, December 23, 2020.
2. Katharine Gammon, "How the Billionaire Space Race Could Be One Giant Leap for Pollution," *The Guardian*, July 19, 2021.
3. Mary K. Jacob, "Inside Kanye West's New $4.5m Home Right Across from Kim Kardashian," *New York Post*, December 27, 2021.
4. Frank Pallotta, "'SNL' Says Goodbye to Kate McKinnon and Pete Davidson, CNN Business, May 22, 2022.
5. *The Tonight Show Starring Jimmy Fallon*, "Pete Davidson Got Stuck Paying for Kid Cudi's Birthday Dinner When Kanye West Crashed," YouTube video (00:06:28), April 19, 2019.
6. Jason Pham, "Kanye's New Girlfriend Did a Sexy Photoshoot with Pete Before His Romance with Kim," StyleCaster, January 5, 2022.
7. "Julia Fox: Dating Kanye Means Lots of Surprises . . . Showering Me With Gifts!!!" *TMZ*, January 6, 2022.
8. "Connecting the Dots: Stalking and Domestic Violence," National Network to End Domestic Violence, February 7, 2020.
9. Ibid.
10. Jackie Wattles, "2021: The Year of Space Tourism," CNN Business, January 3, 2022.
11. Michael Sheetz, "After his Virgin Galactic Spaceflight, Richard Branson Now Hopes to Fly with Elon Musk's SpaceX," CNBC, April 6, 2022.
12. Oliver Gill, "Slash Speed Limit by 10mph to Beat Putin, Says Sir Richard Branson," *Telegraph UK*, April 20, 2022.
13. "Pete Davidson Skipping Ride to Space on Jeff Bezos Rocket: The 'Saturday Night Live' Star Says He Is No Longer Able to Make the Flight," Fox News, March 18, 2022; Derrick Bryson Taylor, "Pete Davidson No Longer Going to Space," *New York Times*, March 18, 2022.
14. Jessica Napoli, "Rickey Gervais Turns Down Chance to Do Comedy in Space: The Comedian Felt It Was Too Dangerous," Fox News, January 12, 2022.

15. Laura Hautala, "Amazon Adjusts 'Time Off Task' Policy That Critics Said Limited Bathroom Breaks," CNET, June 2, 2021.

16. Sharon Zhang, "Bezos's Space Stunt Got Almost as Much TV Time as Climate Crisis in All 2020," Truthout, July 21, 2021.

17. Oxfam, "Carbon Emissions of the Richest 1 Percent More than Double the Emissions of the Poorest Half of Humanity," Oxfam America, September 20, 2020.

18. David Streitfeld, "How Amazon Crushes Unions," *New York Times*, March 16, 2021, updated October 21, 2021.

19. Sharon Zhang, "Treasury Finds Wealthiest 1 percent Dodge Over $160 Billion in Taxes Yearly," Truthout, September 8, 2021.

20. Matthew Gardner, "Amazon Avoids More Than $5 Billion in Corporate Income Taxes, Reports 6 Percent Tax Rate on $35 Billion of US Income," Institute on Taxation and Economic Policy, February 7, 2022.

21. Rich McHugh, "A SpaceX Flight Attendant Said Elon Musk Exposed Himself and Propositioned Her for Sex, Documents Show. The Company Paid $250,000 for Her Silence," Business Insider, May 19, 2022.

22. Shirin Ali, "Scientist Predicts Earth Will Develop Rings Like Saturn," The Hill, November 23, 2021.

23. Jonathan O'Callaghan, "Orbiting Junk Probably Foiled Study of Oldest Known Galaxy," *New Scientist*, March 13, 2021.

24. Joey Roulette, "NASA Delays Spacewalk, Citing Debris Threat to Astronauts," *New York Times*, November 30, 2021.

25. Julia Musto, "China Rocket Debris Falling Toward Earth This Weekend; Point of Impact Still Unknown: 100-foot-long Rocket Core Is Expected to Make an Uncontrollable Re-entry in a Matter of Hours," Fox News, May 8, 2021.

26. Caroline Delbert, "Increased Spaceflight Will Warm Earth's Atmosphere 4 Degrees, Study Finds," *Popular Mechanics*, June 28, 2022.

27. Shi En Kim, "Can the World's First Space Sweep Make a Dent in Orbiting Debris?" *Smithsonian Magazine*, August 25, 2021.

28. Paul D. Williams, "US Will Soon Redeploy Troops in Somalia: The Mission and Key Goals," The Conversation, May 29, 2022.

29. Marshall R. Teague (as Jimmy) quote to Patrick Swayze (Dalton), "Road House," 1989, Movie Quotes; WTF with Marc Maron Podcast, interview with Sam Elliot; Mary Papenfuss, "Jane Campion Hits Sam Elliott Right in the Chaps over His 'Power of the Dog' Dig," Huffpost, March 13, 2022.

30. Bryan Pietch, "George W. Bush Called Iraq War 'Unjustified and Brutal.' He Meant Ukraine," *Washington Post*, May 19, 2022.

31. Tom Brady, Twitter post, March 13, 2022, 4:13 p.m.

32. "Aaron Rodgers Takes 'Full Responsibility' for Comments about COVID-19 Vaccination Status," NFL.com, November 9, 2021.

33. Randy Oliver, "Patrick Mahomes Tells Fiancé Brittany Matthews 'No More Resting Bitch Face' While at Basketball Game," DailySnark, February 17, 2022.

34. Aaron Reiss, "Deshaun Watson Timeline: How Browns QB Ended Up With 11-Game Suspension, $5 Million Fine," The Athletic, August 18, 2022.

35. Ibid.

36. Ben Shpigel, "What to Know About the Allegations Against Deshaun Watson," *New York Times*, June 30, 2022.
37. Rob Maaddi, "NFL Is Adamant About an Indefinite Suspension for Cleveland Browns QB Deshaun Watson," *The Baltimore Sun*, June 30, 2022.
38. Ibid.
39. Rachel Thompson, "Unacknowledged Rape: The Sexual Assault Survivors Who Hide Their Trauma—Even from Themselves," *The Guardian*, August 26, 2021.
40. Ibid.
41. Monica Lewinsky, "Monica Lewinsky's Verdict on the Johnny Depp–Amber Heard Trial: We Are All Guilty: Courtroom Porn and Social Media Have Turned Innocent Bystanders into a Mass of Mudslingers," *Vanity Fair*, May 31, 2022.

CHAPTER 4

Guns, Guns, Guns: Criminal Justice, Mass Shootings, and War
News Abuse in 2021–2022

ROBIN ANDERSEN

In August 2021, the US occupation of Afghanistan ended with images of chaos at the airport in Kabul as people desperately attempted to flee the country. The longest war in US history was known to be unwinnable long before the return of the Taliban, but corporate media and the "papers of record" had enthusiastically backed the war and were held accountable to no one when it failed. A little more than six months later, Russia would invade Ukraine, and once again US media would beat the drums of war and amplify NATO talking points, with weapons-industry talking heads dominating the airwaves. However, as much as corporate news changes, the more it seems to stay the same. Our need to recognize and identify the sometimes familiar, other times changing news practices that mislead, obscure, and promote instead of inform, is what former Project Censored director Peter Phillips had in mind when he coined the term "News Abuse" twenty years ago. Reporting characterized by News Abuse appears seamless, as stories are framed within their own logic and disconnected from information and perspectives excluded by the media's discursive boundaries. Observing how news professionals frame their stories, using hegemonic language and refusing to include alternative voices, is part of recognizing what Phillips defined as News Abuse.

This chapter examines News Abuse in establishment news coverage of policing in the United States and war overseas. In both cases, News Abuse promotes state violence, while downplaying or ignoring its deadly consequences, including the failure of state violence to achieve public safety at home or the stated goals of US policy abroad. US corporate media seldom address deeper connections between the weapons of war, domestic gun rights, and formulations of American exceptionalism embedded in white privilege. Nor do they address connections between the costs of wars abroad and the new wave of domestic austerity advocated by political elites in the United States. In the fragmented world of big journalism, the lack of context is often hidden by the logics of News Abuse identified in this chapter.

WHAT MEDIA WATCHERS HAVE SAID

Media critics who have followed establishment press coverage of the year's biggest stories can help orient us to News Abuse. In the *New York Review of Book*s, Fintan O'Toole assessed the assumptions that prop up establishment news narratives about current wars. "Nowhere is American exceptionalism more evident or more troubling than in compartmentalizing of military atrocities," O'Toole wrote.[1] Pointing out the double standard in war coverage, author and peace activist Medea Benjamin tweeted on May 5, 2022, "How come people don't protest against Saudi oil like they protest Russian oil? Perhaps it's because Yemeni lives 'don't matter'?"[2] And commenting on US information wars with Russia, one of the most outspoken media critics, Caitlin Johnstone, observed, "It's been obvious for a long time that the US empire has been working to shore up narrative control to strengthen its hegemonic domination of the planet."[3] Journalism that understands US military policies within the context of empire is certainly the domain of alternative media. And, writing about the mass killing of children in Uvalde, Texas, Natasha Lennard explained that "policing is not [what we've] been told it is by the police themselves, by those in power, and by the mainstream media culture."[4] Let's begin by looking at how policing has been covered in the establishment media.

CRIME, JUSTICE REPORTING, AND COPAGANDA

Last year, Project Censored identified news coverage of protests by Black Lives Matter (BLM) as an egregious example of News Abuse.[5] Legacy and corporate media portrayed BLM demonstrators across the United States as violent and chaotic, despite subsequent evidence that, in 97 percent of cases, protests were peaceful and non-violent. At the time, alternative and independent media carried very different stories, some with headlines accurately describing "police riots." This year, big media have continued this pro-police bias when reporting on crime, law enforcement, and ongoing struggles to reform the justice system.

Consider, for example, news coverage of a highly anticipated FBI crime-data report, released on September 27, 2021. Newspapers featured sensationalized headlines about one aspect of the multifaceted report. Though major crimes declined overall, the homicide rate rose. *The Washington Post*'s headline screamed, "Killing Soared Nearly 30 Percent in 2020, with More Slayings Committed with Guns."[6] The *New York Times* coverage led with the headline "Murders Spiked in 2020 in Cities Across the United States," and NPR, NBC News, the Hill, and the *Guardian* also focused on the homicide spike.[7] Journalists failed to use the occasion to question the efficacy of policing, or to open a broader dialogue about public safety in the United States. Writing for *The Nation*, Scott Hechinger, a longtime public defender and now executive director of Zealous, identified how journalism got the story wrong.[8]

Without minimizing the terrible loss of each life taken, Hechinger explained that, even though the murder rate rose by 30 percent in 2020 compared to the previous year, homicides were now at historic lows, especially when compared to the 1980s and 1990s. Not surprisingly, establishment journalists jumped on the homicide increase, offering "explanations" primarily from law enforcement, even though ascribing short-term fluctuations in crime data to any particular cause is, according to Hechinger, "impossible."[9]

Current crime reporting is not based on "criminological facts" but continues to repeat familiar narratives that helped drive the mass-incarceration binge. As Hechinger detailed, reporting is marred by "alarmist headlines" and "dehumanizing language" with "overly simplistic stories" that "provoke fear in the public." Indeed, the narrative elements Hechinger described follow the storylines of the docu-cop reality shows that aired on Fox and other networks in the 1980s and 90s, which were often mirrored in local news reporting.[10] Today, the misleading narratives show up across the media, even in prestigious newspapers.

Fear-based coverage of the FBI report excluded the perspectives of public defenders, social workers, health professionals, academics, researchers, and communities with direct experience of the criminal justice system. Foreclosing those voices with editorial selections of "newsworthy" sources is a hallmark of News Abuse. In this case, as Hechinger noted, it allowed police "to use their failures to demand more resources, more funding, more support."[11] The pro-police framework for reporting on crime and justice issues serves to misdirect policy discussions on policing and blocks solutions to corruption, police brutality, and the criminalization of people and communities of color. Such coverage offers no explanatory framework for addressing mass shootings nor for understanding that more police funding will not solve any of these problems.

COPAGANDA

Let's look at the April 12, 2022, shooting that took place on the Brooklyn subway, where twenty-nine people were injured but no one was killed. Despite the number of police officers now patrolling the subway system and the use of surveillance cameras in every subway station in New York City, police did not stop the shooting spree. Instead of questioning police failures and hefty budgets, the NYPD took center stage in reporting the hunt for Frank James, the suspect. *The New York Times* lionized police efforts, saying hundreds of officers were using methods "as modern as scrutinizing video from surveillance cameras and parsing electronic records, and as old-fashioned as a wanted poster."[12] Responding to the fawning press treatment, Josmar Trujillo of Copwatch pointed out that the cops actually failed to find James, while the *New York Times* repeated, "They're going to stop this guy, they're going to catch this guy," though the NYPD did neither.[13]

The *New York Times* also featured Mayor Eric Adams praising New York City's law enforcement officers for eventually arresting the suspect, though James walked around the city for hours, went to McDonald's, and finally called the hotline to give authorities his location. Still, on the sidewalk, New Yorkers had to point the man out to cops to make the arrest. The mayor pronounced the solution to all such crimes, saying, "[If] all goes well, he will never see the outside of a prison cell again."[14] Trujillo called this "copaganda," when police agendas lead in media coverage and cops are foregrounded even in the face of failure. Another writer, Mark Anthony Neal, defined copaganda's active role in countering attempts to hold police accountable for malfeasance as "reinforcing the ideas that the police are generally fair and hardworking, and that 'Black criminals' deserve the brutal treatment they receive."[15]

A different story was told by Adam Gopnik, who described in the *New Yorker* how passengers attended to strangers. "What was most impressive in the immediate post-shooting phone-cam videos was the extraordinary esprit de corps of the straphangers, showing as they did, despite what must have been an urge to run, an amazing degree of care and calm."[16]

THE "FERGUSON EFFECT": BLAMING BLACK LIVES MATTER PROTESTS

A systematic look at media coverage of crime led critic Julie Hollar to identify what has been called the "Ferguson Effect," defined as the supposed fear and resulting retreat from policing "caused" by Black Lives Matter. One *USA Today* headline clearly illustrated this: "Why Violent Crime Surged after Police Across America Retreated."[17] Hollar observed that blaming BLM is popular among police chiefs and their media boosters who seek to "defend against movements challenging police violence" and "deflect blame back onto protesters."[18] Hechinger also pointed to an overwhelming media bias that, "against all evidence to the contrary and the FBI data itself," continues to assert that the increases in homicides could have been "caused by bail reform and protests for racial justice following the police killing of George Floyd."[19]

Today we know, from experience and overwhelming research, that releasing people from jail prior to trial reduces crime for years in the future—and saves tens of millions of dollars in each major city.[20] Yet police point to BLM protests and measures such as bail reform to account for the rise in murders. Speaking on Fairness & Accuracy in Reporting's *CounterSpin*, Alec Karakatsanis, a former civil rights lawyer and executive director of Civil Rights Corps, explained that jailing people "prior to trial just because they can't make a monetary payment actually increases crime by huge margins."[21] It makes people more likely to commit crime by destabilizing their lives, disrupting medical treatment and mental health care, forcing them out of jobs and housing, and often separating them from their children. "Cash bail is actually really harmful to public safety," Karakatsanis explained. Police, prosecutors, and judges may still detain anyone who is a danger to the community or is charged with a serious offense.

Yet the *New York Times* referred to bail reform using the scary, mystifying phrase "the revolving jailhouse door created by bail reform," a not-so-subtle reference to the infamous Willy Horton commercial that fabricated the criminal justice policies of Democratic presidential candidate Michael Dukakis and helped George H. W. Bush get elected in 1988.[22] Ironically, the advertisement, which depicted the entrance to a jail where inmates entered through a revolving door and immediately returned to the streets, was criticized by the *Times* in 2018, when the paper called it part of "the racially charged politics of crime" that "reverberate to this day."[23] There are political consequences to this type of reporting, such as the successful recall of forward-thinking prosecutor Chesa Boudin in San Francisco. As the *Washington Post* gloated, "Boudin's recall proves Democrats have lost the public's trust on crime," though it could have been more accurately called a billionaire-funded, pro-police, media-backed political recall.[24]

THE ROLE OF STATE VIOLENCE AND MASS SHOOTINGS

Much of the police budget in every city is spent on state control measures. According to Alec Karakatsanis, "Cops have tried to surveil, infiltrate, and violently crush every major social, economic, labor, environmental, and racial justice movement since 1900."[25] As a recent example, he pointed to the police reaction to a peaceful climate protest in Los Angeles in April 2022, where scientists had chained themselves to a fence. Video revealed the disproportionate LAPD response to the scientists—about ten cops for each protester.[26]

While corporate media amplify police agendas, other proven measures such as reducing poverty, investing in mental health and substance treatment, education, affordable housing, violence prevention, and restorative justice are rarely mentioned. Corporate "justice" journalism is not just false; it has consequences. It is an insidious and historically rooted contributor to the failed system of policing in our country, "a pro-police worldview deeply ingrained in journalism."[27]

Mass Shootings

On May 14, 2022, a white supremacist sought out the Tops Friendly Market in a predominantly Black neighborhood in Buffalo, after researching the zip code where the most Brown and Black residents shopped, and killed ten people, wounding three others. In spite of the shooter posting a lengthy "replacement theory" diatribe on social media that reflected the ravings of Fox News host Tucker Carlson, police did not stop this shooter either. Only days later, on May 24, 2022, in a massacre at Robb Elementary School in Uvalde, Texas, an eighteen-year-old gunman would kill nineteen grade-school children and two of their teachers. The cops' lack of response for over an hour, a spectacular failure that dumbfounded parents and bystanders, was caught on videotape. Cops aggressively confronted parents with pepper spray and a Taser and handcuffed a mother who wanted to enter the building to save her child.

As corporate media scrambled to account for police actions, Natasha Lennard dismantled the hegemonic police-driven narrative that failed to explain what happened in Uvalde. "The 'thin blue line' does not, as reactionary narratives would have it, separate society from violent chaos," she asserted in the Intercept.[28] Police did not risk their lives going into a hail of gunfire; they "kept themselves safe." Meanwhile, two teachers died trying to protect the children.

Lennard referenced Supreme Court decisions from 1989 and 2005 that affirmed that police departments are not obligated to provide protection to the public.[29] She pointed out that cops don't solve most crimes, nor do they prevent crime.[30] For example, the NYPD's stop-and-frisk policy was not "prevention"; it criminalized poverty and the communities of color forced to live in it.[31] When civilians spotted subway shooter Frank James, he was walking just blocks away from a site where cops were busy destroying a homeless encampment.

Police, White Supremacy, and the Legacy of Slavery

Risking their lives to save innocent people from mass shooters is not what police do. In fact, Lennard asserted, upholding "racial capitalism with violence"—and doing so with impunity—is the role police have played since the country was founded. Municipal policing began with state violence such as "slave patrols and colonial counterinsurgencies." In her book *Loaded: A Disarming*

History of the Second Amendment, Roxanne Dunbar-Ortiz draws similar connections between police and the role of white militias. In an interview broadcast by the Real News Network, Dunbar-Ortiz noted that the Second Amendment was established for white militia settlers, who were self-organized and self-regulated, "to kill Indians and take their land, and later for slave patrols."[32] A former FBI agent, Mike German, wrote a series of articles for the *Guardian* that drew out the connection between law enforcement, the legacy of slavery, and "our government's official sanction of white supremacy."[33] For decades, the Federal Bureau of Investigation has routinely warned that white supremacist and far-right militant groups often have links to law enforcement. "Yet the justice department has no national strategy designed to protect the communities policed by these dangerously compromised law enforcers," German wrote.[34]

White supremacy's connections to gun culture and militarism are also strong. Dunbar-Ortiz explained that the history of mass shootings by lone gunmen killing strangers parallels "the rise of the gun rights movement and ramped-up militarism." An increase in the number of guns and the lack of regulations are contributors, but there is also "a gun culture at work along with a military culture." As the Intercept pointed out, the AR-15 is a weapon of war; it is made to "explode the human body."[35] Military might is a strong selling point, as evident in one AR-15 advertisement for "professional grade weaponry" that featured helmeted men in uniform blasting their way through a building in what journalist Chris Woodyard called "macho-masculinity."[36] Employed now in mass killings, AR-15s are assault rifles, not defensive ones, just as

US military invasions of other counties are aggressive, not defensive. Dunbar-Ortiz also articulated the historical roots of US militarism in settler colonialism, genocide, white supremacy, slavery, and structural inequality, all of which we still grapple with today. The benign US narrative of immigrant progress obscures the reality that the country was founded in violence as a settler state, imperialist since its inception.[37]

As I have detailed, there are connections to be made between guns, mass shootings, state violence, white supremacy, and the culture of war, yet media reports fragment the social, cultural, and political worlds, leaving violence without interconnected causes, motivations, and consequences. If we look at another major event in 2021, the US military withdrawal from Afghanistan, we find that corporate and legacy media celebrated weapons and belligerencies in coverage that also illustrates News Abuse.

THE FAILED FOREVER WARS: PULLING OUT OF AFGHANISTAN IN 2021

When Taliban fighters swept across Afghanistan in a little more than a week and entered its capital, Kabul, on August 15, 2021, without any bloodshed, they surprised the US media, the Biden White House, and the US military. Twenty years earlier, the United States had said the bombing of Afghanistan was necessary to avenge the attacks on the World Trade Center, and thus began the longest war in US history. From the first bombs that hit Afghanistan in 2001, to the smart bombs that "lit up the night sky" over Baghdad, Iraq, in 2003, to Brian Williams' adoration of the "beautiful" bombing of Syria in 2017, TV news anchors have not hidden their admiration for US bombing of the Middle East.[38] But when the US military turned to secret operations by Special Forces, such as the terror of night raids and drone strikes, those deadly brutalities occurred without fanfare or notice.[39]

The war in Afghanistan was promoted with a set of false narratives carefully designed by the military and government and repeated in the press. Military belligerencies are justified with recognizable tropes that are constant in establishment press coverage of war: US wars are a fight between "good versus evil"; "you can't negotiate with terrorists"; and US military might "will always win."[40] Secrecy perpetuated the myth of American moral superiority, enabling an unchallenged war lexicon of "beautiful" bombs accurately targeting terrorists; civilian bodies were simply hidden, remaining unseen, without historical recognition.[41] But US corporate media showed up in full force when Biden pulled out of Afghanistan.

Chaotic Images: The US Evacuation of Kabul

Desperate to get out of the country, those who had worked with the US-backed Afghan government fled to the airport in Kabul, running across the tarmac and swamping the runways. US corporate media covered the chaos with images of hundreds of people jamming the runways and clinging onto aircraft or forcing their way into military transport planes. With the media focusing on the spectacle of the war's end, in three days Afghanistan received more coverage than it had in years. As desperate people crowded the Kabul airport, US corporate media expressed great concern for the lives of those who worked with the American military and its Afghan government. In the twisted logic of war journalism, only some lives are valuable, worthy of safety, security, and dignity. During the US withdrawal of Afghanistan, Gregory Shupak surveyed the editorial pages of five major US newspapers for Fairness & Accuracy in Reporting (FAIR) and noted that not one of them mentioned the 71,000 civilians killed during the course of the US-initiated war: "[C]ivilians evidently aren't significant enough to factor into 'the cost' of the war."[42]

"Intelligence"-Driven Fake News and Blaming Biden

By August 18, 2021, the *New York Times* and many cable news outlets adopted a critical stance on the war's end. President Biden took the blame, with Amanda Marcotte observing in Salon, "The collapse of the Afghan government was portrayed as a massive political liability for Biden."[43] On CNN, Jake Tapper was shocked that Biden "could have been so wrong," directing viewers to watch the "tragic foreign policy disaster unfold before our eyes" and describing the White House as "flat-footed."[44] Yet the CIA, the military, and security agencies were rarely the subjects of criticism, though they demonstrably failed the translators, Afghan security forces, journalists, women, and human rights activists in Kabul.

Unwinnable War

In an unusually critical and candid piece published in

2019, titled "At War with the Truth," the *Washington Post* reported on a trove of documents called the "Afghanistan Papers" that revealed how "senior U.S. officials failed to tell the truth about the war in Afghanistan throughout the eighteen-year campaign, making rosy pronouncements they knew to be false and hiding unmistakable evidence the war had become unwinnable."[45] Yet by August 2021, big journalism seemed to forget the contents of the report. The swift Taliban takeover of Afghanistan should have shattered assertions that military operations always vanquish America's identified enemies.

Without being held accountable for the lies and disinformation that promoted the "forever wars," corporate media launched another call for war, this time in Ukraine. Even before Russia invaded the country, US media were gearing up for sending weapons to Ukraine, handing the news agenda over to "defense" industry promoters.

PROFITS OVER UKRAINE

In the weeks leading up to Russia's invasion of Ukraine, the chief executive officers of Lockheed Martin and Raytheon predicted that the looming war would lead to inflated military budgets and increased sales. Lockheed Martin CEO James Taiclet told investors, "With 'renewed great power competition' comes windfall profits." And Raytheon CEO Greg Hayes predicted that "we're going to see some benefit" from increased "opportunities for international sales."[46] Since the start of 2022, the stock shares of Lockheed Martin and Northrop Grumman have surged in value by nearly 25 percent and 20 percent, respectively, and Raytheon and General Dynamics have enjoyed "almost double-digit growth in their share prices."[47] As billions in profits rolled in, 6 million refugees fled Ukraine and thousands were killed.[48] While bringing misery to millions, weapons companies are the only ones "who win these wars," said Rachel Small, an organizer with World Beyond War.[49] But that point of view was certainly not on the pages or screens of US corporate media.

From the Military to the Arms Industry to US Broadcasts

Corporate media tapped into a bevy of former high-ranking Department of Defense officials and military officers who have become lobbyists, board members, executives, or consultants for the weapons industry.[50] As the Russians invaded Ukraine, a throng of weapons flacks hit the airwaves. An old favorite was retired US combat general Barry McCaffrey, who ordered his infantry division to fire on innocent women and children during the final days of the First Gulf War and who then promoted the endless Iraq War in the years following 9/11 without disclosing his firm's financial interests.[51] McCaffrey has been a mainstay on MSNBC; his defense industry consulting firm is BR McCaffrey Associates LLC.[52] One of CNN's top-choice military talking heads, former CIA director and retired army general David Petraeus, was cheerleading to get MiG fighter jets "into Ukrainian skies."[53] Petraeus is a partner at KKR, a private equity giant with significant military industry business.[54]

Retired army general Wesley Clark, who made appearances on CNN during the First Gulf War and has enjoyed a lucrative career working with defense companies since, was brought back onto the network thirty years later to voice his opinion that this "battle is a long way from over, provided we can continue to provide replenishment to the weapons to the Ukrainians."[55]

When former US defense secretary Leon Panetta appeared on CNN's *Newsroom* for the fourth time, he said, "I think the United States has to provide whatever weapons are necessary to the Ukrainians, so that they can hit back, and hit back now."[56] Panetta is a senior counselor at Beacon Global Strategies;[57] MSNBC did not mention this conflict of interest.[58] Jeremy Bash, who served as chief of staff at the Pentagon and the CIA under President Barack Obama, has been a recurring guest on MSNBC and NBC during the crisis in Ukraine. Days after Putin first launched the invasion, Bash was eager to weigh in, appearing on NBC's *Meet the Press* to tell audiences, "If the United States can train and equip the Ukrainians and, I think, engage in a second *Charlie Wilson's War*, basically the sequel to the movie and the book, which is arming and training a determined force that will shoot Russian aircraft out of the sky, open up those tanks with can openers, like the Javelins, and kill Russians, which is what our equipment is doing, I think this is a huge opportunity to hit Putin very hard."[59] It was a well-rehearsed, gung-ho sales pitch, complete with a war-movie tie-in for a product—the Javelin anti-tank missile—built by Lockheed Martin and Raytheon. No one involved in the broadcast told viewers that Bash's consulting firm has worked for Raytheon.[60]

No Debate, No Anti-War Voices

MintPress News called attention to the defense industry's partnership with Politico, "an internet news giant" employing more than 700 people and reaching an audience of 50 million people a month.[61] Alan MacLeod pointed out that both of Politico's defense and space newsletters "come sponsored by giant military and aerospace contractor Northrop Grumman."[62] Surveying Politico's military news, anti-war activist and writer David Swanson looked at a long article about Biden's proposed 2023 military budget and observed a lack of debate on the increases.[63] Politico referred to a $30 billion funding hike in military spending as "supersizing," the language of extra-large milkshakes and sodas from fast food chains. The proposed increases total $813 billion, including $773 billion for the Pentagon and "tens of billions for nuclear weapons programs overseen by the Energy Department."[64] Politico's coverage ignored the dangers of fighting a superpower with nuclear weapons, and it gave the final say to the top Republican on the House Defense Appropriations panel, Ken Calvert, who simply pronounced, "Non-defense discretionary is going to come down and defense is going to go up at the end of the day. . . . That's it. It's not complicated."[65]

Hawks, Information War, and Atrocity Propaganda Repeated

The war in Ukraine took US military media propaganda to dangerous new levels. Common Dreams observed that journalists were more hawkish at news conferences than

Biden's press secretary, often "cheerleading for escalation in Ukraine," with more weapons and no-fly zones.[66] As part of its "information war" against Russia, the Biden administration released false narratives that were repeated in US establishment media. One fabrication was that Russia might be preparing to use chemical agents in Ukraine, yet three US officials later told NBC, "There is no evidence Russia has brought any chemical weapons near Ukraine."[67] NBC repeated the propaganda, then reported the retraction by quoting an unidentified US official who said, "It doesn't have to be solid intelligence.... It's more important to get out ahead of them [the Russians]."[68] Caitlin Johnstone put it unequivocally: they lied. "They knowingly circulated information they had no reason to believe was true, and that lie was amplified by all the most influential media outlets in the western world."[69]

Johnstone also pointed to another example of corporate media News Abuse, repeating what should have been easily recognized as atrocity propaganda. Lyudmyla Denisova, the Ukrainian parliament's commissioner for human rights, posted an unsubstantiated story about how two Russians raped a one-year-old baby boy until he died.[70] The claims were uncritically parroted by Western media outlets including Business Insider, the Daily Beast, the *Daily Mail,* the *Sun,* Metro, the *Daily Mirror*, and Yahoo News.[71] *Newsweek* headlined another atrocity narrative, claiming, "Russians Raped 11-Year-Old Boy, Forced Mom to Watch: Ukraine Official," without evidence.[72] Denisova was finally relieved of her duties on May 31, 2022.[73]

The Coverage and Debates on Independent Media

While US corporate media single-mindedly called for more war and more weapons, a vibrant debate took place in independent media, addressing Putin's imperial motivations (as opposed to caricatures of his personal ideologies and desires), the role of NATO as a context for the Russian invasion of Ukraine, and Ukraine's right to self-determination. Peace activists and environmentalists called for an immediate end to the war—an existential threat to a planet already in crisis—and argued that no war in our lifetimes has ever benefited humanity or created a more stable and peaceful planet.

The High Costs of Belligerencies Without Negotiations

In April 2022, the Biden Administration unveiled a plan to send Ukraine Lockheed Martin's High Mobility Artillery Rocket System, known as HIMARS, the most advanced weaponry to date. In response, Medea Benjamin warned in Common Dreams that weapons shipments were increasing the likelihood of a full-scale conflict between the United States and Russia.[74] To promote this move, Biden placed an op-ed in the *New York Times* claiming that weapons put Ukraine in the "strongest possible position at the negotiating table," even as Russia's nuclear forces began holding maneuvers.[75] Writing for *Jacobin*, Branko Marcetic reported, "Almost all knowledgeable observers believe the war in Ukraine will have to end with a negotiated agreement. Yet the US, Ukraine's leading patron, has signaled it has no patience for diplomatic efforts that cut against its hope for Moscow's 'strategic defeat.'"[76] Ukrainian professor Ivan Katchanovski agreed, saying, "The US and UK governments show no efforts or desire to achieve peaceful settlement of the armed conflict between Russia and Ukraine." As the conflict continued, Inter Press Service reported that US sanctions against Russia were creating food crises and price increases.[77] Besides contravening the UN Charter, unilateral sanctions are illegal under international law and put "countless civilians" at risk, IPS reported.[78]

In the face of continuing escalation, most corporate news outlets ignored a possible nuclear apocalypse, but, as noted in the Bulletin of the Atomic Scientists, "the doorstep to doom is no place to loiter."[79] The immense environmental damage done by war includes trillions of dollars spent on destruction that could be used for environmental renewal. The enormous fossil fuel footprint of the US Department of Defense makes it the largest institutional user of oil in the world.[80] The horrific human cost of the weapons of war encompasses millions killed and left in misery, the destruction of infrastructure, homelessness, disease, and starvation. The dreadful economic drain and consequent political fallout was identified by Warren Gunnels, staff director for Bernie Sanders when Sanders headed the Senate Budget Committee. Gunnels pointed to the Democratic Party's shift to austerity, tweeting, "'Ending universal free school lunches, enacting the largest Medicare premium hike in history, restarting student loan payments & failing to extend the $300 a month Child Tax Credit, raise the minimum wage or legalize marijuana,' is not a very compelling message."[81] Yet military spending is never cited as a cause for the failure to fulfill domestic programs popular with Americans, such as Medicare for All and raising the minimum wage, nor is it acknowledged as the reason for reductions in school lunch programs that will leave millions of American children hungry.

CONSPIRACY THEORIES, SCAPEGOATING, AND MASS SHOOTINGS

Narratives that obscure connections between the costs of war, domestic austerity programs, and the very real threat of an unlivable planet, go hand in hand with the scapegoating of people of color and mass shootings. Without explanations for the loss of wealth and well-being resulting from war expenditures, conspiracy theories thrive. As Chris Hedges wrote, "The mounting misery of the bottom half of the population ... will find expression through violence."[82] He continued, "People who are Black, Muslim, Asian, Jewish, and LGBTQ, along with the undocumented, liberals, feminists and intellectuals, already branded as contaminants, will be slated for execution." Hedges concluded, "Kill them overseas. Kill them at home.... Violence, in desperation, becomes the only route to salvation."[83] Hedges' point about violence was resonant in the online rant of the eighteen-year-old shooter who murdered innocent Black shoppers at the Tops Friendly Market in Buffalo, New York, in May 2022. The Buffalo shooter's diatribe cited "replacement theory," the conspiratorial belief that low birthrates and immigration are leading to the "genocide" of white people. As the Intercept's Murtaza Hussain noted, the "vision of a bleak, impoverished future" is motivating "an ever-growing number of young men" to undertake "racist massacres across the West."[84]

The toxic discourse of white supremacists is normalized by media treatment of Republicans who nurture these extreme viewpoints. Indeed, as far-right politics takes hold of the GOP, the Southern Poverty Law Center reports, "Republican members of Congress have worked together with open white nationalists and promoted the racist 'great replacement' conspiracy theory that has inspired numerous deadly terror attacks."[85] Yet, as Project Censored pointed out in 2022, legacy news media continue to treat the GOP as a legitimate political party in a democratic system, and the false claims are repeated in what becomes a meaningless back-and-forth.[86]

CONCLUSION

Today, the United States faces an escalating arms race at home and across the globe. There are an estimated 800 million firearms in civilian hands around the world. Half of those weapons are owned by people in the United States, yet the United States accounts for only 5 percent of the world's population.[87] These figures are mirrored in international arms sales and US military spending. The United States spends as much on the military and its weapons as the next nine countries combined.[88]

In-depth corporate journalism could play a vital role in connecting these figures with the causes and contexts of belligerencies and mass shootings, such as white supremacy with deep roots in law enforcement; the use of assault rifles against children and Black and Brown communities; and the rising threats posed by far-right hate groups.

As our nation grapples with how to reimagine public safety in the wake of escalating domestic terrorism, it is time to present the historical, economic, and political factors that have led to violence, belligerencies, and destruction, and to break the symbiosis between police and media known as copaganda. It's time to connect right-wing conspiracies, the politicians who normalize hate and racism, and the support of the powerful gun lobby with the increasing threat of mass shootings. Reports on these issues do occasionally appear in corporate media, but they are presented in isolation and without historical context. Corporate media are currently failing democracy, limiting discussion of life-and-death issues to those calling for war and aggression, excluding any other points of view. Moving away from the practices of News Abuse requires a commitment by news editors and reporters to rethink media frames, the ideological underpinnings that shape them, and the corporate interests that sponsor them.

Special thanks to Lauren Reduzzi, a Project Censored intern, for help with this chapter.

ROBIN ANDERSEN is a writer, commentator, award-winning author, and professor emerita of Communication and Media Studies at Fordham University. She edits the Routledge Focus Book Series on Media and Humanitarian Action. Her forthcoming books are *Death in Paradise: A Critical Study of the BBC Series,* and *Censorship, Digital Media, and the Global Crackdown on Freedom of Expression.* She writes regularly for Fairness & Accuracy in Reporting (FAIR) and is a Project Censored judge.

Notes

1. Fintan O'Toole, "Our Hypocrisy on War Crimes," *New York Review of Books*, May 26, 2022.
2. Medea Benjamin, Twitter, May 5, 2022, 5:38 a.m.
3. Caitlin Johnstone, "US Officials Admit They're Literally Just Lying to the Public About Russia," CaitlinJohnstone.com, April 7, 2022.
4. Natasha Lennard, "Uvalde Police Didn't Move to Save Lives Because That's Not What Police Do," The Intercept, May 27, 2022.
5. Robin Andersen, "False Balance in Media Coverage Undermines Democracy, New Abuse in 2020–2021," Project Censored's *State of the Free Press 2022*, eds. Andy Lee Roth and Mickey Huff (Fair Oaks, CA and New York: Censored Press and Seven Stories Press, 2022).
6. Devlin Barrett, David Nakamura, and John D. Harden, "Killing Soared Nearly 30 Percent in 2020, with More Slayings Committed with Guns," *Washington Post*, September 27, 2021.
7. See, e.g., Neil MacFarquhar, "Murders Spiked in 2020 in Cities Across the United States," *New York Times*, September 27, 2022 , updated November 15, 2021.
8. In addition to identifying how journalism gets the story of criminal justice wrong, Zealous also develops new storytelling devices to address habitual biases in crime reporting. See Scott Hechinger, "A Massive Fail on Crime Reporting by the *New York Times*, NPR," *The Nation*, October 26, 2021.
9. Ibid.
10. Robin Andersen, "Reality TV and Criminal Injustice," in *Exploring Diversity: Readings in Sociology*, eds. David Barnes and Marshall Forman (Needham Heights, MA: Simon and Schuster, 1996), 275–284. For more on this phenomenon, see Barry Glassner, *Culture of Fear: Why Americans Are Afraid of the Wrong Things* (New York: Basic Books, 2018 [2000]).
11. Hechinger, "A Massive Fail."
12. Sean Piccoli and Chelsia Rose Marcius, "Witnesses Describe the Suspect's Arrest: 'He Went Without a Struggle,'" *New York Times*, April 13, 2022.
13. Janine Jackson, interview with Josmar Trujillo, "'The Core of Copaganda Is the Symbiotic Relationship Between Press and Police,'" *CounterSpin* (Fairness & Accuracy in Reporting), May 6, 2022.
14. Piccoli and Marcius, "Witnesses Describe the Suspect's Arrest."
15. Mark Anthony Neal, "Copaganda: How Pop Culture Helped Turn Police Officers into Rock Stars—and Black Folks into Criminals," Inquest, November 13, 2021.
16. Adam Gopnik, "The Subway in Our Collective Imagination Before and After the Brooklyn Shooting," *New Yorker*, April 19, 2022.
17. Jason Johnson, "Why Violent Crime Surged After Police Across America Retreated," *USA Today*, April 9, 2021.
18. Julie Hollar, "NYT Twists Stats to Insist We Need More Policing," Fairness & Accuracy in Reporting, January 22, 2022.
19. Hechinger, "A Massive Fail."

20. Paul Heaton, Sandra G. Mayson, and Megan Stevenson, "The Down-stream Consequences of Misdemeanor Pretrial Detention," *Stanford Law Review*, Vol. 69 (March 2017).

21. Janine Jackson, interview Alec Karakatsanis, "'Crime Surge' Copaganda," *CounterSpin* (Fairness & Accuracy in Reporting), October 1, 2021.

22. Ibid.

23. Peter Baker, "Bush Made Willie Horton an Issue in 1988, and the Racial Scars Are Still Fresh," *New York Times*, December 3, 2018.

24. John Hohmann, "Boudin's Recall Proves Democrats Have Lost the Public's Trust on Crime," *Washington Post*, June 8, 2022; on the right-wing money behind the recall, see Tim Redmond, "What the Boudin Recall Does—and Doesn't—Mean for SF Politics," 48 Hills, June 7, 2022.

25. Alec Karakatsanis, Twitter post, May 23, 2022, 7:13 a.m. Only about 4 percent of police time is spent on what they call "violent crime."

26. People's City Council—Los Angeles, Twitter post, April 6, 2022, 4:25 p.m.

27. Hechinger, "A Massive Fail."

28. Lennard, "Uvalde Police Didn't Move to Save Lives."

29. Ibid., see also Ryan McMaken, "Police Have No Duty to Protect You, Federal Court Affirms Once Again," Mises Institute, December 20, 2018.

30. Only around 2 percent of major crimes are solved by police. See Shima Baughman, "Police Solve Just 2% of All Major Crimes," The Conversation, August 20, 2020.

31. Lennard, "Uvalde Police Didn't Move to Save Lives." Ninety percent of the almost all Black people stopped under the policy were not commit-ting any crime at all. In addition, Lennard pointed out, there is scant evidence that police surveillance reduces or prevents crime.

32. Maximillian Alvarez, "Roxanne Dunbar-Ortiz on Uvalde, the Second Amendment, and the Great American Arms Race, The Real News Net-work, June 2, 2022.

33. Mike German, "The FBI Warned for Years that Police Are Cozy with the Far Right. Is No One Listening?" *The Guardian*, August 28, 2020.

34. Mike German, "The FBI Has a History of Targeting Black Activists. That's Still True Today," *The Guardian*, June 26, 2020.

35. Murtaza Hussain, "AR-15s Were Made to Explode the Human Body. In Uvalde, the Bodies Belonged to Children," The Intercept, May 26, 2022.

36. Chris Woodyard, "AR-15 Speaks to 'Macho-Masculinity,' Gun Control Advocates Say. They Want It to Stop," *Herald-Mail*, March 27, 2017.

37. Roxanne Dunbar-Ortiz, *Not "A Nation of Immigrants": Settler Colonialism, White Supremacy, and a History of Erasure and Exclusion* (Boston: Beacon Press, 2021).

38. "Shocking and Awful," *Channels of War, Program 10*, Deep Dish TV, 2005; Allan Smith, "MSNBC Anchor Brian Williams Sets Off Online Firestorm with Long Soliloquy about 'Beautiful' Footage of Missile Launch in Syria," Business Insider, April 7, 2017.

39. Robin Andersen, *"Act of Valor*: Celebrating and Denying the Brutalities of Endless and Global US War," *Democratic Communiqué*, Vol. 26 No. 2 (Fall 2014), 22–38.

40. For historical perspective, see, Deepa Kumar, "Play It Again, (Uncle) Sam: A Brief History of US Imperialism, Propaganda, and the News," in *Censored 2015: Inspiring We The People*, eds. Andy Lee Roth and

Mickey Huff (New York: Seven Stories Press, 2014), 295–314. See also Robin Andersen, *A Century of Media, A Century of War* (New York: Peter Lang, 2006).

41. Jim Naureckas, "Rumsfeld Remembered as 'Complex,' 'Energetic'—Not as Killer of Multitudes," Fairness & Accuracy in Reporting, July 2, 2021. See also Andrew Roth, Zoe Huffman, Jeffrey Huling, Kevin Stolle, and Jocelyn Thomas, "Covering War's Victims: A Content Analysis of Iraq and Afghanistan War Photographs in the *New York Times* and the *San Francisco Chronicle*," in *Censored 2008*, eds. Peter Phillips and Andrew Roth with Project Censored (New York: Seven Stories Press, 2007), 253–271; available online at projectcensored.org.

42. Gregory Shupak, "As Kabul Is Retaken, Papers Look Back in Erasure," Fairness & Accuracy in Reporting, August 19, 2021.

43. Amanda Marcotte, "The Afghanistan Blame Game Begins—And the Media Immediately Ignores What Triggered This Disaster," Salon, August 16, 2021.

44. Josh Feldman, "Jake Tapper Calls Out Biden for Recent Comments on Afghanistan: 'Seems Shocking' He 'Could Have Been So Wrong,'" Mediaite, August 15, 2021.

45. Craig Whitlock, "At War with the Truth," *Washington Post*, December 9, 2019.

46. Kenny Stancil, "'Shut Down This War Machine': Peace Activists Block Entrances to Major Weapons Fair in Canada," Common Dreams, June 1, 2022.

47. Ibid.

48. "Ukraine Civilian Deaths 'Thousands Higher' than Official Toll: UN," Al Jazeera, May 10, 2022.

49. "Hundreds Protest, Block Entrance to North America's Largest Weapons Fair," World Beyond War, June 1, 2022.

50. An investigation by the Project on Government Oversight (POGO) about defense contractors hiring former Pentagon officials found, from 2008 to the present, "over 380 within two years of leaving the Department." See Mandy Smithberger, "Brass Parachutes: The Problem of the Pentagon Revolving Door," POGO, November 5, 2018.

51. See Seymour Hersh, "Overwhelming Force," *New Yorker*, May 22, 2000 (published online May 14, 2022); Barry R. McCaffrey, "A General's View of Iraq," *Los Angeles Times*, April 3, 2007; and David Barstow, "One Man's Military-Industrial-Media Complex," *New York Times*, November 29, 2008.

52. "Experience Brings Perspective," BR McCaffrey Associates, undated [accessed June 10, 2022].

53. "State of the Union: Interview with Rep. Michael McCaul (R-TX); Interview with U.S. Secretary of State Antony Blinken; Interview with Former CIA Director David Petraeus; Interview with Nadya Tolokonnikova," CNN, March 6, 2022.

54. "Team: David H. Petraeus," Kohlberg Kravis Roberts (KKR), undated [accessed June 10, 2022]. Petraeus also sits on the board of directors at Optiv, which designs cybersecurity technology for the Department of Defense. See, "Who Is Optiv Federal?" Optiv Federal, undated [accessed June 10, 2022].

55. Leslie Wayne, "After Retirement Clark Has Forged a Lucrative Career," *New York Times*, November 10, 2003.

56. The former CIA director also said, "I think we need to understand that there is only one thing that Putin understands, and that's force." See "Interview with Former U.S. Secretary of Defense Leon Panetta; Interview with State Department Spokesman Ned Price; Russian Missiles Hit Train Station. Transcript," CNN, April 8, 2022.

57. Beacon Global Strategies describes itself as "a strategic advisory firm specializing in international Policy, Defense, Cyber, Intelligence, and Homeland Security." See "A Global Perspective," Beacon Global Strategies, undated [accessed June 10, 2022]. *The New York Times* reported that Raytheon has been a client. See Kenneth P. Vogel and Eric Lipton, "Corporations and Foreign Nations Pivot to Lobby Biden," *New York Times*, November 17, 2020.

58. MSNBC also failed to include disclosures when it interviewed former Homeland Security secretary Jeh Johnson, who now serves on the board of directors of Lockheed Martin—the biggest defense contractor in the world. See Aditi Ramaswami and Andrew Perez, "The Defense Industry's Ukraine Pundits," The Lever, April 12, 2022.

59. *Meet the Press* (NBC), February 27, 2022. Bash was hired by NBC as a national security analyst in 2017.

60. Bash is also a founder and managing director at Beacon Global Strategies. See Ramaswami and Perez, "The Defense Industry's Ukraine Pundits."

61. Alan MacLeod, "Politico's Defense News, Brought to You by Northrop Grumman," MintPress News, February 18, 2021.

62. Ibid.

63. David Swanson, "U.S. Military Spending Is Undebatable Because Indefensible," World Beyond War, June 6, 2022. Swanson wrote that the spending spree on weapons has now expanded to countries such as Spain, Thailand, Germany, Japan, and Netherlands, "with either no debate at all or with all debate shut down by a single word: Russia." In many cases, when nations increase their military spending, it's understood as fulfilling a commitment to the US government.

64. Connor O'Brien, "The Push to Supersize Pentagon Spending Ratchets Up," Politico, June 4, 2022.

65. Ibid.

66. Jake Johnson, "Corporate Media Accused of 'Cheerleading' for US Escalation in Ukraine," Common Dreams, March 18, 2022.

67. Ken Dilanian, Courtney Kube, Carol E. Lee, and Dan De Luce, "In Break with the Past, US Is Using Intel to Fight an Info War with Russia," NBC News, April 6, 2022.

68. Ibid.

69. Johnstone, "US Officials Admit They're Literally Just Lying."

70. Caitlin Johnstone, "On Russians 'Raping Babies'," Consortium News, May 23, 2022. Narratives of killing and harming innocent babies have been used as war propaganda since its inception and were instrumental in demonizing Germans in World War I. See, Andersen, *A Century of Media, A Century of War*, Chapter One.

71. Caitlin Johnstone, "Official Behind Media Reports of Russian Atrocities Fired by Ukrainian Parliament," Consortium News, June 1, 2022.
72. Adam Staten, "Ukraine Official Fired over Handling of Russian Sexual Assault Claims," *Newsweek*, May 31, 2022
73. Ibid.
74. Jake Johnson, "'Slippery Slope . . . Just Got a Lot Steeper': US to Send Ukraine Advanced Missiles as Russia Holds Nuke Drills," Common Dreams, June 1, 2022.
75. Joseph R. Biden Jr., "President Biden: What America Will and Will Not Do in Ukraine," *New York Times*, May 31, 2022; "Russia's Nuclear Forces Holding Manoeuvre Drills—Report," Reuters, June 1, 2022.
76. Branko Marcetic, "The Biden Administration Is in No Rush to Help Ukraine Negotiate an End to the War," *Jacobin*, May 30, 2022.
77. Jomo Kwame Sundaram and Anis Chowdhury, "US Leads Sanctions Killing Millions to No End," Inter Press Service (IPS), June 7, 2022.
78. Ibid.
79. "At Doom's Doorstep: It Is 100 Seconds to Midnight," Bulletin of the Atomic Scientists, January 20, 2022.
80. "War Threatens Our Environment," World Beyond War, undated [accessed June 10, 2022].
81. Warren Gunnels, Twitter post, June 5, 2022 8:46 a.m.
82. Chris Hedges, "America's Gun Fetish," ScheerPost, June 6, 2022.
83. Ibid.
84. Murtaza Hussain, "Racist 'Replacement' Conspiracy Is Undergirded by a Real Resource Scarcity," The Intercept, May 17, 2022.
85. Republicans in Congress have scapegoated the Asian American community, celebrated a vigilante who killed two protesters at a Black Lives Matter demonstration, and defended insurrectionists. They have also enacted a historic number of voter-suppression bills to disenfranchise voters of color and people in poverty. They have rallied their base against inclusive and anti-racist education and introduced a slew of bills that would promote discrimination against transgender people and gut the teaching of Black history. Attempts to ban books are on the rise, targeting in particular titles that address race, sexuality, and gender. See, "The Year in Hate & Extremism Report 2021," Southern Poverty Law Center, March 9, 2022.
86. Andersen, "False Balance in Media Coverage Undermines Democracy."
87. Alvarez, "Roxanne Dunbar-Ortiz on Uvalde."
88. "The United States Spends More on Defense than the Next Nine Countries Combined," Peter G. Peterson Foundation, June 1, 2022.

CHAPTER 5

Media Democracy in Action

Contributions by LEE CAMP (*Redacted Tonight*),
SAM HUSSEINI (Institute for Public Accuracy), ALLISON
BUTLER (Mass Media Literacy), NOLAN HIGDON (Critical
Media Literacy Conference of the Americas) and
AFSANEH RIGOT (Article 19)

Introduction by MISCHA GERACOULIS

*Within democratic societies, divisions are growing
as a result of the spread of opinion media following the "Fox
News model" and the spread of disinformation circuits that
are amplified by the way social media functions.*
—REBECCA VINCENT, DIRECTOR OF OPERATIONS
AND CAMPAIGNS, REPORTERS WITHOUT BORDERS[1]

Those who work on behalf of press freedom caution that we've entered a new globalized era of polarization in which the media figure prominently. At one end are journalists who've been treated as criminals simply for doing their job; at the other end are the purveyors of fake news and the online platforms that profit from the havoc they wreak.

Rebecca Vincent's synopsis of the 2022 *World Press Freedom Index*, the annual assessment of journalism in 180 nations and territories, produced by Reporters Without Borders (RSF), cited "a two-fold increase in polarization amplified by information chaos" and "a globalized

and unregulated online information space that encourages fake news and propaganda" fueling "divisions within
countries, as well as polarization between countries at the
international level."[2]

As Vincent asserted, the "Fox News model" has
impacted all media, including online spaces, as well as
public engagement and, some say, democracy itself. Nora
Benavidez, the human rights attorney who is also an
expert on free speech and the First Amendment, iden-
tifies Fox and Meta (Facebook's owner) as two leading
examples of media that profit from lies, organized disinformation campaigns, and propaganda, at the expense of
democratic societies around the world.[3]

Calculating some of this cost is Article 19 senior
researcher Afsaneh Rigot, whose contribution to this
chapter draws attention to harms perpetrated against
many of the world's most vulnerable and marginalized
citizens by digital technologies, including social media,
messenger apps, and dating apps. While social media are
increasingly documented as potent means to organize
criminal activity, such as the January 6 Capitol insurrection and the spate of mass shootings in the United States,
Rigot's research documents human rights violations in
nations of the Middle East and North Africa, where law
enforcement officials exploit technology use by LGBTQ+
people to target, entrap, and arrest them.

The "Fox News model" disrupts venerable norms of civil
debate and ethical journalism, replacing them with dehumanizing monologues, self-aggrandizing callouts, and
intolerant cancellations. Broad media illiteracy combined
with naïve reliance on corporate fact-checkers makes inter-
preting information an exercise in futility. By contrast, as

Benavidez argues, we are most likely to counter the proliferation of disinformation and misinformation by engaging in critical thinking.[4] The importance of asking critical questions is spotlighted by journalist Sam Husseini in his article for this chapter. He explains how confronting powerful officials—including elected politicians and military officers—with tough, potentially unpopular questions is a fundamental civic duty for journalists.

Allison Butler, who teaches communication at University of Massachusetts Amherst, and co-directs the nonprofit organization Mass Media Literacy, would likely agree with Husseini's focus on the importance of critical questioning. In her article, Butler describes how Mass Media Literacy teaches critical media literacy skills for media users, especially students, educators, and scholars. Emphasizing that a *critical* component is necessary to reading the word as well as the world, Butler sees the significance of critical media literacy extending beyond school classrooms. In effect, the theory and practice of critical media literacy is advanced as integral to a just, equitable, and democratic society.

This chapter also features Nolan Higdon, who teaches in the Education Department at University of California, Santa Cruz, and the department of history at California State University, East Bay, describing the aims of critical media literacy in the context of the Critical Media Literacy Conference of the Americas (CMLCA). He highlights some of the ways that conference participants "interrogate" media together. In his words, this engagement is "predicated on respect, decency, humanity, integrity, empathy, and sympathy"—hallmarks of civil discourse that contrast starkly with the deriding, divisive

Fox model of communication. This isn't to say that critical media literacy or the CMLCA encourages groupthink; disagreement is part and parcel of democracy. It's also quite different from incitement. In this new era of polarization, the CMLCA assumes a position of inclusivity, connection, and collaboration to address major issues that threaten "planetary life." Indeed, as Higdon and the conference demonstrate, without the power of press freedom and democratic practices, humankind is hard pressed to stand up against injustices of any kind.

Comedian Lee Camp, who endorses freedom of expression through comedy and performance, brings attention to the public's increasing distrust in journalism, and addresses threats to the safety of journalists and truth tellers, intellectual freedom, and democracy. Camp's article focuses on how the suspension of freedoms of information and expression has resulted in scapegoating, blacklisting, and media takedowns that he and other critics experienced in 2022 for speaking out against war.

Similar to Reporters Without Borders' goals to champion the vital role of the Fourth Estate and leave no freedom-of-information breach unreported, Project Censored promotes independent journalism, opposes censorship, and maintains that, as Reporters Without Borders puts it, journalism is a common good for humanity and an immunization against disinformation. By upholding the work of the journalists and practitioners featured here—who inform, check, and balance infractions on freedom of expression, and who advocate for critical education along with other human rights and civil liberties—this year's Media Democracy in Action chapter offers lucid direction for navigating this new era of polarization.

MISCHA GERACOULIS is a journalist and educator who serves as a contributing editor at *The Markaz Review* and on the editorial board of the Censored Press. Her teaching and research are focused on the intersections among human rights education, critical media literacy, and ethics. She dedicates her introduction to the Palestinian American journalist Shireen Abu Akleh, born January 3, 1971, killed May 11, 2022.

THE COMEDY SHOW *REDACTED TONIGHT* GETS REDACTED BY US EMPIRE

LEE CAMP

As a twelve-year-old growing up in Richmond, Virginia, when I began jotting down whimsical observations, dreaming of becoming a professional comedy writer getting paid to insert fart observations into columns about gardening or pop culture, I never thought that one day the US government with its corporate proxies in the Big Tech national security complex would shut down my television show due to the ostensible danger it posed. At age seventeen, when I started performing stand-up comedy about cats and dogs and dating (edgy stuff), I never imagined that Big Tech would one day globally ban eight years of my work, ranking my comedy TV show as more threatening to Americans' delicate virgin ears than many Nazi videos or channels educating teenagers on how to most effectively choke someone unconscious. When I was twenty-one and handing out fliers to bleary-eyed tourists in Times Square, begging them to come to the comedy club, I didn't think that one day I would be the most censored comedian in the United States. I'd previously learned about George Carlin and Lenny Bruce—thrown behind bars for words they had spoken onstage—and thought to myself, "Thank goodness we've evolved past those barbaric times when our government persecuted people for speech."

Clearly, I suffered from a failure of imagination.

In March 2022, the US government (either directly or indirectly) shut down the entire network that aired my television show, *Redacted Tonight with Lee Camp*. The network was RT America, and yes, it was funded by Russia. However, the reason I was willing to have my program at that network (which was based in Washington, DC) for eight years was exactly because they never censored me and never told me what to say. I wrote all my own material and was never once told to cut anything. It was the only network where I could be fully and clearly anti-war, anti-imperialist, and anticapitalist. For those who don't know, no mainstream media outlet in the United States would be caught dead with a host espousing true anti-war and anticapitalist sentiments. Phil Donahue, Jesse Ventura, and Chris Hedges are just a few of the well-known people who lost their media jobs for being anti-war. Although RT America has not stated clearly why it shut down, we do know it happened nearly overnight and that, within the span of about five days, major corporations, including DirecTV, Sling TV, Dish, YouTube, Roku, and Spotify, either pulled the plug on or deleted the archives of all RT America programs—making it fairly clear to me that they were told to do so by someone with that kind of power.

Soon after RT America shuttered, all eight years of my show's YouTube videos were banned globally. This amounted to more than 500 episodes and much more than 1,000 videos erased in the modern-day equivalent of book burning. The digital destruction of wide breadths of content and knowledge also hit every other RT America show, including those hosted by Pulitzer Prize winner Chris Hedges, fearless journalist Abby Martin, former governor of Minnesota Jesse Ventura, and US political prisoner Julian Assange.

Within days of the cancellation of my show and the banning of all my YouTube videos, my podcast *Moment of Clarity* was also deleted from Spotify. As far as I know, this makes me the most censored comedian working in America today. And is it for preaching hateful messages of violence? Is it for mocking the less fortunate or demanding the oppression of those who are different from me? Is it for calling for the bombing and murder of foreign peoples?

No.

All of those ideas are generally accepted and at times even standard US government policy. My censorship is instead due to the fact that I'm anti-war and anti-imperialist. It's because I reveal the truth behind the so-called "mainstream," corporate media propaganda, outing the war crimes of our insanely wealthy, powerful, and morally bankrupt government.

Perhaps more shocking than the censorship is the utter silence of the corporate media. They see no reason to defend freedom of the press for journalists or outlets they consider to be enemies of the US state. And anyone calling out the war crimes of the United States (including, for example, the fact that the "War on Terror" has killed 6 million people during the past twenty years) should, in their minds, be shut down, cut off, and silenced. In the case of Julian Assange, they even see it as acceptable to imprison and torture him.

Every time I start to feel shocked or startled that this is happening in our country today, I must remind myself that this is nothing new for the United States. Countless socialists, anarchists, leftists, civil rights icons, and more have been arrested, beaten, maligned, and otherwise attacked. During World War I, German Americans who had nothing to do with the battle overseas were harangued and persecuted in numerous ways. Speaking out against US involvement in that war was considered a crime, and presidential candidate Eugene Debs was sentenced to ten years in prison for such speech. During World War II, innocent Japanese Americans were rounded up and put in internment camps. In the 1960s and '70s, numerous Black Panthers were framed and locked away for their political ideas, some of them tasting freedom again only very recently.

Entertainers have been abused and blacklisted as well. The Smothers Brothers lost their hit television show for coming out against the Vietnam War. Lenny Bruce, Jim Morrison, Billie Holiday, and so many others found themselves chased by the government because they exposed the ruling elite in one form or another.

Shutting down speech that goes against the war machine, or reveals the racism at the heart of the American system, or exposes the capitalist gods of profit has a long, storied history in the United States—a history that is rarely, if ever, taught in schools. The slogan "The Land of the Free" comes with a giant asterisk.

The question is: When will we all decide we've had enough and fight for true freedom of speech?

LEE CAMP is the former creator, host, and head writer of the TV comedy news show *Redacted Tonight with Lee Camp*. Camp is a former writer for the Onion and the Huffington Post, and the author of *Bullet Points & Punch Lines*. Camp is also a comedian who continues to host the show *Moment of Clarity* at *LeeCamp.com*.

QUESTIONING POLITICOS AT NEWS CONFERENCES—AN UNDERUTILIZED ANTIDOTE TO CENSORSHIP?

SAM HUSSEINI

In my career as a journalist, I have tried—forcefully, but within the parameters of the profession—to question politicians about the most critical issues of the day.

In June 2017, at the National Press Club, I asked Joint Chiefs of Staff chairman Joseph Dunford: "What's the legal justification for targeting Syrian government forces?"[5] He claimed that the Authorization for Use of Military Force (AUMF) enacted after the September 11 attacks in 2001 established the US government's authority. Legal expert Francis Boyle and I put out a news release through the Institute for Public Accuracy, where I am senior analyst and communications director, debunking that claim. This story was picked up the following day by the *New York Times*, with Charlie Savage citing my question and quoting a senator taking issue with General Dunford's false claim.[6] Thus, with a sharp question and a scrappy media infrastructure, the Fourth Estate could meaningfully challenge the war makers.

In February 2020, just before the COVID-19 pandemic,

I asked the Centers for Disease Control's principal deputy director, Anne Schuchat, also at the Press Club, if it was "a complete coincidence" that the outbreak happened in the one city in China with a BSL4 lab, and whether we shouldn't be having "at least some of the discussion about the ethics of some of the research that happens" in such labs. I went on to write several investigative pieces on the issue.[7]

Unfortunately, with much of the "independent media," including *Democracy Now!*, buying the establishment line that lab origin was a ridiculous theory, my questioning did not have an overt, clear impact in this case.[8] Still, it serves as an early historical marker: journalists cannot claim ignorance about the possibility of a lab origin for COVID-19, and I suspect the questions I raised did cause some internal debate. My questioning would eventually be picked up by journalists such as Nicholson Baker, who, a year later in *New York Magazine*, would reassess the warped conventional wisdom on the issue of pandemic origins.[9] But the lack of a meaningful push in real time may have foreclosed the possibility of altering public perspective about the threats at a time when global public opinion could have been engaged in a truly historic way.

The Washington Stakeout

In an attempt to get more regular access to officials, from 2006 to 2011, under the banner of the Washington Stakeout, I tried to ask tough questions of politicos as they left the Sunday morning chat shows. After the financial crisis of 2008, I asked deficit-hawk congressional representatives why there was a tax on bandages, but not on complex Wall Street transactions. I asked 9/11 Commission co-chairs Lee Hamilton and Thomas Kean if US interventionist policy did not cause resentment in Arab countries. I asked Chuck Schumer if the US should pay reparations to Iraq for the invasion. I asked Colin Powell when he found out that the "evidence" he cited for Iraq's weapons of mass destruction (WMDs) had been based on a false confession extracted through torture.

Doing the Washington Stakeout was joyful but exhausting. I had to determine which of the guests would actually be coming into the studio, try to figure out appropriate questions for them, and then zoom around with cameraperson in tow from one studio to the next. My friend Matthew Bradley volunteered to do much of the work, including all the tech work. I paid the cameraperson a pittance out of my pocket. Pickup by independent outlets such as the Real News Network happened sometimes, but it was spotty.

During the Arab uprisings in 2011, I asked Saudi Ambassador Turki bin Faisal Al Saud about the legitimacy of the Saudi regime. It was aggressive questioning, but informed by my understanding at that critical time that the Gulf States, through their money and big media, were effectively singling out secular states, including Syria and Libya, which had been targeted by the US establishment. The Press Club executive director suspended me from the Press Club for aggressive questioning. I appealed to the ethics committee, which overturned the suspension. It was something of a victory, but raised my profile such that politicians quit stopping for me as they left the Sunday morning talk shows. This effectively killed the Washington Stakeout.

After the Washington Stakeout, I was able to get into the State Department during President Donald Trump's administration. When they nominated Gina Haspel to head the CIA, I asked repeatedly whether the State Department deemed waterboarding torture (which cables show Haspel had overseen at a secret base in Thailand).[10] Spokesperson Heather Nauert would not answer, as my sustained questioning made evident.

Perhaps the most well-known attempt was during the Trump-Putin summit in Helsinki in 2018. In the context of major media obsession with the highly dubious "Russiagate" narrative, I held up a sign that read "Nuclear Weapons Ban Treaty," which was backed by 122 countries but subject to a block by the United States and Russia—effectively threatening the world to maintain their "superpower" monopoly. Instead of getting my question in, I got dragged out of the hall and was locked up until the media centers closed at midnight.[11] This generated some media attention. The big networks called to have me on as a guest—but then all cancelled. Jim Acosta of CNN, who presents himself as First Amendment champion, portrayed me as a protester trying to cause a commotion rather than a journalist. At least CNN's Christiane Amanpour correctly noted, "For all we know, [the sign] could have been a question—it sounds pretty innocuous."[12]

Asking the Tough Questions

There are numerous hurdles to this work, including access, accreditation, and distribution. The Congressional Press Galleries have convoluted requirements that examine a journalist's income; working for a nonprofit might nix requests for accreditation, but it is completely at the galleries' whim. The Senate Press Gallery committee is chaired by Leo Shane III of *Military Times*. The challenges to gaining access, let alone getting the opportunity to pose tough questions, are many.

What may be needed is a far more ambitious project than the Washington Stakeout: a wiki that gives critical information on various political figures and the topics and issues about which they ought to be challenged. Thus, other independent journalists as well as activists, students, and regular citizens would have tools to challenge those in power. Such content could also be provided on a PDF so that it could be printed, copied, and distributed at events.

The benefits of such work could be enormous. Questioning officials helps focus on actual journalistic work, rather than succumbing to the circular firing squad to which left media are prone. It's easier to bicker over bread crumbs or preach to the choir than to roll up your sleeves and ask tough questions of political figures. Doing so, however, might help build a mass audience for independent media and get critical information onto more mainstream outlets.

To be effective, we need insightful political instincts combined with some minimal media infrastructure that provides a platform for posing challenging questions and informing the public about the results in a timely manner. Independent outlets, Big Tech platforms such as Twitter, or a combination of the two could fulfill this role. Unfortunately, attempts to do so by "independent" media have been minimal at best.

As it currently stands, "tough questions" are more likely to originate from establishment media staking out more hawkish, militaristic positions than those of the White House. That is one circumstance that desperately needs to be questioned.

SAM HUSSEINI is an independent journalist. His work can be read on Substack at husseini.substack.com/. His previous writings, including those referenced in this piece, are available at husseini.org.

MASS MEDIA LITERACY: PROVIDING RESOURCES AND DISMANTLING ISOLATION THROUGH CRITICAL MEDIA LITERACY

ALLISON BUTLER

Mass Media Literacy (massmedialiteracy.org) is a grassroots organization based out of Massachusetts with representation in California, Vermont, and New Hampshire. We work with teachers, librarians, and community organizers to bring critical media literacy to teacher education, curriculum development, and classrooms. With our world becoming increasingly digitized and organized by corporate media organizations, with the vast majority of our lives structured around and via media use, we can no longer afford (if we ever could) to circumvent learning about the media. We believe that sustainable education in critical media literacy is needed across the K-12 curriculum and that students of media literacy deserve structured opportunities to access, analyze, and produce a variety of media. Pre-service teachers deserve critical media literacy education as part of their teacher preparation. Classroom teachers deserve continuing education in critical media literacy so that the work is infused throughout their lesson plans and curriculum development.

Mass Media Literacy is focused on the *critical* in critical media literacy. Our work is action-oriented, participatory, and dialogic in the Freireian sense of reading the world and reading the word. Our work is grounded in social justice, highlighting ways for teachers and students to make change in their communities and "talk back" to the corporate media. By examining media ownership, production, and distribution, our work pays close attention to the power structure and dynamics of "mainstream" media.

Mass Media Literacy is committed to making critical media literacy available for all, and we maintain an uncompromising independence. We are financially supported by the Media Education Foundation (mediaed. org) and do not accept any corporate money for our work. Over the years, we have worked directly in classrooms with both teachers and students, have presented at school and public libraries, and have worked with the Massachusetts Teachers Association (massteacher.org) and the New England Library Association (nelib.org) on providing professional development and continuing education for K-12 teachers. We have built broad introductory lessons on critical media literacy; class- and topic-specific lessons that align with common core and state standards; and timely, topical issues such as net neutrality, how to evaluate "fake news," and culturally responsive news literacy lessons that centralize the stories and treatment of marginalized communities.

Our work is primarily focused directly within learning spaces. But Mass Media Literacy is also committed to building research and scholarship on critical media literacy. Whenever possible, we make our work available for any teacher to adapt to their classroom needs, and we work with individual teachers to craft lessons that work for their spaces.

While the vast majority of our work thus far has taken place in Massachusetts and New England, we see our work as reproducible across the nation. For example:

- ◙ For over a year, Mass Media Literacy worked with a team of 10th grade teachers to build critical media literacy work into their lessons, across subjects matters including English, math, social studies, and science. The media literacy trainers started with the teachers' goals, cross-referenced those with the state standards and common core expectations, and built media-focused lessons. This work could be replicated and adapted across any grade or subject. Either remotely or in person, Mass Media Literacy trainers can work with teachers and administrators to build critical media literacy lessons and activities for long-term, sustainable infusion.

- ◙ After the 2016 election, Mass Media Literacy developed an interactive presentation on how to evaluate and make sense of news and "fake news," which was initially presented to the New England Library Association, then adapted for middle school and high school students and public libraries. Updated versions of this presentation have since been shared at community organizations, in person and via local community access channels.

While we aim for our work to be sustainable and infused across curricula, Mass Media Literacy is also interested in addressing timely current events. We will work with teachers and community organizers on interactive presentations that address topics of interest and/or time-sensitive issues. All our work is designed to be shared with our audience so that they may adapt anything for their purposes.

◼ Mass Media Literacy builds culturally responsive news literacy curricula focused on the representation of marginalized communities in the news. Our initial curricula are focused on the treatment of Black bodies in the wake of the 2020 #BLM protests. We presented this work to the Massachusetts Teachers Association conference. The work is currently being expanded to address the presentation of multiple racial/ethnic intersections in the news, for example, representations of Asians and Asian Americans amid the chaos of the COVID-19 pandemic, of Native Americans amid the climate crisis, and of Latinx amid questions of immigration and COVID-19–era labor relations.

Overall, Mass Media Literacy aims to bring critical

media literacy to as many places as possible, to support teachers, students, and community members in growing their own knowledge of media institutions and how they operate. Over the course of our work, we have found that the most frequently repeated concern of teachers is that they feel they are alone and without resources when trying to bring critical media literacy to their classrooms. Our goal is to dismantle that isolation, to provide teachers with resources and long-term support in their work. The second most frequent concern we hear is that teachers, schools, and libraries cannot afford to hire support; at Mass Media Literacy, we have no expectation for financial profit from this work. We will work within a budget that makes the most sense for the person, or group, doing the asking. We believe that the knowledge and practice of critical media literacy knowledge is inherently democratic, and we want to do our part to support equitable access and opportunity.

ALLISON BUTLER, PHD, is a senior lecturer, director of undergraduate advising, and the director of the Media Literacy Certificate Program in the department of communication at the University of Massachusetts, Amherst, where she teaches courses on critical media literacy and representations of education in the media. Butler co-directs the grassroots organization Mass Media Literacy (massmedialiteracy.org), where she develops and runs teacher trainings for the inclusion of critical media literacy in K-12 schools. She serves as the vice president on the Board of the Media Freedom Foundation. Butler holds an MA and a PhD from New York University and is the author of numerous articles and books on media literacy, most recently, *Educating Media Literacy: The Need for Teacher Education in Critical Media Literacy* (Brill, 2020) and *Key Scholarship in Media Literacy: David Buckingham* (Brill, 2021).

CRITICAL MEDIA LITERACY CONFERENCE OF THE AMERICAS

NOLAN HIGDON

The third annual Critical Media Literacy Conference of the Americas (CMLCA) took place October 21–23, 2022, in Oakland, California. CMLCA brought together educators, scholars, and activists to explore and share pedagogical approaches that run counter to prevailing neoliberal education. While media literacy discourse is often dominated by acritical perspectives, which refuse to critique the production process behind the pedagogy, the CMLCA evaluates, investigates, interrogates, and analyzes not only media, but also the media education process itself. This is known as a *critical* approach to media literacy. As the organizers of the CMLCA explain:

> The goal of critical media literacy is to engage with media through critically examining representations, systems, structures, ideologies, and power dynamics that shape and reproduce culture and society. It is an inquiry-based process for analyzing and creating media by interrogating the relationships between power and knowledge. Critical media literacy is a dialogical process for social and environmental justice that incorporates Paulo Freire's (1970) notion of praxis, "reflection and action upon the world in order to transform it." This pedagogical project questions representations of class, gender, race, sexuality, and other forms of identity and challenges media messages that reproduce oppression and discrimination. It

celebrates positive representations and beneficial aspects of media while challenging problems and negative consequences, recognizing media are never neutral. Critical media literacy is a transformative pedagogy for developing and empowering critical, caring, nurturing, and conscientious people.[13]

To achieve its goals, the CMLCA proudly rejects funding from corporate sources, instead relying on universities—such as California State University East Bay, Instituto Provincial de Educación Superior "Paulo Freire," Mount St. Mary's University, University of California, Los Angles, University of Southern California—and nonprofit institutions including the Action Coalition for Media Education, Mass Media Literacy, Project Censored/Media Freedom Foundation, the Union for Democratic Communication, and Youth Be Heard.

The CMLCA is not a traditional conference. Rather than focus on individual achievement, the conference seeks to build a community of individuals focused on helping each other and global citizens engage with media from a critical perspective. At CMLCA, presenters do not talk at attendees; instead, presenters and attendees are integrated into the learning process through spaces of constructive discourse. They participate not only in paper presentations but also in workshops, roundtables, and salons. The conference values human-to-human interaction predicated on respect, decency, humanity, integrity, empathy, and sympathy.

CMLCA was created by scholars, practitioners, and activists who apply the tools of critical media literacy "to interrogate 'texts' presented in diverse formats (oral, visual, spatial, aesthetic, object-based, cultural or multimodal), particularly if they maintain systems and ideologies of power, or reproduce social, economic, political, cultural, linguistic, or environmental inequity. A CML approach interrogates media content, illuminating the discriminatory and subjugating messages for the purpose of raising consciousness to increase solidarity efforts towards humankind and planetary life."[14]

The objective of the annual multilingual conference is "to expand the conceptual horizons on the meaning and purpose of current actions, silences, and eco-discourses related to the control or containment of the eco-crises and the potential actions to care for planetary life. We are interested in exploring the interconnected systems of land, water, air, life and culture."[15]

CMLCA's democratic approach to education is situated at a critical moment in human history, when climate change and environmental degradation threaten our survival. Indeed, our global community has been ravaged by neoliberal capitalism, and in its wake instability, inequity, and suffering threaten our collective existence. As a result, the 2022 conference theme—"Critical Literacies, Multimodalities, and Care for Life"—called on critical media literacy practitioners, scholars, and activists to think beyond their discipline, institution, or region, to situate critical media literacy in the context of our global environment.

The conference organizers invested a great deal of labor to ensure that the conference would be free of charge for participants. The generosity of universities, nonprofits, and volunteers has enabled the conference to be free for all attendees. This is a crucial difference between CMLCA and other, corporate-sponsored media literacy conferences, which charge exorbitant registration fees and seek to turn a profit rather than utilize the tools of CML to improve educational outcomes and our global community. Attendees will be met by a global and inclusive community eager to collaborate with one another.

NOLAN HIGDON is a lecturer at Merrill College and the education department at University of California, Santa Cruz, and co-founder of the Critical Media Literacy Conference of the Americas. His latest publications include *Let's Agree to Disagree: A Critical Thinking Guide to Communication, Conflict Management, and Critical Literacy* (co-authored with Mickey Huff, Routledge, 2022) and *The Anatomy of Fake News: A Critical News Literacy Education* (University of California Press, 2020).

DESIGN FROM THE MARGINS PROMOTES BETTER TECH FOR ALL

AFSANEH RIGOT

Our communication and social media technologies have become weaponized against at-risk groups, creating harms and human rights abuses that are transnational in scope. From Russian police coercing protesters into unlocking their phones to search for evidence of dissent, to Egyptian courts using dating apps to prosecute queer people, to facial recognition technologies that perpetuate racial biases against Black Americans, there is undeniable evidence of real digital harms and physical dangers caused by technologies that treat the needs of vulnerable populations as "edge cases."[16]

Tech developers typically dismiss "edge cases," because they are difficult to solve and impact fewer people, an approach that reflects the prevalence across the tech industry of the "move fast and break things" ethos that Mark Zuckerberg enthusiastically pushed at Facebook. But "edge cases" are powerful indicators for understanding deep flaws in our technologies. This is why I refer to these cases—the people, groups, and communities who are the most impacted and least supported—as *decentered*. By understanding who is most impacted by social, political, and legal frameworks, we can also understand who is most likely to be victimized by specific technologies. Often, the most marginalized are those most criminalized: these are the decentered cases. We need to move toward building and designing tech based on the needs of those most marginalized. When we fail to protect them, we all remain unprotected.

My work focuses on pushing back against the "move fast, break things" mindset that informs so much of our everyday technology. I developed Design From the Margins (DFM) on the premise that our tech should center users who are also members of marginalized or criminalized communities—the very people that tech developers often dismiss as "outliers" or "edge cases."[17] From a DFM perspective, our technologies, tools, products, and platforms are most robust when success is defined in terms of how well each protects its most vulnerable and disenfranchised users: the decentered. And, as an added benefit, technology that has recentered the extremes will *always* be generalizable to the broader usership.

The DFM framework developed from years of documenting the impact of technology on specific decentered groups and noting the increasing weaponization of new communications technologies by law enforcement. In 2016, for example, I led a research project with local organizations in Iran, Lebanon, and Egypt that focused on how LGBTQ people in those nations used dating apps such as Grindr and Hornet, which made them vulnerable to abuse and arrests.[18] One aim of this report was to identify what technology companies need to do to address the risks faced by people using their apps and platforms.

Take, for example, the case of a queer Syrian refugee in Lebanon, stopped by police at a checkpoint. When police search the person's phone, an officer spots the icon of a dating app, Grindr, which outs the individual as queer in the officer's eyes. Further inspection of the phone reveals what the officers deem to be "queer content." The individual is taken in for further interrogation and subjected to verbal and physical abuse. They now face sentencing under Article 534 of the Lebanese penal code and potential fines, imprisonment, and even denial of their immigration status.

But what if this person could have easily hidden the Grindr app's logo? Based on recommendations from my research, Grindr developed stealth modes to make this option a reality. Choices such as Grindr's Discreet App Icon were game changers. It allowed people to make the Grindr app icon on their phones look like a calendar app or some other harmless alternative. This feature was created solely based on these "extreme" cases, but it has proven so popular with users globally that Grindr now offers its Discreet App Icon not only in "high-risk" countries but around the world. People everywhere have personal reasons to maintain their privacy.

Based on further recommendations from my research, Grindr introduced a variety of new features that were unprecedented for a dating app.[19] Due to their importance and popularity, most of these features are now deployed to Grindr's millions of users worldwide.[20] These changes provide immediate safety to users in highly risky contexts, protecting them from harassment, arrest, and physical harm, but they also provide benefits to all kinds of users worldwide, from New York City to São Paulo.

From 2020 to 2022, I worked to document the legal prosecution of LGBTQ people in Egypt, Lebanon, and Tunisia, with a focus on how authorities used LGBTQ people's private digital data as evidence against them.[21] Police not only entrapped LGBTQ people on queer dating apps, aided by informants, but also gathered and collected incriminating evidence from LGBTQ people's devices. All of the interviewed lawyers and a majority of the court files mentioned evidence taken as screen shots from WhatsApp. Previously, WhatsApp had introduced disappearing messages with a seven-day option. The app users whose cases I studied required better, faster options. Responding to my research, in December 2021, WhatsApp rolled out improved disappearing message options, including a twenty-four-hour vanish option and a default setting to allow all users to employ disappearing messages.

This might seem like a small change, but it has already produced a big shift in how people use WhatsApp.[22] The messaging service now offers improved functionality to all kinds of people who prefer to keep their digital conversations private. During an April 2022 event sponsored by Harvard University's Belfer Center for Science and International Affairs, WhatsApp's public policy manager for Europe, the Middle East, and Africa indicated that the company is committed to developing additional security based on DFM principles.[23]

We expect our architects to design buildings and bridges to withstand the most extreme conditions and heavy loads, so why shouldn't we expect tech engineers to design the equivalent—sensitive, resilient technologies that protect and benefit all users?[24] Our digital tech is better and safer, more innovative, robust, and secure for *everyone* when designers start by considering the needs and concerns of the most marginalized and impacted users. It's challenging to convince Big Tech companies of this, but there's now sufficient evidence to show not only that Design From the Margins is necessary, but also that it works.

AFSANEH RIGOT is a senior researcher at Article 19. Her work on Design From the Margins was developed while she was a 2021–2022 fellow in the Technology and Public Purpose program at Harvard University.

Notes

1. "RSF's 2022 World Press Freedom Index: A New Era of Polarisation," RSF (YouTube), May 2, 2022. The complete text of Reporters Without Borders (RSF)'s 2022 *World Press Freedom Index* report is available through its website.
2. Ibid. Readers of Project Censored's yearbook may not be surprised to learn that the United States has dropped from 17th in RSF's 2002 ranking to 42nd in this year's *World Press Freedom Index*.
3. See, for example, Nora Benavidez and Kate Coyer, "Facebook Ought to Be Protecting Democracy Worldwide Every Day," *Boston Globe*, April 14, 2022.
4. Ibid.

5. "Bombing Syria: * Impeachable * Carve-Up Agenda," Institute for Public Accuracy, June 19, 2017.

6. Charlie Savage, "Senators Wrestle with Updating Law Authorizing War on Terrorist Groups," *New York Times*, June 20, 2017.

7. Sam Husseini, "Did This Virus Come From a Lab? Maybe Not—But It Exposes the Threat of a Biowarfare Arms Race," Salon, April 24, 2020; Sam Husseini, "The Long History of Accidental Laboratory Releases of Potential Pandemic Pathogens Is Being Ignored in the COVID-19 Media Coverage," Independent Science News, May 5, 2020; Sam Husseini, "Peter Daszak's EcoHealth Alliance Has Hidden Almost $40 Million in Pentagon Funding and Militarized Pandemic Science," Independent Science News, December 16, 2020.

8. Amy Goodman, interview with Peter Daszak, "'Pure Baloney': Zoologist Debunks Trump's COVID-19 Origin Theory, Explains Animal-Human Transmission," *Democracy Now!*, April 16, 2020.

9. Nicholson Baker, "The Lab-Leak Hypothesis: For Decades, Scientists Have Been Hot-Wiring Viruses in Hopes of Preventing a Pandemic, Not Causing One. But What If . . . ?" *New York Magazine*, January 4, 2021.

10. Julian E. Barnes, and Scott Shane, "Cables Detail C.I.A. Waterboarding at Secret Prison Run by Gina Haspel," *New York Times*, August 10, 2018.

11. Sam Husseini, "I Came as a Journalist to Ask Important Questions," *The Nation*, July 17, 2018.

12. Sam Husseini, "Trump and Big Media: Clash or Collusion?" Consortium News, November 11, 2018.

13. "Conferences," Critical Media Project, undated [accessed May 31, 2022].

14. "Call for Proposals," Critical Media Project, undated [accessed May 31, 2022].

15. Ibid.

16. Afsaneh Rigot, "If Tech Fails to Design for the Most Vulnerable, It Fails Us All," *Wired*, May 15, 2022.

17. Afsaneh Rigot, "Design From the Margins: Centering the Most Marginalized and Impacted in Design Processes—From Ideation to Production," Technology and Public Purpose Project (Harvard Kennedy School, Belfer Center for Science and International Affairs), May 13, 2022.

18. Afsaneh Rigot, "Apps, Arrests and Abuse in Egypt, Lebanon and Iran," ARTICLE 19, February 2018.

19. See, e.g., John Paul King, "Grindr Rolls Out New Features for Countries Where LGBTQ Identity Puts Users at Risk," *Washington Blade*, December 13, 2019.

20. "Grindr Introduces Discreet App Icon Feature for All Users," PR Newswire, February 20, 2020.

21. Afsaneh Rigot, "Digital Crime Scenes: The Role of Digital Evidence in the Persecution of LGBTQ People in Egypt, Lebanon, and Tunisia," Berkman Klein Center for Internet & Society, Harvard University, March 7, 2022.

22. Although Signal remains a more secure alternative to WhatsApp, it is not currently available in every nation; and, realistically, due to the ubiquitous nature of WhatsApp (which is owned and promoted by Meta), WhatsApp remains the everyday communications app of choice for people around the world.

23. "Design From the Margins: Centering the Decentered," Belfer Center for Science and International Affairs, Harvard Kennedy School, April 12, 2022.
24. Thanks to my colleague Jessica Fjeld for this metaphor. Note, however, that some structures are still designed on the basis of aesthetics and usability, regardless of what we might expect of their engineering.

Acknowledgments

State of the Free Press 2023 is a product of the commitment, coordination, and contributions of many more people than those listed in the book's table of contents. We appreciate the opportunity to recognize many of them here.

We are grateful to Elizabeth Bell for editing this year's volume. It takes a keen eye and topical expertise to edit a book like this one, and the final product is greatly improved as a result. We also thank our former editor, Michael Tencer, for his past work and his ongoing support of the Project's endeavors.

This is the second Project Censored yearbook to be jointly published by the Censored Press—the publishing imprint of Project Censored and its nonprofit sponsor, the Media Freedom Foundation—and Seven Stories Press. We are grateful to T. M. Scruggs and John and Lyn Roth, early and ongoing supporters of the Censored Press, who helped us make the crucial shift from vision to reality, and the all-star team that comprises the Censored Press editorial board, including Nora Barrows-Friedman, Mischa Geracoulis, Veronica Santiago Liu, Dan Simon, and T. M. Scruggs.

At Seven Stories Press, we thank Dan Simon, publisher and editorial director; Jon Gilbert, operations director; Ruth Weiner, publicity director and co-publisher of Triangle Square Books for Young Readers; Claire Kelley, library and academic marketing director; Tal Mancini, production editor; Lauren Hooker, senior editor; Allison Paller, web manager; Stewart Cauley, art director; Elisa Taber, assistant editor and academic manager; Eva Sotomayor and Anastasia Damaskou, publicists; Silvia Stramenga, rights director and editor of foreign literature; and Catherine Taylor, publicity manager at Seven Stories Press UK—all of whom have our respect and gratitude for their steadfast commitment to co-publishing the Project's yearbook.

Anson Stevens-Bollen created the book's cover illustration, which features a viral media bot, its mass audience, and a few who know better. Readers familiar with his previous yearbook covers, dating back to *Censored 2019*, will know to inspect the image closely for telling detail. Anson's original story icons once again add visual pop to the Top 25 story list.

Books like ours need a team of keen-eyed proofreaders. This year they include Mischa Geracoulis, Gavin Kelley, Steve Macek, Lauren Reduzzi, Troy Patton, and Matthew Phillips.

Vital financial support from donors sustains Project Censored and our work. This year we are especially thankful to Cooper Atkinson, Sharyl Attkisson, Laura Borst, John Boyer, Allison Butler, Sandra Cioppa, James Coleman, Jan De Deka, Dmitry Egorov, Martha Fleischman, Larry Gassan, Leonard C. Goodman, Michael Hansen, Nolan Higdon, Derek Kerr, William Kuerdig, Sheldon Levy, James March, James McFadden, Harry Mersmann, Margaret Neeley, David Nelson, Peter Phillips, Aaron Placensia, Allison Reilly, Krista Rojas, Howard R. Rosenberg, John and Lyn Roth, T. M. Scruggs, Bill Simon, David Stanek, Roger Stoll, Lana Touchstone, Elaine Wellin, Derrick West and Laurie Dawson, Michelle Westover, and Montgomery Zukowski.

We thank Craig Aaron and everyone at The Free Press for their support of Project Censored's educational programs.

The Media Freedom Foundation board of directors, identified below, provides invaluable counsel and crucial organizational structure. Emeritus president and director Peter Phillips continues to be an inspiration and one of the Project's most resolute allies.

Our longtime director of communications and outreach, Adam Armstrong, manages the Project's website, social media channels, and multimedia content. Adam works tirelessly to ensure the Project's research and reports engage a global audience.

We are incredibly fortunate to work with Lorna Garano of Lorna Garano Book Publicity. Lorna brilliantly promotes Project Censored and its work, expanding the Project's circle of allies and supporters and amplifying our influence.

We wholeheartedly thank Nolan Higdon for continued outreach and increasing the Project's public visibility; James Preston Allen, Paul Rosenberg, Terelle Jerricks, and the team at *Random Lengths News*, as well as the Association of Alternative Newsmedia; Jason Houk at KSKQ, and the folks behind Independent Media Week; our allies in the Union for Democratic Communications and the Action Coalition for Media Education; Anthony Fest, longtime senior producer of the Project's weekly public affairs program, and Eleanor Goldfield, whom we welcome as the show's new co-host and associate producer; Bob Baldock and Ken Preston, as well as Ephraim Colbert, José Gonzalez, and Kevin Hunsanger, at KPFA Pacifica Radio in Berkeley, CA; Davey D and *Hard Knock Radio*; Abby Martin of *The Empire Files* and Media Roots; Mnar

Adley, Alan MacLeod, and all at MintPress News and *Behind the Headlines*; Eleanor Goldfield of *Act Out!*; Maximillian Alvarez, Kayla Rivera, and the staff at The Real News Network; Maya Schenwar and Alana Yu-lan Price at Truthout; Eric Draitser and *CounterPunch Radio* as well as Jeffrey St. Clair and the crew at *CounterPunch*; the team at Common Dreams; Norman Stockwell of *The Progressive*; Jordan Elgrably, Mischa Geracoulis, and *The Markaz Review*; Natalie Pompilio and Eils Lotozo at *Haverford*, the magazine of Haverford College; Julianna Forlano of *actNOW*; John Baxter and Angela Dexter of the Jefferson Exchange; John Fugelsang of *Tell Me Everything*; Kevin Gosztola at Shadowproof and the *Unauthorized Disclosure* podcast; Matthew Crawford and *The Curious Man* podcast; Michael Moore and the *Rumble* podcast; Shad Reed of *West Coast Styles*; Jeff Schechtman of WhoWhatWhy?; Nicole Sandler and the *Nicole Sandler Show*; Chris Cook of *Gorilla Radio*; Susan Tchudi and Steve Tchudi of *Ecotopia* on KZFR; Aaron Good and the *American Exception* podcast; John Collins, Amna Al Obaidi, and the team at Weave News; Mitch Jeserich of *Letters and Politics* on KPFA and KPFK; Susan Zakin and *Journal of the Plague Years*; J. G. Michaels at *Parallax Views*; Robert Tomaszewski and all at KPCA in Petaluma; Chase Palmieri of Credder; Steve Brown and the Society for Investigative Journalism; Krish Mohan of *Taboo Table Talk*; James McFadden, Phoebe Anne Sorgen, and the Alameda County Greens; Michael Welch of *The Global Research News Hour*; Alison Trope of USC's Critical Media Project; Jeff Share; everyone behind the Critical Media Literacy Conference of the Americas; Lee Camp of *Redacted Tonight*; Sharyl Attkisson of *Full Measure*; Arlene Engelhardt and Mary Glenney, hosts of *From a Woman's Point of View*; Dana Porteous of *The Creatives* podcast; Greg Ruggiero; Peter Kuznick; David at *The David Talbot Show*; Sonali Kolhatkar of *Rising Up with Sonali*; Frank and Emily Dorrel, Rachael Bruhnke; Jodie Evans and CodePink; Sam Husseini and the Institute for Public Accuracy; *Highbrow Magazine*; *LitHub*; *Ms. Magazine*; Rebecca Strong; Theresa Mitchell of *Presswatch* on KBOO; Max Tegmark at Improve the News; Matt Taibbi, Steven Jay, and Jeff Van Treese of *Mobilized* on Free Speech TV; Karen Hunter of the *Karen Hunter Show*; Andrew Keen at *Keen On*; Julian Vigo of *Savage Minds*; Robert Scheer of ScheerPost and *Scheer Intelligence* podcast (KCRW); *The Chris Hedges Report*; Marcel Reid, Michael McCray, and all at the Whistleblower Summit & Film Festival in Washington, D.C.; Sue Buske of the Buske Group; Tracy Rosenberg at Media Alliance; the Alliance for Community Media West; Toadstool Books, New Hampshire; Cary Harrison of *Reality Check* on KPFK; Karen Ballerini at the Sonoma County Library, Lumacon, and teachers Nathan Libecap and Mike Watt; Betsy Gomez and the Banned Books Week Coalition, including Christopher Finan and our allies at the National Coalition Against Censorship and the American Library Association's Office for Intellectual Freedom; Ralph Nader and all at the Center for Study of Responsive Law; and Hektor Haarkötter, Daniel Müller, Jörg-Uwe Nieland, Yosuke Buchmaier, Filiz Kalmuk, and Peter Ludes, at the German Initiative on News Enlightenment.

At Diablo Valley College, Mickey thanks everyone who continues to support his work in the Journalism Department, including Adam Bessie, Mark Akiyama, Adam Perry, Michael Levitin, Nolan Higdon, Rosa Leither,

Charleen Earley, Donna Smith, John Corbally, Matthew Powell, Bridgitte Shaffer, Albert Ponce, Sangha Niyogi, and everyone in the Social Justice Studies Program and the Faculty Senate; John Freytag, Jason Mayfield, Jeffrey Michels, Beth Arman, Catherine Franco, Douglas Phenix, Nikki Moultrie, dean of social sciences Obed Vazquez and administrative assistant Lisa Martin; as well as college president Susan Lamb. Mickey also thanks his students, who are a constant reminder of future possibilities, for the inspiration they provide.

Mickey thanks his family, especially his wife, Meg, for her amazing work, counsel, and care, and their children, for patience, moral support, sense of humor, and their love of a good argument. Andy could not do what he does without the support and love of Elizabeth Boyd.

Finally, we thank you, our readers and supporters, who continue to cherish a truly free press, to expose and oppose censorship, and to champion a more open, just society. Together, we make a difference.

MEDIA FREEDOM FOUNDATION/PROJECT CENSORED BOARD OF DIRECTORS

PROJECT CENSORED 2021–22 JUDGES

ROBIN ANDERSEN. Writer, commentator, and award-winning author. Professor Emerita of Communication and Media Studies at Fordham University. She edits the Routledge Focus Book Series on Media and Humanitarian Action. Her forthcoming books are *Death in Paradise: A Critical Study of the BBC Series*, and *Censorship, Digital Media, and the Global Crackdown on Freedom of Expression*. She writes regularly for Fairness & Accuracy in Reporting (FAIR).

AVRAM ANDERSON. Electronic Resources Management Specialist, California State University, Northridge. A member and advocate of the LGBTQI+ community researching LGBTQ bias and censorship. Co-author of *The Media and Me: A Guide to Critical Media Literacy for Young People* (2022) and "Censorship by Proxy and Moral Panics in the Digital Era," in *Censorship, Digital Media, and the Global Crackdown on Freedom of Expression* (2023). They also contribute to the *Index on Censorship*, *In These Times*, and Truthout.

JULIE ANDRZEJEWSKI. Professor Emeritus, St. Cloud State University. Served as director of the Social Responsibility master's program, and president of the faculty union. Publications include *Social Justice, Peace, and Environmental Education* (co-edited, 2009) and, most recently, a book chapter, "The Roots of the Sixth Mass Extinction" (in *Animal Oppression and Capitalism*, Vol. 2, 2017). She is currently co-chair of Indivisible Tacoma and organizer of the WA Indivisible Town Hall Series.

OLIVER BOYD-BARRETT. Professor Emeritus of Media and Communications, Bowling Green State University and California State Polytechnic University, Pomona. Most recent publications include *Conflict Propaganda in Syria: Narrative Battles* (2022), *Media Imperialism: Continuity and Change* (2020), *RussiaGate and Propaganda* (2020), and *Western Mainstream Media and the Ukraine Crisis* (2017).

KENN BURROWS. Faculty member at the Institute for Holistic Health Studies, Department of Health Education, San Francisco State University. Founder and director of the Holistic Health Learning Center and producer of the biennial Future of Health Care conference.

ELLIOT D. COHEN. Editor and founder of the *International Journal of Applied Philosophy*. Recent books include *Making Peace with Imperfection* (2019), *Counseling Ethics for the 21st Century* (2018), *Logic–Based Therapy and Everyday Emotions* (2016), and *Technology of Oppression: Preserving Freedom and Dignity in an Age of Mass, Warrantless Surveillance* (2014).

BRIAN COVERT. Journalist, author, and educator based in Japan. Worked for United Press International (UPI) news service in Japan, as staff reporter and editor for English-language daily newspapers in Japan, and as contributing writer to Japanese and overseas newspapers and magazines. Contributing author to past *Censored* editions. Teaches journalism at Doshisha University in Kyoto.

GEOFF DAVIDIAN. Investigative reporter, war correspondent, legal affairs analyst, editor, photojournalist, data analyst, and educator. Founding publisher and editor of the *Putnam Pit*, *Milwaukee Press*, and ShorewoodNewsroom.com. Contributor to Reuters, magazines, newspapers, and online publications.

MISCHA GERACOULIS. Educator, journalist, contributing editor at *The Markaz Review*, and board member at the Censored Press. Teaching and research are focused on the intersections among human rights education, critical media literacy, and ethics. The Armenian genocide, diaspora, displacement, refugee crises, and imprisoned journalists are among the other topics of her research and publications.

ROBERT HACKETT. Professor Emeritus of Communication, Simon Fraser University, Vancouver. Co-founder of

NewsWatch Canada (1993), Media Democracy Days (2001), and OpenMedia.ca (2007). His eight books on media and politics include *Journalism and Climate Crisis: Public Engagement, Media Alternatives* (with S. Forde, S. Gunster, and K. Foxwell-Norton, 2017) and *Remaking Media: The Struggle to Democratize Public Communication* (with W. K. Carroll, 2006). Winner of 2018 SFU award for community impact. He writes for thetyee.ca, nationalobserver.com, rabble.ca, and other media.

NOLAN HIGDON. Lecturer at Merrill College and in the Education Department at University of California, Santa Cruz. Founding member of the Critical Media Literacy Conference of the Americas. His recent publications include *The Anatomy of Fake News: A Critical News Literacy Education* (2020); *Let's Agree to Disagree: A Critical Thinking Guide to Communication, Conflict Management, and Critical Media Literacy* (2022), with Mickey Huff; and *The Podcaster's Dilemma: Decolonizing Podcasters in the Era of Surveillance Capitalism* (2022), with Nicholas Baham III.

KEVIN HOWLEY. Professor of Media Studies at DePauw University. Prior to joining academia, he worked in community media as a trainer and producer. In addition to his record of peer-reviewed scholarly publication, he has worked as a news-paper columnist, radio broadcaster, and video producer. His current research and teaching interests include participatory media, multimodal writing, and critical utopianism.

NICHOLAS JOHNSON. * Author, *How to Talk Back to Your Television Set* (1970), and nine more books, including *Columns of Democracy* (2018) and *What Do You Mean and How Do You Know?* (2009). Commissioner, Federal Communications Commission (1966–1973); Professor, University of Iowa College of Law (1981–2014, media law and cyberlaw). More at nicholasjohnson.org.

CHARLES L. KLOTZER. Founder, editor, and publisher emeritus of *St. Louis Journalism Review* and *FOCUS/Midwest*. The *St. Louis Journalism Review* has been transferred to Southern

Illinois University, Carbondale, and is now the *Gateway Journalism Review*. Klotzer remains active at the *Review*.

NANCY KRANICH. Instructor, School of Communication and Information, and special projects librarian, Rutgers University. Past president of the American Library Association (ALA), member of ALA's Freedom to Read Foundation Roll of Honor, and convener of the ALA Center for Civic Life. Author of hundreds of publications, including *Libraries and Democracy: The Cornerstones of Liberty* (2001); "Adventures in Information Policy Wonderland" (2019); and "Libraries: Reuniting the Divided States of America" (2017).

MARTIN LEE. Investigative journalist and author. Co-founder of Fairness & Accuracy In Reporting, and former editor of FAIR's magazine, *Extra!* Director of Project CBD, a medical science information nonprofit. Author of *Smoke Signals: A Social History of Marijuana—Medical, Recreational, and Scientific* (2012), *The Beast Reawakens: Fascism's Resurgence from Hitler's Spymasters to Today's Neo-Nazi Groups and Right-Wing Extremists* (2000), and *Acid Dreams: The Complete Social History of LSD: The CIA, the Sixties, and Beyond* (with B. Shlain, 1985).

PETER LUDES. Visiting Positions in Sociology at the Universities of Newfoundland and Amsterdam; Professor of Culture and Media Science at the University of Siegen (Germany) and Visiting Positions at Harvard, Mannheim and Constance; Professor of Mass Communication, Jacobs University, Bremen, 2002–2017. Visiting Research Professor in Comparative Cultures at the University of Cologne, since 2018. Founder of the German Initiative on News Enlightenment (1997) at the University of Siegen. Recent publications on brutalization and banalization (2018) and collective myths and decivilizing processes (2020, with Stefan Kramer).

WILLIAM LUTZ. Professor Emeritus of English, Rutgers University. Former editor of the *Quarterly Review of Double-*

speak. Author of *Doublespeak: From Revenue Enhancement to Terminal Living: How Government, Business, Advertisers, and Others Use Language to Deceive You* (1989), *The Cambridge Thesaurus of American English* (1994), *The New Doublespeak: Why No One Knows What Anyone's Saying Anymore* (1996), and *Doublespeak Defined* (1999).

CONCHA MATEOS. Senior Lecturer in Visual Studies, Department of Communication Sciences, Universidad Rey Juan Carlos, Spain. Journalist for radio, television, and political organizations in Spain and Latin America. Academic researcher and activist. Coordinator for Project Censored research in Europe and Latin America.

DANIEL MÜLLER. Head of the Postgraduate Academy at the University of Siegen, in Germany. Researcher and educator in journalism, mass communication studies, and history at public universities for many years. Has published extensively on media history, media–minority relations in Germany, and on nationality policies and ethnic relations of the Soviet Union and the post-Soviet successor states, particularly in the Caucasus. Jury member of the German Initiative on News Enlightenment.

JACK L. NELSON.* Distinguished Professor Emeritus, Graduate School of Education, Rutgers University. Former member, Committee on Academic Freedom and Tenure, American Association of University Professors. Recipient, Academic Freedom Award, National Council for Social Studies. Author of 17 books, including *Critical Issues in Education: Dialogues and Dialectics*, 9th ed. (with S. Palonsky and M. R. McCarthy, 2021) and *Human Impact of Natural Disasters* (with V. O. Pang and W. R. Fernekes, 2010), and about 200 articles.

PETER PHILLIPS. Professor Emeritus of Political Sociology, Sonoma State University. Director, Project Censored, 1996–2010. President, Media Freedom Foundation, 2010–2016. Editor or co-editor of fourteen editions of *Censored*. Author of *Giants: The*

Global Power Elite (2018). Co-editor (with Dennis Loo) of *Impeach the President: The Case Against Bush and Cheney* (2006).

MICHAEL RAVNITZKY. Attorney, writer, editor, engineer, and Freedom of Information Act expert who has developed tools to broaden access to public records in the public interest.

T. M. SCRUGGS. Professor Emeritus (token ethnomusicologist), University of Iowa. Print, audio, and/or video format publications on media in Nicaragua and Venezuela, as well as on Central American, Cuban, Venezuelan and US music and dance. Involvement with community radio in Nicaragua, Venezuela, and the United States, including the KPFA (Berkeley, CA) Local Station Board and Pacifica National Board. Executive producer, *The Resurrection of Victor Jara* and other documentaries. Board member, The Real News Network and Truthout.

PAUL STREET. Researcher, award-winning journalist, historian, author, and speaker. Author of ten books to date: *This Happened Here: Neoliberals, Amerikaners, and the Trumping of America* (Routledge, October 2021); *Hollow Resistance: Obama, Trump and the Politics of Appeasement* (CounterPunch, 2020); *They Rule: The 1% vs. Democracy* (2014); *Crashing the Tea Party*, with Anthony R. DiMaggio (2011); *The Empire's New Clothes* (2010); *Barack Obama and the Future of American Politics* (2009); *Racial Oppression in the Global Metropolis* (2007); *Still Separate, Unequal* (2005); *Segregated Schools: Educational Apartheid in Post–Civil Rights America* (2005); and *Empire and Inequality* (2004). He writes regularly for *CounterPunch*.

SHEILA RABB WEIDENFELD.* Emmy Award–winning television producer. Former press secretary to Betty Ford and special assistant to the President; author, *First Lady's Lady*. President of DC Productions Ltd. Creator of snippetsofwisdom. com. Director of community relations of Phyto Management LLC and Maryland Cultivation and Processing LLC.

ROB WILLIAMS. Founding president of the Action Coalition for Media Education (ACME). Teaches media, communications, global studies, and journalism at Champlain and Saint Michael's Colleges and Northern Vermont University. Author of numerous articles on critical media literacy education. Publisher of the *Vermont Independent* online news journal. Author of *The Post (Truth) World* (2019) and *Media Mojo!* (2020), and co-editor of *Media Education for a Digital Generation* (with J. Frechette, 2016) and *Most Likely to Secede* (with R. Miller, 2013), about the Vermont independence movement.

Special thanks to **NANCY SNOW**, who has served as a judge since 2005 and is now retiring from that role.

*Indicates having been a Project Censored judge since our founding in 1976.

How To Support Project Censored

Nominate a story

To nominate a *Censored* story, forward the URL to andy@projectcensored.org or mickey@projectcensored.org. The deadline to nominate stories for the next yearbook is March 31, 2023.

Criteria for Project Censored news story nominations:

1) A censored news story reports information that the public has a right and a need to know, but to which the public has had limited access.

2) The news story is recent, having been first reported no later than one year ago. Stories submitted for *State of the Free Press 2024* should be no older than April 2022.

3) The story is fact-based with clearly defined concepts and verifiable documentation. The story's claims should be supported by evidence—the more controversial the claims, the stronger the evidence necessary.

4) The news story has been published, either electronically or in print, in a publicly circulated newspaper, journal, magazine, newsletter, or similar publication from either a domestic or foreign source.

Make a tax-deductible donation

We depend on tax-deductible donations to continue our work. Project Censored is supported by the Media Freedom Foundation, a 501(c)(3) nonprofit organization. To support our efforts on behalf of independent journalism and freedom of information, send checks to the address below or donate online at projectcensored.org. Your generous donations help us to oppose news censorship and promote media literacy.

Media Freedom Foundation
PO Box 1177
Fair Oaks, CA 95628
mickey@projectcensored.org
andy@projectcensored.org
Phone: (707) 241-4596

About the Editors

MICKEY HUFF is the director of Project Censored and president of the nonprofit Media Freedom Foundation. To date, he has co-edited fourteen editions of the Project's yearbook. He is also the co-author, with Nolan Higdon, of *Let's Agree to Disagree* (Routledge, 2022), a practical handbook on critical thinking and civil discourse, and *United States of Distraction* (City Lights, 2019). Huff is a professor of social science, history, and journalism at Diablo Valley College, where he co-chairs the history program and is chair of the Journalism Department. In 2019 he received the Beverly Kees Educator Award from the Society of Professional Journalists' Northern California chapter. Huff is the host and executive producer of *The Project Censored Show*, the Project's weekly syndicated public affairs radio program. A musician and composer, he lives with his family in Fair Oaks, California.

ANDY LEE ROTH is the associate director of Project Censored and co-editor of thirteen editions of the Project's yearbook. He coordinates the Project's Campus Affiliates Program, a news media research network of several hundred students and faculty at two dozen colleges and universities across North America. His research and writing have been published in a variety of outlets, including *Index on Censorship*, *In These Times*, *YES! Magazine*, Truthout, *Media, Culture & Society*, and the *International Journal of Press/Politics*. He earned a PhD in sociology at the University of California, Los Angeles, and a BA in sociology and anthropology at

Haverford College. He lives in Winthrop, Washington, with his sweetheart and their extraordinary, nineteen-year-old cat, Eddie.

For more information about the editors, to invite them to speak at your school or in your community, or to conduct interviews, please visit projectcensored.org/press-room.

Index

Blair, Payton, 87

The Blaze (media website), 56-57

Blint-Welsh, Tyler, xvi

Bloomberg Law (legal website), 41

Bloomberg, Michael, 134, 135

Bloomberg News (media website), 25, 96, 119

Blue Gold, 125

Blue Origin (spaceflight company), 154, 158

Boebert, Lauren, 43, 44

Boghosian, Heidi, xiii-xviii

Boyle, Francis, 213

Bolivia, 126-27

Boston Globe, 5

Boudin, Chesa, 182

Bowen, Alyssa, 80-81

Boyd, Elizabeth, 27

BP (oil and gas company), 97

Brady, Tom, 166-67, 170

Bradley Foundation, 48, 81

Bradley, Matthew, 215

Branson, Richard, 149, 154, 155, 161

The Brass Check, 3-4

Braun, Mike, 61

Brazil, 117

Breaking The Set, 11

breastfeeding, 114, 131-36

Brennan Center for Justice, 69, 83, 84

Bridgforth, Bonnie, 91

Brookings Institution, 89

Brooklyn subway shooting (2022), 179

Bruce, Lenny, 210, 212

Buffalo shooting (2022), 183, 196

Bulletin of the Atomic Scientists, 195

Bureau of Safety and Environmental Enforcement (BSEE) (US), 97-99

Burns, Jennifer, 136

Burrows, Kenn, 68

Bush George, H.W., 182

Bush, George W., 11, 165

Business Insider, 45, 49, 58, 158, 193

Butler, Allison, 16, 46, 92, 99, 207, 218-22

Buxbaum, Amy Grim, 23-111

BuzzFlash, 71, 73

California, 98, 138-39

California State University, *see also* Sonoma State University
East Bay, 207, 224
Long Beach, 171

Callow, Lily, 77

Calvert, Ken, 192

Cambridge Analytica, 64

Camp, Lee, 11, 16, 208, 209-13

Campaign Legal Center, 60

Campbell, Alexia Fernández, 35-37

Campion, Jane, 162, 163

Canada, 66, 85

Canadian Dimension, 125

cancer, 39, 40, 116, 119

Capital Gazette, xiv

carbon emissions, 45, 66, 71-72, 149, 157, 160, 195, *see also* climate crisis

Carbon Tracker (climate change nonprofit organization), 33

Cargill, 120-21

Carlin, George, 210

Carlson, Tucker, 183

Carpenter, John, 157

⌈CP⌋ THE CENSORED PRESS

The Censored Press is the publishing imprint of Project Censored and its nonprofit sponsor, the Media Freedom Foundation. Building on the Project's yearbook series, website, weekly radio show, and other educational programs, the Censored Press advances the Project's mission to promote independent investigative journalism, media literacy, and critical thinking.

The Censored Press benefits from a robust partnership with Seven Stories Press, the Project's longtime publisher and stalwart ally, which prints and distributes Censored Press titles. In Fall 2022, the two presses released *The Media and Me: A Guide to Critical Media Literacy for Young People*, written by Project Censored and the Media Revolution Collective and illustrated by Peter Glanting. In early 2023, the Censored Press and Seven Stories Press will publish *Going Remote: A Teacher's Journey*, a graphic memoir written by Adam Bessie and illustrated by Peter Glanting; and *Guilty of Journalism: The Political Case Against Julian Assange*, by Kevin Gosztola, with a foreword by Abby Martin.

The generosity of several founding donors ensures that the Censored Press will be a sustainable publishing imprint, but your additional support will allow us to undertake even more publishing projects and provide new opportunities for reporting, teaching, and thinking critically.

https://censoredpress.org/